Twelve Greeks and Romans Who Changed the World

Twelve Greeks and Romans Who Changed the World

Carl J. Richard

Barnes & Noble

NEW YORK

2006 Barnes & Noble Publishing

ISBN-13: 978-0-7607-8256-9
ISBN-10: 0-7607-8256-3

Printed and bound in the United States of America

1 3 5 7 9 10 8 6 4 2

For Amos E. Simpson, who has inspired so many students with a love of history.

Gladly would he learn and gladly teach.
—Geoffrey Chaucer, *The Canterbury Tales*

Contents

Preface

This book is not a monograph, a specialized work intended solely for academics and focused on the technical points of ancient history, but a broader work with two goals: to contribute to the restoration of a sensible, balanced view of Western civilization, and to assert the importance of Greco-Roman culture as the foundation of that civilization. Based on the notion that history can be fun without being frivolous, this work contains both serious analysis and, in imitation of the classical historians themselves, anecdotes intended to illustrate the personal qualities of the Greeks and Romans who contributed most to Western civilization.

This work focuses so intently on the *contributions* of the twelve Greeks and Romans—on how they changed the world—that it cannot truthfully be called a collection of biographies. In the case of some of these individuals (Homer and Thales, for instance), so little is known of their lives that real biographies are impossible. But even in the other cases, I have left out biographical details that have little relevance to the individuals' most influential achievements. In place of these details, I have devoted much space to the historical context in which these twelve individuals lived, information I consider more useful to the task at hand, especially for those readers who are not specialists in classical history.

The fact that all twelve of the Greeks and Romans highlighted in this book are male is not an example of chauvinism, but a consequence of the regrettable fact that the Greeks and Romans, like nearly all other ancient peoples, rarely granted women direct political power. One does not have to endorse all aspects of Greco-Roman culture to appreciate its contribution to Western civilization. Nevertheless, the reader will find even within the pages of this work several examples of powerful women, such as Artemisia, Aspasia, Olympias, and, of course, Cleopatra.

I have tried to balance political and military leaders with artists and intellectuals. One of the long-term consequences of classical historiography was the equation of history with politics and war, an equation not successfully challenged until the 1960s. But in recent years, the old myth that history was *nothing but* battles has been replaced with the equally unfortunate tendency to disregard battles entirely, whether based on a distaste for war or on the false assumption that military success is entirely a function of economic power. Military leadership is certainly worth studying because it has played a crucial role in determining which civilizations have triumphed, just as political leadership is worth studying because it has established social conditions that have been either conducive or detrimental to artistic and intellectual achievement.

I would like to express my gratitude to Professors Thomas McGinn of Vanderbilt University, Amos E. Simpson of the University of Louisiana, Lafayette, and David Tandy of the University of Tennessee, Knoxville, all of whom sacrificed precious time from their busy schedules to read an earlier version of this work and to offer valuable advice on its improvement. Additionally, I would like to thank Vaughan Baker, my department head, for her highly constructive suggestions concerning the format of this work. Furthermore, I would like to thank my editor, Mary Carpenter, for her continual encouragement and sage advice. But, above all, I would like to thank my precious wife, Debbie, my best friend, for her unceasing prayers and support. When Aristotle was asked, "What is a friend?" he replied, "One soul dwelling in two bodies."

Introduction

The British poet Percy Shelley once wrote, "We are all Greeks." All of the languages of the modern West, including English, contain numerous Greek words. The Greeks deduced the core of modern scientific and mathematical knowledge and developed the very method that has allowed modern scientists to surpass them. They established the Western forms of drama, poetry, prose, art, and architecture. By articulating all of the principal metaphysical and ethical problems and proposing a dazzling variety of solutions, their philosophers set the terms for all subsequent philosophical discourse. They invented research-based historical writing. They formulated the theories of popular sovereignty, natural law, and mixed government that undergird modern democratic government. The Greeks, writes the historian H. D. F. Kitto, taught the world what the human mind was made for. It is the combination of the Greek emphasis on reason and the Judaic emphasis on ethical monotheism that has given the Western mind its distinctive shape.

Like the Hebrews, the Greeks distinguished themselves from other peoples. While the Hebrews divided the people of the world into Jews and Gentiles, the Greeks separated them into Greeks and "barbarians." The Greek word "barbaros" was not necessarily a pejorative term. On the contrary, the Greeks admired many aspects of the Egyptian and Persian civilizations and recognized their own intellectual debt to the Near East. In differentiating themselves from others, the Greeks simply noted an important fact: no one else thought as they did.

Yet, if one could ask an ancient Greek what distinguished him from the barbarian, he would not place the astonishing triumphs of the Greek

1

mind first. Rather, he would say, "The barbarians are slaves; we Hellenes are free men." By this, he would mean that, whatever his system of government (and the Greeks adopted many different systems), he was free from arbitrary rule. The concept of popular sovereignty, the idea that the people must consent to the form of government, whether monarchy, aristocracy, or democracy, was a powerful force in ancient Greece. Even monarchs based their rule not on divine right (as in the Near East), but on the argument that the people consented to that form of government. State affairs were considered public affairs, not the private concern of a despot. Above all, law governed the Greeks. The poet Pindar wrote: "Law is the king of all, both of the mortals and of the immortals." Even the gods were considered subject to law. Citizens were treated as members of a common society, not as helpless subjects. Arbitrary government offended the Greeks, and most barbarian societies possessed arbitrary government. Barbarian kings did not rule according to law, but according to their own wills. The Greeks did not prostrate themselves before their kings, considering this practice an affront to human dignity.

Although the Romans were generally not as innovative as the Greeks, it is arguable that their contribution to Western civilization was as great, if not greater. In addition to the Romans' distinct contributions to administration, engineering, and law, they also brought Greek theories down to earth, modified them, and transmitted them throughout the Western world. Without Roman conquest, Greek ideas would probably not have gained a hearing in most of the West. Furthermore, without the Roman sense of social responsibility to temper the individualism of Hellenistic Greece, classical culture may not have survived. (The record of the Hellenistic kingdoms was not a hopeful one.) Like many marriages, the marriage between Greek and Roman culture was, in some ways, a union of opposites. Their offspring, Western civilization, possessed a balance that aided its survival. Whichever parent the child favors more remains, as always with such questions, a matter of eternal dispute.

But today, at the very point in history when Western civilization has reached the apex of its influence in the world, it has become fashionable within the academic community to blame it for all that is wrong with the modern age. In a sense, this is nothing new: the criticism of one's own culture is a hallmark of the Western tradition, going back at least as far as Socrates. Ironically, this means that no one is more Western than the Western academics who criticize Western civilization. Furthermore, there are legitimate reasons to criticize the Western world. Westerners have sometimes been racist and imperialist. But so have non-Westerners, a fact overlooked by some academics, who romanticize non-Western cultures. The same academics tend to minimize or ignore the important artistic, philosophical, scientific, and political contributions Western civilization has made to the world.

In order to restore a balanced perspective to the study of Western civilization—an appreciation for both its glories and its faults—it may be useful to study twelve Greeks and Romans who contributed most to its formation and, in so doing, changed the world as a whole. Each of these individuals, like all others who lived before and after them, possessed both virtues and vices. Their legacies include both significant achievements and tragic errors.

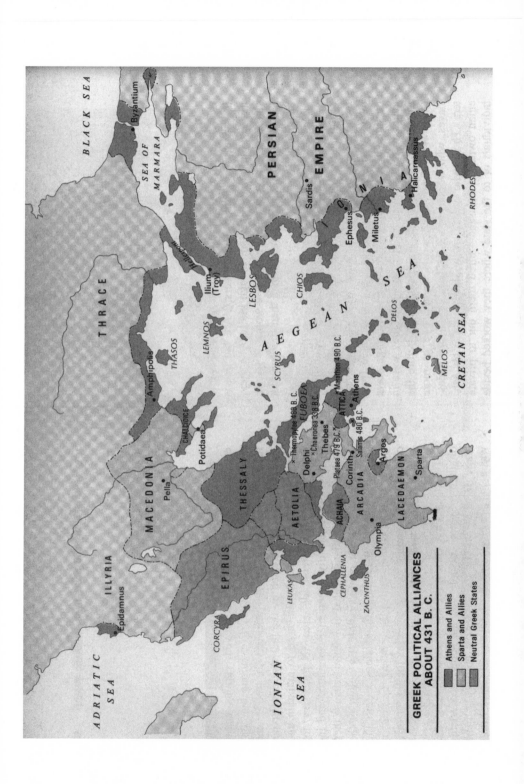

GREEK POLITICAL ALLIANCES ABOUT 431 B. C.

Athens and Allies
Sparta and Allies
Neutral Greek States

1

Homer: Founder of Western Literature

The founder of Western literature—and, many still believe, the greatest wordsmith the world has ever known—was, according to Greek legend, a blind poet from the island of Chios. Homer's epic poems not only shaped the work of subsequent Greek and Roman poets, but also influenced the development of Greek drama, which, in turn, was the progenitor of television programs and films, the most popular forms of modern entertainment. Homer also influenced numerous medieval and modern poets and novelists.

GREECE BEFORE HOMER

The Mycenaeans

Around 2000 B.C., the Mycenaeans, an Indo-European people, infiltrated the Greek mainland from the north and established several different kingdoms, the most powerful of which was Mycenae. By 1600 B.C., the Mycenaeans had assimilated the mysterious locals, called "Pelasgi" by later Greeks, while themselves borrowing some elements from the Minoan civilization in Crete. For instance, the Mycenaeans adapted Linear B, a syllabic written language, from the Minoans' Linear A. Though applied exclusively to administrative and technical matters, Linear B, which contained forty characters, possessed the clarity and control that distinguished later Greek thought. The language, like its descendant, classical Greek, possessed clear rules, yet was flexible enough to express different shades of meaning.

Mycenaean tablets contain the names of many of the later Greek gods. Like the Minoans, the Mycenaeans preferred figurines of the gods and small shrines to great statues or temples. But the Mycenaean religion was more patriarchal than that of the Minoans. Although the Mycenaeans and the Minoans both possessed a god named Zeus, the Mycenaean Zeus differed substantially from the Minoan Zeus. The Minoan Zeus was subordinate to the Mother Goddess, who was either his mother or his consort. Furthermore, the Minoan Zeus was not immortal; in fact, he had died. (Cretans later scandalized other Greeks by showing them the tomb of Zeus.) By contrast, the Mycenaean Zeus whom the later Greeks inherited was the most powerful of all gods—a sky god whose messenger was the rainbow and whose chief weapon was the thunderbolt.

Although Mycenaean palaces reveal their cultural debt to the Minoans, their society differed in important ways. Since Mycenaean cities, such as Mycenae, Pylos, and Tiryns, were more susceptible to invasion than the island of Crete, they were invariably fortified with the massive "Cyclopean walls" of Homeric fame. (Later Greeks were so astonished by the gigantic walls they believed that the giant Cyclopes of Greek mythology must have erected them.) Springs connected to the cities by tunnel and various warehouses allowed the Mycenaeans to withstand sieges. Each palace was organized around a *megaron*, a huge hall containing a large central hearth surrounded by four columns. A bathroom near the front door allowed the lord or his guests to bathe on arrival. Its stone floor slanted down into a drain. The palace was a complex of royal apartments, store rooms, servants' quarters, chariot sheds, and altars.

Mycenaean kings seem to have possessed great power over their prosperous kingdoms. Their palaces and burial grounds, gigantic beehive tombs carved into the hills and mountains, have yielded heaps of gold, silver, and ivory objects. The Mycenaeans acquired this tremendous wealth through trade (a royal monopoly) and piracy. As late as the Homeric Age (c. 730 B.C.), no shame was attached to piracy. Homer's Achilles notes dispassionately: "Cattle may be had for the raiding." Mycenaean tombs were filled with bronze weapons and frescoes depicting their occupants waging war and hunting. They also contained clay figurines of women and animals. The Mycenaeans traded widely with Egypt, Palestine, Anatolia, Syria, Sicily, southern Italy, Cyprus, Crete, and the Aegean islands.

The Dark Ages (1180–750 B.C.)

The collapse of Mycenaean civilization remains shrouded in mystery. While it is relatively clear that Mycenae and Tiryns were burned in the 1190s or 1180s B.C., and that other Mycenaean and Minoan cities were burned at about the same time, it is not clear who (or what) destroyed these cities. The most persuasive theory, advanced by Robert Drews, is that the Mycenaean cities were destroyed by raiders who had learned how to use javelins and slashing swords to defeat the Mycenaeans, who relied heavily on charioteers wielding composite bows. The raiders looted and destroyed the centers of Mycenaean civilization and returned home. Drews suspects that the raiders who sacked the Mycenaean cities of southern Greece were actually the more primitive inhabitants of northern Greece, Greeks who spoke the Aeolic dialect and who had previously served as mercenaries for the southern Greeks. Furthermore, Drews believes that it was these northern Greeks—rather than the Mycenaeans of southern Greece, who spoke the Ionic dialect—who had sacked Troy, the famous city situated on what is now called the Turkish Straits, a few decades earlier.

In any case, the destruction of the Mycenaean centers led to the collapse of civilization—centralized government, wide trade, monumental architecture, and writing—for centuries. War, probably combined with disease, decimated the population. A Cyprian poet later claimed that the Trojan War had resulted from overpopulation. Zeus had decided to alleviate the burden that so large a population placed on the earth. While the Greeks seem to have maintained some contact with Syria and Phoenicia during the Dark Ages, exchanging olive oil for metals, such trade was minimal. Subsistence agriculture became the order of the age. Many Mycenaeans from the destroyed cities fled to the mountains of Arcadia and to the islands of Cyprus; within several generations, these speakers of the Ionic dialect had also settled various Aegean islands and western Asia Minor, a region of the Greek world that became known as Ionia. These migrations created a vacuum in southern Greece that was eventually filled by the Dorians, a collection of primitive Greek speakers from northern Greece. The Dorians migrated into southern Greece in the late twelfth or early eleventh century B.C.

Composed at the beginning of the so-called Archaic period that followed the Dark Ages, Homer's *Iliad* recounts traditions concerning the events of the late Mycenaean Era but, to some extent, superimposes on them the lifestyle of the Dark Ages. The Dark Ages were aristocratic. Kings were but the first among equals; they could not order other aristocrats around. The chief characteristic expected of the nobles was *arete* (virtue), which the Greeks defined as warrior qualities, such as manliness, strength, skill, and valor. Although peasants were considered incapable of arete, they possessed certain rights. They assembled and voted on important matters, such as the decision to go to war.

Although the Dark Ages interrupted civilization in Greece for over four centuries by temporarily diminishing communication with the civilizations of the ancient Near East, they also contributed an independence of thought to the new Greek culture that emerged around 750 B.C. Though willing to learn from other peoples, the Greeks were now able to craft their own distinctive civilization from preexisting elements.

The collapse of the Mycenaean civilization forced each community to defend itself against raiders. Congregating on an *acropolis* (a fortified hilltop), the people of each valley joined together in common defense. The acropolis became the residence of a king, a place of assembly, and a religious center. Since the chaos rendered trade and communication over mountains difficult, Greek poleis were isolated and self-sufficient. By the time trade flourished again and marketplaces arose beneath each acropolis, the polis had become the fundamental political and social unit of Greece. Once formed, the poleis benefited from the fact that the major powers of the Near East were too distracted by local concerns to challenge the Greeks until the fifth century B.C.

Writing returned to Greece near the end of the Dark Ages. While the language was a descendant of the Mycenaean tongue, the new alphabet in which it was expressed was adapted from Phoenician script, which consisted of twenty-two consonants. The new Greek alphabet contained twenty-four letters, including symbols for vowel sounds. The small number of letters made possible the rapid spread of literacy. In fact, the whole alphabet was inscribed on some pots during the eighth century B.C. Unlike the Mycenaeans, classical Greeks used writing for a great variety of purposes. One early sample of classical Greek is found on an Athenian pot: "Whoever dances the best will get me." Another sample of early Greek writing, discovered on a rock outcrop at the back of a gymnasium, consists of adolescent graffiti.

THE *ILIAD* AND THE *ODYSSEY*

The Greeks also used writing to record traditional epic poems. The recitation of poetry was a common occupation for the blind. But Homer's descriptions are so vivid it is unlikely that he was born blind. He probably composed the *Iliad* around 730 B.C., and the *Odyssey* about 710 B.C., though the texts of both poems were probably not entirely fixed until about 650 B.C. In both poems, Homer wove together previous oral traditions, perhaps even borrowing some traditional lines of verse, to produce unique works of genius.

While the *Iliad* is set during the Trojan War, the *Odyssey* recounts the hero Odysseus's adventures in attempting to return home following the war. As the ancient critic Longinus put it: "Homer in the *Odyssey* is like the setting sun; the grandeur remains, but not the intensity." The *Iliad* remains the most revered poem in Western literature, the *Odyssey* the most beloved. The *Odyssey* presents a more favorable image of the poor and demonstrates a greater concern with ethics than does the *Iliad*. From the *Iliad* to the *Odyssey*, the emphasis shifted from the physical prowess of Achilles to the intelligence, patience, self-control, ingenuity, intellectual curiosity, and loyalty of Odysseus. Zeus punishes the monstrous Cyclops for his violation of the cardinal rule, hospitality to strangers, by allowing Odysseus to blind him. The Cyclops had eaten some of Odysseus's men, an act that identified him as a particularly bad host, according to Homeric rules of etiquette. This new emphasis on hospitality to strangers was probably a response to the growth of trade, which required more frequent travel. Commoners were no longer mere objects of ridicule, as in the *Iliad*, but potentially worthy of respect. In the *Odyssey*, the faithful Eumaeus is presented as a noble and virtuous herdsman who helps Odysseus reclaim his throne. This development was perhaps connected with the rise of a Greek middle class as the result of the expansion of trade during the Archaic period.

In both the *Iliad* and the *Odyssey*, Homer portrays women in an uncommonly favorable light. Though Helen, the unfaithful wife of Menelaus, is depicted as the cause of the Trojan War, Hector's wife Andromache is portrayed as a woman of virtue. In the *Odyssey*, Homer's female characters, especially the ingenious and faithful Penelope, possess well-developed personalities. By contrast, Homer's contemporary, Hesiod (like most later Greeks), viewed women as cunning and dangerous creatures who must be controlled. In the *Works and Days*, Hesiod wrote: "He who trusts a woman trusts trickery." Hesiod attributed human suffering to the curiosity of Pandora, who had, against expressed warnings, opened a box of evils, thereby unleashing them on the world.

While the Homeric epics probably contain a few lines added by professional reciters who lived shortly after the time of their composer, the theory that "Homer" was actually a long series of different composers is contradicted by the poems' thematic and stylistic unity. Some modern critics have even argued persuasively that certain passages of the poems once thought to violate thematic unity are actually essential to that unity.

What qualities made Homer a literary genius? First, like subsequent Greek artists, Homer focused his attention squarely on his human characters. Nothing interests human beings more than humanity. Homer reflected this interest even when portraying the gods, who seemed little more than extraordinarily powerful humans. When Homer described a trait of nature, he did so with astonishing skill, but only to compare it with some human action.

Second, like all artistic geniuses, Homer combined the unique with the universal. In the *Iliad*, Agamemnon's quarrel with Achilles is a unique dispute between two unique men over unique grievances. But Homer's theme is universal: because these two proud men have a foolish quarrel, many men must die—and that is the way of the world.

Third, Homer was never wordy. Homer always told his story, made his point, and moved on. He did not preach; he merely painted his portrait in such a way as to suggest certain conclusions, trusting in the intelligence of his audience. All of the action in the *Iliad* occurs at the very end of the Trojan War. The poem ends with the funeral of the Trojan hero Hector, killed by Achilles in revenge for Hector's slaying of Achilles' dear friend Patroclus, though Achilles knew that he was destined to die soon after killing Hector. Homer does not even describe the actual fall of Troy due to the admission of Odysseus's Trojan Horse. To end the story with the reader knowing that Troy is about to fall and Achilles to die conveys a far greater sense of tragedy than tediously recounting these events. The *Iliad* is not about the Trojan War. It is about the fatal effects of *hubris* (foolish pride).

Fourth, Homer was a master of suspense—an impressive distinction for a poet whose subject matter consisted of well-known stories. Homer's technique for maintaining suspense consisted of disclosing his overall narrative plan in increments, each increment shedding only a little more light. While revealing the general direction and ultimate goal of the action—in the *Iliad*, enough to convey the sense of impending calamity that lies at the heart of tragedy—he left the precise route in darkness.

Fifth, Homer's descriptions were vivid. John A. Scott notes: "The greatness of Homer consists in this, that he saw things and people exactly as they are and could describe all these in such clear and simple language that we can see them too. This is the reason that a child can comprehend him, and that the wisest man knows that the greatness of Homer, with its simplicity, lies just beyond his grasp."

Sixth, Homer displayed great humanity. Even hard-bitten scholars sometimes cannot keep their voices from breaking when reading Homer's account of Hector's farewell to his wife and child before going away to die in battle. Similarly, Odysseus's tearful reunion with his faithful wife Penelope, after a twenty-year absence (ten fighting the Trojans and ten attempting to return), is touching, especially in light of the misogyny that characterized much of Greek culture. A deeply devoted family man, Odysseus declares: "The best thing in the world is a strong house held in serenity where man and wife agree." Rather than simply noting the death of a warrior, Homer states: "And no longer would the children call him 'poppa' as they sat before his knees." Rather than make the Greek hero Diomedes say, "Ill-fated are those who oppose my strength," Homer has him say, "Ill-fated are those whose sons oppose my strength." Those (like Thomas Paine) who conclude that Homer was a warmonger have not read him carefully. Homer was neither a warmonger nor a pacifist. He treasured the noble qualities of the warrior (courage, fortitude, ingenuity, and self-discipline), but was equally aware of the terrible grief that war brought. To Homer, one man's glory was another's sorrow, and he felt the sorrow as deeply as the glory.

Seventh, Homer displayed an intense curiosity and an infectious love of life. Odysseus was the personification of Homer's curiosity about humans and their creations. Indeed, Odysseus's curiosity constantly led him and his men to grief, as when he stayed in the Cyclops's cave in order to see what kind of creature lived in such a place. Life could be enjoyed only by facing up to its many dangers. Given the choice between a long and obscure life and a short and glorious one, Achilles made the Greek choice. When facing execution, Socrates later used Achilles as an example of why he could not change his ways in order to avoid death.

HOMER'S LASTING INFLUENCE

Just as the Scriptures united the Hebrews, Homer's epics united the Greeks, answering questions about the gods and settling disputes concerning ethics. Despite their quarrels and wars, the Greeks knew that they were bound together by their love and reverence for Homer. Homer was the centerpiece of Greek education, nourishing the imaginations of Greek poets, dramatists, historians, philosophers, sculptors, politicians, and ordinary people for generations. No Greek who lived after Homer could escape his influence, so deeply were his poems imbedded in Greek culture. Hence, Homer played at least an indirect role in all of the great achievements of classical Greece. When Plato reached dizzying heights of eloquence, it was because he strove unceasingly to equal Homer.

Homer's plots, themes, and dialogue profoundly influenced the development of Greek drama. Aeschylus, one of the greatest of the Greek tragedians, called his own plays "crumbs from the great table of Homer." Aeschylus's *Persians* (472 B.C.), a dramatic account of the Greek victory in the Persian Wars, was thoroughly Homeric, attributing the outcome of the wars to Persian hubris. Yet, like Homer, Aeschylus depicted the horror of war even in victory. Also in imitation of Homer, Aeschylus and the other dramatists often utilized their audience's knowledge of Greek myths to great emotional effect, developing a tragic contrast between the audience's knowledge of the characters' impending doom and the characters' blithe ignorance of their own fates.

Homer is called the "Founder of Western Literature" not merely because he was its first and greatest author, but also because he exerted a

direct influence on nearly every great literary figure that followed. The
Roman poet Virgil's brilliant *Aeneid* was a self-professed attempt to rival
the blind bard of Chios. Geoffrey Chaucer claimed that Homer was "high
on a pillar" among poets. Michelangelo exulted: "Whenever I read
Homer, I look at myself to see if I am not twenty feet high." John Milton
praised Homer in *Paradise Regained*. John Dryden argued: "[Virgil and
others] are only so far true heroic poets as they have built upon the foundations of Homer." Alexander Pope contended regarding Homer: "No
man of a true poetical spirit is master of himself while he reads him. . . .
Be Homer's words your study and delight. / Read them by day and
meditate by night. / Thence your judgments, thence your maxims bring,
/ and trace the Muses upward to their spring." Samuel Johnson declared:
"Nation after nation, and century after century, has been able to do little
more than transpose Homer's incidents, new-name his characters, and
paraphrase his sentiments." Thomas Jefferson exulted: "I thank on my
knees Him who directed my early education for having put into my possession this rich source of delight; and I would not exchange it for anything which I could then have acquired, and have not since acquired."
He called Homer "the first of poets, as he must ever remain until a language equally ductile and copious shall again be spoken." Jefferson
added: "When young any composition pleases which unites a little
sense, some imagination, and some rhythm, in doses however small. But
as we advance in life these things fall off one by one, and I suspect that
we are left at last with only Homer and Virgil, and perhaps with Homer
alone." Johann Wolfgang von Goethe, Alfred Lord Tennyson, John Keats,
Henry David Thoreau, Oliver Wendell Holmes, Matthew Arnold, Eliza-
beth Barrett Browning, and Gilbert K. Chesterton all issued similar testi-
monials to Homer's power. Samuel Coleridge wrote of the *Odyssey:*
"Strongly it bears us along in swelling and limitless billows, nothing before and nothing behind us but the sky and the ocean." Ralph Waldo
Emerson noted: "Every novel is a debtor to Homer. . . . That wit and joy
might find a tongue and earth grow civil, Homer sung." Even Walter
Bagehot, a noted English economist, claimed: "A man who has not read
Homer is like a man who has never seen the ocean. There is a vast and
famous object of which he has no idea." Finally, E. K. Rand concluded:
"Just how many years ago Homer lived . . . nobody can tell us. That he
will live forever is a certainty."

When Emerson wrote that every novel was a debtor to Homer, he
meant that there have been no new plots since Homer. The universals of
the human condition have remained the same; only the particulars have
changed. Indeed, there is a remarkable similarity between the *Odyssey*
and the original *Star Trek* television series. In both cases, a captain leads
his ship and men through numerous adventures and hazards, all the

while encountering strange and alien creatures. The captain is intelligent but extremely vain and too curious by half, and his curiosity frequently leads to the deaths of his followers, who are expendable characters. In Homer a sense of wonder is provided by a mythic past, in *Star Trek* by a mythic future. Thus does Homer continue to influence popular culture, even a modern culture he would not have understood.

Dessiné d'après un Hermès, trouvé à Tivoli, et Gravé par Ambroise Tardieu.

2

Thales: Founder of
Western Science

It was Thales of Miletus who began the quest to discover the natural causes that regulate the physical universe. Though he and his Greek successors made some mistakes, they advanced scientific knowledge far beyond what could have been expected, considering the primitive state of the technology at their disposal. Even when their theories proved invalid, the Greeks identified and clearly stated for later scientists many of the fundamental problems of science, such issues as the constituents of matter, the nature of change, the movement of the planets, reproduction, and heredity. More importantly, they developed the scientific outlook and the scientific method that have enabled modern scientists to alter human existence radically.

THE ACHIEVEMENT OF THALES

Thales (625–546 B.C.) has often been called the "Father of Philosophy." *Philosophia* is a Greek word meaning "love of wisdom." Greek philosophers were not merely what we call philosophers today (those who study metaphysics, ethics, logic, epistemology, and so on), but also scientists, political theorists, and sometimes even poets. No branch of knowledge was excluded from consideration. The concept of specialization was alien to the Greeks, though this was partly due to the fact that there was much less to learn in each field than there is today. Greek philosophers were the original "Renaissance men." (Indeed, Renaissance figures later modeled themselves on the Greeks and Romans.) Greece stood in sharp contrast to the Near East, where science was the exclusive province of a powerful class of priests who had inherited their positions and whose economic and ideological reliance on their religion and its dogmas invariably hindered inquiry. By contrast, Greek scientists were laymen, to whom science was an avocation—men who could think and act independently, and who considered all questions open to debate.

It was no accident that Miletus, the leading center of trade in Ionia, was also the birthplace of philosophy. The Greeks of Miletus traded with the Phoenicians, the Lydians, and Miletus's own colonies in the Mediterranean and Black Seas, which numbered about seventy. Interaction with other cultures probably encouraged a willingness to depart from conventional patterns of thought.

Thales was the first to emphasize the role of physical laws in the operation of the universe. Though most Greeks never shared this emphasis, and even Thales believed in omnipotent and immortal gods, such an emphasis proved essential to the progress of science. According to legend, Thales collected sufficient astronomical knowledge to predict a total solar eclipse during the year 585 B.C., to determine the solstices, and to divide the year into 365 days. He knew enough geometry to calculate both the distance of a ship at sea and the height of an object by its shadow. He made the famous statements, "Know thyself," "Virtue is refraining from doing what we blame in others," and "The whole world is the native country of a wise man."

One story about Thales alleges that he was looking up so intently at the sky one day that he fell into a well (the beginning of the eccentric professor stereotype), but Aristotle relates a more plausible tale concerning the ancient scientist. According to Aristotle, Thales once decided to teach a lesson to his fellow citizens, who criticized him for wasting time on idle pursuits like science. Using his knowledge to predict a bumper olive crop, Thales quietly bought all of the olive presses in Miletus and in several neighboring city-states. Since everyone who needed a press to make olive oil had to come to Thales, he earned a fortune. Thales had made his point: A true philosopher could make money if he considered it worth the effort.

Like all other scientists, ancient and modern, Thales was not immune from error. Thales' greatest mistake was his contention that the earth was composed of water, on which the land floated. Although the Egyptians had advanced the same theory, they had based it on religious beliefs. By contrast, Thales based his theory on logic, however faulty: water was a special substance because it existed in all three states, because it was peculiarly abundant, and because it was vital to all organisms; therefore, it must be the primary element. The foundation for Thales' error was the belief in a simple universe that only seemed complex, a belief shared by most Greek philosophers.

THALES' GREEK SUCCESSORS

Anaximander (c. 611–547 B.C.)

Thales' student Anaximander wrote *About Nature*, the first work of prose in Western history. Anaximander was one of the first to draft a map and to construct a globe. He claimed that the earth was one of numerous worlds suspended in space. Anaximander computed the size of the Sun and its distance from the earth with only slight error. He contended that thunder and lightning were caused by blasts of wind, not by Zeus's thunderbolts. Anaximander originated the concept of evolution, suggesting that all living creatures had come from the water as it had been evaporated by the Sun and that humans had evolved from fish. Anaximander formulated the theory after observing the mammalian characteristics of some sea creatures.

Pythagoras (c. 582–500 B.C.)

Around 530 B.C., Pythagoras, the son of a gem-engraver in Samos, moved to Croton, a colony in southeastern Italy, in order to escape the tyranny of the dictator Polycrates. (The historian Herodotus once wrote of Polycrates: "He robbed all men indiscriminately, for he said that his friends were more grateful if he gave them their property back than they would have been if he had never taken it.") It was Pythagoras who first coined the term "philosopher." He believed that the universe operated largely according to mathematical laws. His response to those like Heraclitus who claimed that the world was in constant flux was to declare that mathematics was eternal, perfect, and incorruptible. Beneath the apparent complexity and chaotic flux of the universe lay a foundation of simplicity and immutable order. Pythagoras and his followers exerted a tremendous influence on Plato and, through him, on Western philosophy in general. Their emphasis on number as the informing principle of the universe proved crucial to the development of science.

The Pythagoreans' astronomical theory was neither geocentric (earth centered) nor heliocentric (sun centered). They held that a ball of fire that they called Hestia (the name of the goddess of the hearth) occupied the center of the universe, around which the earth, the Moon, the five observable planets, the Sun, and the stars circled. They added that there was a "counter-Earth" beneath our Earth—or, in some accounts, on the other side of the Sun—and that the movement of the heavenly bodies formed a harmony, an "actual music of the spheres," which, to human ears, accustomed to it from birth, was silence. While this was not a heliocentric theory, it was revolutionary in removing the earth from the center of the universe.

The Pythagoreans were among the first to *prove* that the sum of the squares of the legs of a right triangle equals the square of the hypotenuse—the so-called Pythagorean theorem, a theorem previously employed by the Babylonians. They were also the first to prove mathematically that the pitch of a stringed instrument equals the length of the string, thereby demonstrating that even music was guided by mathematical laws.

Xenophanes (late sixth and early fifth century B.C.)

Like his teacher Pythagoras, Xenophanes of Colophon left Ionia for southern Italy. A poet as well as a philosopher, Xenophanes is often called the "Father of Geology and Paleontology," because he was the first to formulate a theory of extensive geological change. Xenophanes based the theory on the existence of seashells in the mountains of Malta and the imprint of seaweed and fish in the stone quarries of Syracuse. He also claimed that clouds were created by water vapor carried up into the air.

Xenophanes held that even in religious matters, rational investigation was more reliable than revelation: "The gods have not revealed to humankind all things from the beginning; it is by seeking that humans eventually discover what is better." Xenophanes doubted that the gods resembled humans: "Man made gods and furnished them with his own body, voice, and garments. . . . If horses and lions had hands . . . they would make portraits and statues of their gods in their own image. . . . The Ethiopians say that their gods are dark-skinned and snub-nosed, while the Thracians claim theirs to be blue-eyed and red-haired." Xenophanes accepted the Greek gods as lesser deities but also envisioned: "One great God, both among the gods and among men, neither similar in shape nor in mind to mortals. . . . He sees all, and knows all, and hears all, and moves everyone away from troubles. He remains the same forever, being changed by nothing, for it is not fitting that he change now one way, now another." Xenophanes complained: "Homer and Hesiod have attributed to the gods all kinds of things which are considered disgraceful and a cause of censure to humankind, namely theft, adultery, and deceiving one another. . . . We commend the man . . . who seeks virtue and does not harangue us with the ancient myths of noisy wars of Titans, Giants, [and] Centaurs. These things are worth nothing."

Empedocles (fifth century B.C.)

A poet, statesman, orator, tragedian, magician, and physician, Empedocles of Acragas in Sicily not only reiterated Anaximander's theory of evolution, but also proposed an early form of the theory of natural selection to explain its operation. He argued that chance alone determined the physical attributes of different species and that their adaptability determined whether they survived or became extinct.

Leucippus and Democritus (fifth century B.C.)

In opposition to Empedocles' hypothesis that the four basic elements of the universe were earth, air, fire, and water, Leucippus of Miletus first proposed the atomic theory, a theory further developed by his student Democritus of Abdera shortly thereafter. The theory claimed that all matter consisted of minute, indivisible, indestructible *atoms* (the very word means "indivisible"), which differed in shape, size, and weight, but not in quality. Different arrangements of these opposed but interlocking atoms produced different substances. An infinite number of atoms were dispersed throughout an infinite universe. The creation of worlds was caused by the collision and aggregation of falling and swerving atoms in space. Leucippus and Democritus also argued that the universe, which was composed of matter and void alone, operated entirely according to natural laws. Leucippus was famed for his powers of perception. According to one legend, he once greeted a maidservant with "Greetings, maiden." The next day he greeted her with "Greetings, woman"—evidently perceiving that she had been seduced during the night. He also wrote treatises on poetry, music, agriculture, painting, and "fighting in armor."

Anaxagoras (fifth century B.C.)

Around 480 B.C., Anaxagoras of Clazomenae moved to Athens, where he became a teacher to Pericles, Euripides, and probably Socrates as well. Anaxagoras asserted that the Sun was not the god Hyperion, but only a mass of white-hot metal "larger than the Peloponnesus," a theory that he formulated after a meteorite landed at Aegospotami near the Turkish Straits in 468 or 467 B.C. He added that the stars were also hot stones, like the Sun, but were too far away for the earth to feel their heat. The Moon was made from the same material as the earth, and its light was a reflection of sunlight. He even suggested that there were dwellings on the Moon, as well as hills and ravines. There were other worlds, populated by other civilizations. Winds were caused by the rarefaction of the air by the Sun.

Hippocrates (fifth century B.C.)

Hippocrates of Cos is called the "Father of Medicine" for three reasons. He was the first to claim that all illnesses resulted from natural causes. Either Hippocrates himself or one of his students wrote concerning the supposedly supernatural illness of epilepsy: "It seems to me that this disease is no more divine than any other. It has a natural cause just as other diseases have. Men think it supernatural because they do not understand it. But if they called everything which they do not understand supernatural, why, there would be no end of such things!" The author added that an epileptic goat, when dissected, was found to be "full of fluid and foul-smelling, convincing proof that the disease and not the deity is harming the body." Although the Hippocratics did not doubt that the gods were the ultimate cause of all things, they believed that the gods worked through natural causes, rather than through direct intervention in the world. A Hippocratic physician wrote: "Each illness has a nature and a power of its own, and none is so invulnerable that it is beyond medical treatment." The physician then railed against those who sold magical cures.

Second, Hippocrates and his followers emphasized the importance of testing medical theories. It was fine for those who studied the impenetrable mysteries of the heavens and the inner earth to rely on mere hypothesis, but medicine was a "craft" and had to be based on empirical data. The Hippocratics opposed the simplistic assertion of a single cause for all illnesses (e.g., heat, cold, dryness, or moisture). They were careful to record their patients' symptoms and responses to each treatment. The degree of detail found in their case histories remained unequaled until the sixteenth century. Their *Airs, Waters, and Places* laid the foundation of epidemiology (the study of disease) by examining the impact of climate on health. They also studied anatomy, physiology, gynecology, pathology, and surgery. They practiced preventative medicine by encouraging a healthy diet and lifestyle.

Third, the Hippocratic school drafted a famous oath for physicians, in which each promised to respect (and, if necessary, lend money to) his teacher, to share his knowledge and skills with others who had taken the oath, to put his patients' health above all other concerns, including his own life (e.g., in the case of contagious diseases), and to preserve doctor-patient confidentiality. Physicians also swore not to give drugs to women in order to induce abortion, not to assist anyone in committing suicide, and not to use their positions to seduce patients, members of their families, or their servants. A modern version of the Hippocratic Oath is still administered to doctors in many countries.

Though Hippocrates was the son of a priest of Asclepius, the god of healing, his teacher Democritus exerted a greater influence on him, as manifested in Hippocrates' rejection of supernatural explanations for disease. The Hippocratics published fifty-eight works on medicine.

Modern historians have criticized Hippocrates and his followers for their errors. The most serious mistake of the Hippocratics was their disastrous theory of the four body humors. According to this theory, the body was composed of four liquids (blood, phlegm, black bile, and yellow bile) that were perfectly balanced. Illness was the product of an imbalance between the liquids. Followers of Hippocrates (Hippocratic oafs?) interpreted the theory to support leeching. Since sick patients possessed too much blood, they should be drained in order to restore the balance of humors. But no one is infallible, and the physician Galen later captured the spirit of Hippocrates when he wrote: "There was but one sentiment in his soul, and that was the love of doing good, and in the course of his long life, but a single act, and that was the relieving of the sick."

Herophilus (c. 335–280 B.C.)

By dissecting the bodies of criminals provided by the Hellenistic kings of Egypt (some sources allege that the criminals were still alive at the time), Herophilus, the "Father of Anatomy," learned that the brain was the center of the nervous system and that the arteries carried blood rather than air, as was generally believed. He was the first to measure the pulse and to attribute it to the pumping of the heart, correcting the popular idea that it was an innate faculty of the arteries. He also expanded knowledge of the structure and function of the eye, the duodenum, and the reproductive organs.

Erasistratus (c. 304–250 B.C.)

Herophilus's colleague Erasistratus of Ceos, the "Father of Physiology," distinguished sensory from motor nerves, expanded knowledge of the digestive system, and outlined the roles of the four major heart valves. Both Herophilus and Erasistratus challenged the predominant view that the heart was the seat of intelligence, rather than the brain, but failed to displace that dogma.

Euclid (late fourth, early third century B.C.)

Around 300 B.C., Euclid of Alexandria published the *Elements*, one of the most important books ever written because it systematized the theorems of plane and solid geometry, putting into irrefutable form propositions only loosely proved by his predecessors. Euclid also wrote treatises on astronomy, optics, and musical theory.

Aristarchus (c. 310–250 B.C.)

Aristarchus of Samos created a valid method for estimating the distances of the Sun and Moon from the earth; only inadequate mathematics and instruments prevented success in this endeavor. More significantly, Aristarchus espoused the heliocentric theory, the theory that the earth rotated on its axis once per day and revolved around the Sun once per year. He also correctly explained the absence of parallax, the lack of variation in the relative positions of the stars when observed from different points on the earth's surface, by hypothesizing that the stars were situated at extreme distances from the earth.

Archimedes (287–212 B.C.)

Archimedes, who had studied at Alexandria but lived in Syracuse, was the first to write a detailed work on electrical discharges in the atmosphere. He also calculated the value of pi, the ratio of a circle's circumference to its diameter, with greater accuracy, invented a terminology for expressing numbers up to any magnitude, and laid the foundations for integral calculus. He gave rigorous deductive proofs of the principles behind leverage, boasting, "Give me a place to stand, and I will move the earth." He proved that the volume of a sphere is two-thirds that of the cylinder that circumscribes it. A classic absent-minded professor, he often forgot to bathe. When dragged to the public baths, bathed, and oiled by friends, he drew geometric figures on his arms with the oil. When Archimedes discovered the law of hydrostatics (which explains flotation), by noticing the water he displaced in the public bath, he ran naked through the streets shouting, "I have found it!" Archimedes also invented the compound pulley, the windlass, and the hydraulic screw for raising water.

When the Romans attacked Syracuse, Archimedes unleashed a terrifying array of gadgets on them. Catapults hurled stones weighing ten talents (830 pounds) at the Romans, crushing their battering rams. Grappling poles, connected to levers and pulleys and thrust from the city walls, seized some of their ships and turned them upside down or dashed them against the cliffs. Meanwhile, beams extending over the city walls dropped boulders or lumps of lead on Roman siege engines mounted on boats, while small catapults discharged iron darts at the sailors from close range. Grappling hooks, let down from cranes, lifted Roman soldiers up high and dashed them to the ground, killing them. The Romans grew so terrified they believed that the gods were fighting against them. They soon bolted at the sight of a simple rope or beam protruding from the walls. One legend, perhaps apocryphal, claims that Archimedes even formed a giant piece of polished glass into the first laser gun in history, using it to concentrate reflected sunlight at the Roman fleet, thereby burning many ships. Nevertheless, despite the damage inflicted by Archimedes on Roman ships during the daytime, the Romans returned to capture Syracuse at night. A Roman soldier killed Archimedes when he failed to respond to a shout as he contemplated a diagram in the sand. Archimedes was so engrossed in his calculations he did not even realize that the city was under attack.

Eratosthenes (c. 276–196 B.C.)

Director of the famous Library at Alexandria and tutor to Ptolemy IV Philopator, the Hellenistic king of Egypt, Eratosthenes of Cyrene has been called the "Father of Geography." He published *Geographica,* which contained a great map of "the inhabited world" (Europe, the Near East, and India), a work motivated by Alexander the Great's conquests. The map was the first to contain parallel lines of latitude and longitude. Eratosthenes was the first to suggest that sailors could reach India from Europe by sailing west. He was wrong only because the Americas lay between Europe and India, as Christopher Columbus later discovered. Eratosthenes also calculated the circumference of the globe with an error of less than 1 percent. Having noted that the noonday Sun on the day of the summer solstice completely illuminated a well at Syene (now called Aswan) and, hence, was directly overhead, the following year he dispatched an assistant to measure the angle of a shadow cast at Alexandria at precisely the same time. The angle was 7.2 degrees. Assuming that the earth was a perfect sphere, and knowing the exact distance between the two cities, he employed the rules of geometry to calculate the circumference of the globe. The slight error was due to the fact that the earth is not a perfect sphere. (The Greeks had long known that the earth was round due to the shape of its shadow on the Moon during a lunar eclipse.) An able astronomer, Eratosthenes also compiled a catalog of over one thousand stars that indicated the location and brightness of each.

Hipparchus (c. 190–120 B.C.)

Unfortunately, Aristarchus was unable to convince his colleagues of the validity of the heliocentric theory. The prevailing theory throughout the ancient and medieval periods was the geocentric theory that Hipparchus of Nicaea first introduced into scientific circles in an elaborate form. The geocentric theory held that the earth lay at the center of the universe and that the planets, the stars, and the Sun revolved around it. Hipparchus could make the theory conform to observation of the planets only by hypothesizing the existence of epicycles, smaller orbits within the planets' larger orbit around the earth. Not until the sixteenth century would Nicolaus Copernicus revive the heliocentric theory after reading about Aristarchus at the University of Padua.

Nevertheless, Hipparchus improved astronomical observation techniques through the astrolabe, a device for measuring the positions of heavenly bodies, whose reinvention in the seventeenth century allowed large-scale European exploration of the rest of the world. In addition, Hipparchus compiled a sizable star catalog, measured the lunar month and solar year with remarkable accuracy (erring by only six and a half minutes on the solar year), discovered the progression of the equinoxes, and tried to establish an international commission for the observation of a lunar eclipse throughout the Mediterranean world in order to determine longitudes. Finally, he was most responsible for the development of trigonometry.

Strabo (c. 63 B.C.–A.D. 24)

Strabo of Pontus in northern Asia Minor compiled a new map of the known world based on his own extensive travels. His was the first map to reflect the importance of projection, the distortions that occur when one attempts to reproduce a round surface onto a flat surface.

Dioscorides (c. 40–90)

An army surgeon, Pedanius Dioscorides compiled a list of drugs and the plants from which they were made. His work *On Medical Matters* was the first authoritative text on botany and pharmacology.

Claudius Ptolemy (c. 100–170)

Claudius Ptolemy of Alexandria attempted to chart the heavens and the earth. His map of the Roman world was extremely accurate and well projected, employing lines of latitude and longitude. Nevertheless, his underestimation of the size of the planet and overestimation of the size of Asia later led Columbus to believe that he could reach India in only six weeks by traveling westward across the Atlantic Ocean. Even more famous among Ptolemy's errors was his support for the geocentric theory, a theory that became the basis of medieval astronomy.

These mistakes aside, Ptolemy contributed much to ancient mathematics and science. He improved trigonometry. He constructed astrolabes and sundials. His *Optics* explored the refraction and reflection of light.

Galen (c. 129–199)

Galen of Pergamum rose from humble beginnings to become the physician for a school of gladiators and, later, for the Roman emperor Commodus. Galen explained the mechanism of respiration, demonstrated that veins and arteries carried blood, showed that an excised heart would continue to beat outside the body, and proved that injuries to one side of the brain produced disorders in the opposite side of the body. He noted the functions of the bladder and the kidney and identified seven pairs of cranial nerves. He demonstrated that the brain controls the voice and described the heart valves. He dissected goats, pigs, and monkeys to learn how different muscles were controlled at different levels of the spinal cord. Galen was also one of the few ancient physicians to note the influence of the mind on the body.

Unfortunately, Galen's biological and medical encyclopedia helped enshrine the Hippocratic doctrine of the four body humors. Hence, Galen recommended the use of leeches, in some instances, to drain "excess blood." Ironically, modern historians of medicine believe that Galen's recommendation may actually have cured some Romans. Since the Roman diet was iron-poor, the withdrawal of moderate amounts of blood may have starved some disease-causing bacteria without killing the patient. Other patients, especially in the Middle Ages, when Galen's encyclopedia became the standard medical authority and leeching was carried to extremes, were not so fortunate.

It is a tragic irony that the astronomical and medical theories of Ptolemy and Galen, theories their formulators intended only as a basis for further investigation, were later used to stifle it. As the historian A. R. Burn once put it: "It was not the fault of these two great observers and thinkers that later centuries chose them to represent ancient and unquestionable authority. If their work had not existed, something, probably less good, would have been found."

THE INFLUENCE OF THE GREEKS ON MODERN SCIENCE

It is no accident that modern science began during the Renaissance, when Greek manuscripts became widely available in western Europe for the first time in the many centuries since the fall of the Roman Empire. With a few notable exceptions, including Copernicus's rediscovery of the heliocentric theory of Aristarchus, what modern scientists learned from their Greek predecessors was not so much scientific fact as the scientific outlook and the scientific method. They derived from the Greeks a confidence in the human ability to decipher the physical laws that governed the universe, as well as a willingness to formulate, debate, and test unorthodox theories. These traits, when combined with the modern willingness to use science to produce technology, have allowed modern scientists to extend, improve, and, to the dismay of some, complicate human life within a remarkably brief period of history.

3

Themistocles: Defender of Greek Civilization

Themistocles, the leader of democratic Athens during the Persian Wars, saved Greek civilization by thwarting the Persian invasion of Greece. It was Themistocles who convinced the Athenians to use the silver produced by the mines of Laurium to construct the Athenian fleet that defeated the Persians at the crucial Battle of Salamis. It was also Themistocles who organized the city-states in defense of Greece. Finally, it was Themistocles' cunning ploy that forced the Greeks to stand and fight at Salamis, where the narrowness of the strait helped produce a Greek victory. The Persian Wars decided the fate of Western civilization. Had the Persians been able to incorporate the Greek poleis into their vast empire, they might have crushed the spirit of the Greeks. The achievements of classical Greece would not have survived to form the basis of Western culture. Furthermore, the Greeks' miraculous victory over the Persians filled them with a supreme confidence that further unleashed their genius.

BACKGROUND: SPARTA AND ATHENS

Sparta

During the Archaic period, Sparta and Athens developed the distinct political and social institutions that made them the two superpowers of Greece. Sparta was situated in Laconia (or Lacedaemon), the southeastern portion of the Peloponnesus, the peninsula of southern Greece. Watered by the Eurotas River, Laconia consists of some of the most fertile land in Europe—in sharp contrast to the poor soil of most of the rest of Greece.

It appears (though this remains shadowy) that some time in the tenth or ninth century B.C. the Spartans conquered a neighboring polis called Helos and enslaved its population. Though the Spartans did allow some of the conquered peoples, whom they called *perioikoi* (those dwelling around), local self-government and freedom from forced labor, they reduced the majority, called *helots*, to serfdom. The perioikoi produced war materials and other items for the Spartans and sometimes even served as reserves in the Spartan army. The Spartans paid for the supplies and allowed the perioikoi to sell surplus goods to other poleis. In a sense, the perioikoi lived more comfortably than Spartan citizens, who were not allowed to trade with other poleis. By contrast, the helots, though allowed to keep half of their crops, were owned by the state; some worked directly for the state but most were assigned to the land of an individual Spartan and could not depart from it. Even those allotted to individual Spartans could be conscripted by the state at any time and could be freed only by the state.

In the late eighth century B.C., when the Spartans faced overpopulation like the rest of Greece, they decided to solve the problem by conquering fertile Messenia to the west, rather than by colonizing distant shores of the Black and Mediterranean Seas, as many other city-states were doing. (The Spartans established only one colony, at Taras, on the southern tip of Italy.) The Spartans invaded Messenia, annexed its territory, and added its citizens to the helot population. The annexation of all of one polis's territory by another was rare in Greece, not only because the Greeks valued the smallness of their poleis, but also because such a policy would require a standing army. Indeed, the significance of the Spartans' military expansionism is that it left them a small minority in their own country, rulers over a vast population of oppressed helots. Thus, Sparta could not hope to develop along the same lines as the other Greek poleis. The constant need to suppress the helot population necessitated the development of rigid social discipline and a military state.

The implications of the Spartan policy of conquest became apparent only after the Messenian revolt of the mid-seventh century B.C. In this bloody rebellion, the Messenians, with the aid of Arcadia, almost gained their independence and nearly annihilated the Spartans in the process. It was during this period that the Spartan poet Tyrtaeus wrote these stirring lines:

> For a good man to die falling beside the front-line fighters, in defense of his country, is a noble thing. . . . Since a wanderer receives no recognition, neither honor nor respect nor mercy, let us fight with all our might for this land, and die for our children. . . . Flee not, leaving behind, fallen on the ground, the elders whose knees are no longer nimble. For it is a disgrace when an older man, his hair already white and gray of beard, falls in the front line and lies before a younger man. . . . So let every man bite his lip and, with both feet firmly on the ground, take his place for battle.

Having finally suppressed the bloody rebellion of the Messenians, the Spartans, now acutely aware that they comprised but a small minority in their own country, decided that they must change their society into a disciplined military machine or be enslaved by their own helots. At the height of Spartan power, a mere 9,000 Spartan citizens ruled nearly 100,000 helots.

Spartan legend claimed that a lawgiver named Lycurgus had introduced the unique Spartan political and social systems around 750 B.C., based on the institutions that then prevailed in Crete. Lycurgus had then made the Spartans take a solemn oath not to make any change in his constitution until he returned from a voyage to Delphi, and then purposely starved himself to death there and even had his ashes scattered in the sea, so that he could never return to Sparta in any form. The truth is that the Spartans established their distinctive institutions in the late seventh century B.C. in the wake of the Messenian revolt, and Lycurgus is almost certainly a mythical figure.

Though complex, the Spartan political system was largely a gerontocracy, an oligarchy ruled by a council of elders. The Gerousia, an assembly of Sparta's two kings and twenty-eight elders, the latter elected by the popular assembly from aristocratic families, possessed much of the city's legislative and some of its judicial and executive power. Members of the Gerousia held lifetime terms.

Sparta's dual monarchy, controlled by two families reputedly descended from the demigod Heracles, was designed to prevent dictatorial rule and to allow one king to stay at home and preside over religious rituals while the other waged war. Rivalry between the two kings generally prevented them from effectively checking the Gerousia.

The Spartans also possessed a popular assembly, the Apella, which consisted of all citizens aged thirty and over. But the Apella was the laughingstock of Greece. It decided only those few matters presented to it by the Gerousia and could not even debate these issues. Voting in the assembly was accomplished by banging on one's shield, with the louder side winning. A group of officials shut up in a nearby shed had to decide which clamor was louder.

Each year, five *ephors* (overseers) were chosen by a procedure akin to the lot. The ephors' job was to spy on the kings, each of whom was required to have an ephor at his side at all times, to initiate legislation in the Gerousia, to execute some of the laws passed by the Gerousia and Apella, to negotiate with foreign governments, to call up the army and decide who would march, to disburse government funds, to serve as moral censors, and to judge civil suits and (with the Gerousia) criminal trials. They could fine or arrest kings, pending trial. Each year the ephors issued an official declaration of war against the helots, which served as the legal basis for the execution of any troublemaker among them. Each month the kings took an oath not to exceed their authority, and the ephors took an oath not to overturn the monarchy. But the provision that ephors could not serve again after their single year in office greatly undermined their power.

Sparta was famed more for its unique social system than for its system of government. When a Spartan child was born, the ephors inspected him for signs of illness. If the child was weak or deformed in any way, he was hurled from the top of Mount Taygetus, a crude form of genetic engineering.

At seven, Spartan girls began athletic training, scandalizing most Greeks by running about in revealing skirts. The girls' training, which included running, wrestling, and hurling the discus and javelin, was considered unusually rigorous. The Spartans hoped to make their women physically fit so that they might better endure childbirth and produce healthier babies. First and foremost, girls were trained to be the mothers of warriors. On special occasions, standing nude before dignitaries, they sang songs in praise or ridicule of specific boys (also nude), as a powerful incentive to the latter's good conduct.

So successful was the girls' indoctrination that Spartan mothers became notorious for their patriotism and martial ardor. When a Spartan woman asked about a battle and was informed that all five of her sons had been killed, she replied testily, "That isn't what I asked you, vile slave, but rather how our country was doing." Spartan mothers told their sons departing for battle: "Come back with your shield—or on it!"

At the age of seven, boys were taken from their mothers and trained at a boot camp. The "herds" of boys were taught to read (but "no more than was necessary"), count, sing patriotic songs, and recite Homer. They were not taught lyric poetry or philosophy because such subjects "softened men." The carefully selected superintendent of the camp maintained a strict discipline with the aid of brutal older boys. The young boys were taught to steal most of their food from gardens and mess halls, as training in endurance and stealth; they were beaten if caught. They walked barefooted, received only one cloak per year, bathed only a few days per year, and slept on beds of reed. They were trained in running, swimming, and dancing (for dexterity). Spartan athletic training was so rigorous the Spartans generally won the most prizes at the Olympic Games. The boys marched silently in a mass, keeping their hands in their cloaks, their eyes fixed on the ground before them. They were encouraged to play a savage game of "king of the mountain," a game in which the "king," a boy at the top of a hill, must maintain his position by fighting off all challengers and preserve his "reign" at all costs.

At twenty, Spartan males went into concealment—the *krypteia*, from the same root as "crypt," "cryptic," and "cryptography"—with nothing but a dagger. Only at night could they leave their hiding places to secure provisions and to kill any helots who were out after curfew.

At twenty-one, Spartan males joined a *synousia*, an "association" or brotherhood of fifteen men in the army. Each male had to be accepted unanimously by the brotherhood. Since a rejection meant social death, this rule served as a powerful incentive for Spartan boys to display courage, reverence, and obedience daily. Few ever had to be rejected. The soldiers of the brotherhood spent all of their time together, eating in a common mess hall, and sleeping in a common barracks. Because Spartan men were professional soldiers, they were forbidden to perform manual labor of any kind. Helots furnished by the polis farmed their land, part of which was provided by the state, part by inheritance. Soldiers contributed grain from their farms to their own mess hall. To fail to do so, or to reject training, meant the loss of citizenship. Soldiers were not allowed to carry torches after dark, so that they might learn to travel fearlessly at night. Each year the 300 best warriors were chosen to fight beside the king. Anyone who was not selected could challenge one of the 300 to a fight for his position. Those who behaved cowardly in battle were deprived of citizenship and were made to wear cloaks with colored patches and to shave only one cheek as badges of their dishonor. When one Spartan soldier ran from battle, his grandmother killed him. Even the Spartans' statues of the gods depicted them armed.

At thirty, Spartan males became full citizens and joined the popular assembly. Between this time and age forty-five, they were expected to marry. They generally married women approximately eighteen years of age, in contrast to most other Greek men, who married girls soon after they reached puberty. Those males who failed to marry by forty-five were fined and ordered to walk naked through the marketplace on a certain winter day every year, singing a song about how their shame was justified since they had disobeyed the law. For their failure to provide little warriors for the state, such men were also deprived of the respect normally accorded to elders. Even Dercyllidas, one of the best Spartan generals, was denied his rightful seat at a social gathering by a young man. The young man explained, "You have not fathered a son who will offer his seat to me." Marriage was effected by forcibly carrying off the bride (more training in warrior skills). Once married, Spartan males continued to live in the barracks with their brethren and were technically forbidden to visit their wives, though, in actuality, they were expected to do so. It was understood that the husband would periodically sneak away to his wife, in the dead of night, all the while trying not to get caught (more stealth training). Some men fathered children before ever seeing their wives in the daylight. Some Spartan males shared their wives with other "virtuous" men, with the blessing of the state. A Spartan husband would not think of denying his wife to another male, nor would the wife consider refusing such a request, if the suitor were an honorable man. The point was to produce more children, but without the passionate feuds that resulted from surreptitious sex. By institutionalizing adultery, the Spartans hoped to rob it of its power to destabilize society.

At forty-five, Spartan males could return to their wives and homes. There they lived for the rest of their lives.

At sixty, Spartan males could retire from military service if they wished. The elders of noble families became eligible for election to the Gerousia. Newly elected members of the Gerousia received the dubious privilege of a double mess of porridge when dining in public mess halls. They generally gave the extra serving to a friend or family member as a token of honor.

Sparta lost no opportunity to teach each generation its vital role in the survival of the polis. At festivals, a choir of old men sang, "We were once valiant young men," a choir of young men sang, "But we are the valiant now; put us to the test, if you wish," and a choir of boys sang, "But we shall be far mightier."

Like all other social systems, the Spartan system possessed distinct advantages and disadvantages. The deleterious effects of the system are obvious to the modern individualist. First, the Spartan fear of foreign ideas, a fear stemming from the need to preserve their unique system, hurt the Spartans intellectually and economically. Spartans were forbidden to trade and travel, lest foreigners corrupt them. Soldiers patrolled the polis's borders to discourage visitors. When a foreigner asked a Spartan how many Spartan citizens there were, he replied, "Enough, my friend, to keep out undesirables." The few invited visitors were escorted around by a guard and sometimes expelled without explanation. As a result, in sharp contrast to Athens, Sparta left posterity no art, even in the broadest sense of the term. Even Spartan history has come down to us from the Athenians, since the Spartans did not write history. When an Athenian politician criticized Sparta for its lack of education, a Spartan king replied proudly, "Your point is correct, since we are the only Greeks who have learned nothing wicked from you Athenians." While Athens possessed an intelligently controlled currency, accepted even by the primitive tribes of northern Europe, the Spartans used unwieldy iron bars for that purpose because they feared the seduction of wealth.

Second, the need to maintain discipline caused the Spartans to feed and clothe themselves miserably. The very word "spartan" has come to mean "bare" or "unadorned." After tasting the infamous black porridge of Sparta, a Sybarite who had the misfortune to be a guest at a public mess hall there, declared, "Now I understand why you Spartans do not fear death!" Spartan law decreed that the ceiling in every house be constructed using only an ax, and the doors with only a saw, the object being to encourage frugality in furniture and cutlery (who would adorn a shack with golden goblets and velvet chairs?). As a result of this practice, an astonished Spartan king who visited a lavish dining hall in Corinth asked his host if the timber there grew square. The Spartans were proud of their ability to survive on horrendous food and shabby clothing. One of their kings, Agesilaus II, claimed that the greatest benefit of the Spartan system was the "contempt for luxury" it inspired. When Agesilaus met outdoors with a Persian satrap (provincial governor) to negotiate peace, the satrap arrived with embroidered rugs and soft cushions to keep from soiling his splendid robes, while the Spartan king plopped himself down on the grass. The Spartans' pride in their frugality could sometimes be obnoxious. Once, when the Athenian philosopher Diogenes the Cynic saw Rhodians parading about in fine clothes at the Olympics, he scoffed, "Affectation!" But when he saw the Spartans parading about in their rags soon after, he declared, "More affectation!" Aristotle noted that while the Spartans' single-minded pursuit of courage had provided them with essential security, it had deprived them of "the ability to live in a way that has real value." By sacrificing personal freedom so completely to the considerations of security, they had defeated the whole purpose of security, which was to defend that degree of freedom necessary to self-fulfillment. By the very means with which they sought to avoid enslavement at the hands of foreigners, the Spartans had enslaved themselves.

Finally, the collectivized Spartan system left individual Spartans with personality deficiencies. The historian Plutarch, who admired the Spartans, compared them with bees because they were incapable of leading private lives, being "organic parts of their community, clinging together around their leader, forgetting themselves in their enthusiasm, and belonging wholly to their country." Spartans became notorious for their lack of humor. When a man asked a Spartan if he wished to hear him imitate a nightingale, the Spartan declined, saying, "I have heard the nightingale herself." The very word "laconic," derived from Laconia, became a synonym for "terse."

But the Spartan system possessed advantages as well. First, it encouraged a selflessness lacking in most individualistic societies. When an old man looking for a seat at the Olympics was jeered away by other Greeks, the Spartans rose up en masse, even the elders, to offer him a seat. The old man sighed, "All Greeks know what is right, but only the Spartans do it."

Second, the Spartans' lifelong discipline produced skilled, rugged, courageous, and patriotic soldiers. By 550 B.C., the Spartan army was the best in Greece. Combined with the Athenian navy, the Spartans later saved Greece from enslavement by the Persians. So strenuous was Spartan training that their soldiers considered war a vacation from its rigors. The Spartans were the only people who actually relaxed their discipline in wartime. Plutarch noted that Spartan troops marched to the sound of flutes in perfect order, with calm and confidence, neither fearful nor reckless, "as if some divine force had taken charge of them." When asked why Sparta had no walls, King Agesilaus II pointed to Spartan soldiers and said, "These are the Spartans' walls." King Agis remarked that Spartans did not ask how many the enemy were, only where they were located. A Spartan with a crippled leg

Chapter 3

refused to leave the army, saying, "What's needed to fight our foes is a man who stands his ground, not one who runs away." The Spartans became famous for their patriotism. When a foreigner tried to curry favor with King Theopompus by claiming that in his own polis he was called a "friend of Sparta," Theopompus replied sternly: "Stranger, it would be more honorable for you to be called a friend of your own city."

Finally, the Spartan system produced strong, independent women. As the mothers of warriors, Spartan women possessed a much higher status in society than Athenian women. In Sparta, only women who died in childbirth and soldiers who died in battle were permitted headstones above their tombs. Since Spartan males lived in the barracks and spent all of their time preparing for war, the women had to oversee the helots. As the managers of Spartan farms, living without male supervision, Spartan women developed practical skills and an independent caste of mind.

The Spartans did not lack admirers, even in the rival city of Athens. Socrates and his disciples Plato and Xenophon greatly admired their frugality, discipline, stability, courage, and patriotism. Above all, they admired the Spartans for having rationally devised their own unique lifestyle, rather than meekly continuing a traditional way of life. Whatever one thought of the Spartan system, it was not a mindless copy of any other. Yet one contemporary made the telling observation: "Despite the universal praise for such a code of behavior, not a single city is willing to copy it."

By 500 B.C., the Spartans had established the Peloponnesian League, an alliance of Peloponnesian (and a few other) poleis sworn to mutual defense and determined to suppress democracy in the region. The Spartans feared the instability they associated with democracy above every other danger. Legend had it that when a man urged Lycurgus to create a democracy in Sparta, the lawgiver had replied, "Make your own household a democracy first." The man withdrew his request.

Athens

Attica, the territory of Athens, did not unite until approximately 700 B.C., when as many as twelve small poleis combined to form it, a development vital to Athenian greatness. Yet before the sixth century B.C., Athens was still only a minor polis.

Like most other Greeks of the Archaic period, the Athenians possessed an oligarchic system of government by the seventh century B.C. A council of nobles called the Areopagus, who possessed lifetime tenure, held the legislative and judicial power. Members of the Areopagus were former *archons* (rulers), aristocratic magistrates annually elected by the popular assembly to execute the laws of the Areopagus. The six lesser archons recorded official decisions and guarded public documents. The king archon conducted religious ceremonies, the polemarch served as the military leader, and the eponymous archon presided over the Areopagus. Like the Spartan Apella, the Athenian popular assembly, called the Ecclesia, possessed little power.

As in the rest of Greece, Athenian aristocrats abused their power. According to Athenian legend, in 621 B.C. an aristocrat named Draco, who was perhaps a mythical figure (the name means "snake"), drafted Athens's first written law code. Later dubbed "the code written in blood," Draco's laws were particularly harsh toward the lower classes, whence comes the word "draconian." The code mandated death for a wide variety of crimes, including idleness and the theft of fruit. Those unable to pay their debts could be enslaved and sold abroad or forced to sell their children. As in the rest of Greece, the aristocratic monopolization of land turned small farmers into serfs or colonists and the landless into slaves. Furthermore, the aristocratic system of government barred the rising middle class from representation in the political system. Athens was ripe for revolution.

In 594 B.C., Athenian aristocrats took bold action to prevent such a revolution. They appointed a man named Solon sole archon for a year and charged him with the duty of revising the laws. Solon had become famous for his poems, which had opposed the greed and injustice of the aristocrats. He immediately repealed the Draconian laws, canceled all debts, forbade the practice of enslavement for debt, freed those already enslaved for debt, and repurchased those sold abroad. Perhaps Solon's greatest long-term reform was to persuade nobles to produce olives instead of grain. Athenian soil was poorly suited to grain production but perfect for olive cultivation. The deep roots of olive vines could find moisture in the soil during the summer. Instead of attempting self-sufficiency and failing, as Athens had in the past, Athenians now turned to trade for their sustenance. The Athenians exported olive oil and pottery and imported grain. Trade increased Athens's wealth and stimulated creativity by bringing Athenians into contact with foreign cultures. In addition, olive production created more jobs for the poor. Solon also encouraged foreign craftsmen to settle in Athens by offering them citizenship. The offer of citizenship to foreigners on a large scale was unprecedented in the ancient world. Furthermore, Solon constructed state-owned pottery factories in order to diversify Athens's exports and to prevent the poor from becoming entirely dependent on the aristocratic olive producers. Formed from excellent clay, Athens's pottery was soon sought after by the whole of the Mediterranean world. Solon declared that each citizen must teach his son a trade and to write. Solon established the right of any citizen to initiate legal proceedings (even on behalf of another) and forced families to rely on the law when family members were murdered, rather than engaging in blood feuds. Solon turned the Areopagus into a mere judicial body, transferring its legislative functions to the new Council of 400, in which the rising middle class was represented. At the same time, the archonship was opened to the low-born wealthy. These reforms, which doubled the number of those able to hold office, had the important psychological effect of basing status on wealth rather than birth. Athens was still not a democracy, but Solon had taken the first steps in that direction.

Few were happy with Solon's reforms. Many nobles were angered by Solon's cancellation of debts, and many of the poor by his refusal to redistribute land. Solon compared himself to "a wolf beset by hounds."

At the end of his year as archon, Solon wisely departed Athens for ten years on the pretext of pursuing his commercial interests. When asked if he had provided the best laws for the Athenians, he replied, "The best that they would accept." He went to Egypt, where a priest told him of the fabled island of Atlantis. Solon also journeyed to Lydia, a kingdom in Asia Minor ruled by Croesus. Croesus sought to impress Solon. After showing Solon his vast treasure, Croesus asked: "Who is the most fortunate of men?" Croesus expected that Solon would answer, "Croesus." Instead, Solon nominated a rich old Athenian who had lived to see his grandson and who had died an honorable death, defending his polis in battle. Still hopeful, Croesus asked who was the second most fortunate of men. But Solon replied that the second most fortunate were two brothers from Argos. These simple shepherds were former Olympic victors who had died in their sleep, after putting themselves to the yoke and carrying their elderly mother, a priestess of Hera, five miles to a temple for worship on an important festival day. Solon claimed that since no one could foresee the future no one could be considered fortunate until he had died an honorable death. This amounted to a prophecy, since the Persians conquered Croesus's kingdom soon after. Legend has it that, while lying on the pile of wood his Persian executioners were about to set ablaze, Croesus shouted, "Solon, Solon, Solon!" Perplexed, the Persian king Cyrus halted the execution and questioned Croesus about the identity of "Solon," imagining he must be a god. When Croesus told him the story of Solon's visit, Cyrus, moved by a realization of the vicissitudes of fortune, felt sympathy for Croesus and released him, treating him as an honored guest and advisor for the rest of his life. Throughout Western history, the name "Solon" has been used as a synonym for a statesman possessing wisdom and virtue.

Unfortunately, Solon's reforms did not extinguish class tensions in Athens. These tensions proved so great that in 590–589 B.C., and again in 586–584 B.C., popular unrest prevented the appointment of archons. By taking advantage of the strife and chaos, an aristocrat named Pisistratus, a second cousin of Solon's, was able to seize dictatorial power three times. In 561 B.C., Pisistratus used a dispute between the plains and coastal people of Athens to assume power. Pisistratus formed a party of disgruntled poor.

Then he came into the city one day, bearing wounds that he claimed the coastal people had inflicted. (His critics believed they were self-inflicted.) Due to his status as a war hero, Pisistratus was able to secure permission to maintain a force of bodyguards, fifty men armed with clubs. He then used this force to seize power. When the plains and coastal people settled their differences, they drove Pisistratus out of Athens. On the second occasion, Pisistratus sent heralds ahead to announce that he was coming with Athena, the patron goddess of Athens. He then arrived with a five-foot, ten-inch woman, clad in shining armor and riding in a chariot. Her real name was Phye. While it is doubtful that many Athenians were actually taken in by this prank, most regarded it as a good joke and accepted Pisistratus as their dictator again. Pisistratus cemented his power by marrying the daughter of Megacles, an important leader. But Pisistratus soon quarreled with Megacles, who was infuriated by the discovery that Pisistratus was having "unnatural sex" with Megacles' daughter. Pisistratus was again driven from Athens and spent ten years (556–546 B.C.) mining gold in Thrace. Pisistratus returned and seized power in Athens yet again, with the aid of Thracian and Macedonian mercenaries. This time Pisistratus was able to maintain dictatorial power from 546 to 527 B.C., forcing many aristocrats to flee the polis and holding their sons as hostages on several different islands.

Pisistratus was an energetic dictator. He divided the lands of the fleeing aristocrats among the poor and provided for the aged and the disabled. He reduced taxes from 20 to 10 percent and gave low-interest loans to small farmers. These farmers bought better plows and oxen, thereby increasing productivity. He rebuilt Athens through ambitious works projects. He constructed beautiful temples on the Acropolis. The greatest of these structures, the Temple of Athena, later destroyed by the Persians before it could be completed, would serve as the model for the Parthenon. Pisistratus built a great aqueduct to supply Athens with water. He conquered fertile portions of Thrace, the valuable silver mines of the Hellespont (the land on either side of the Turkish Straits), and the island of Salamis. He transformed Athens from a minor polis into a cultural center through the patronage of artists, sculptors, potters, and poets, both foreign and domestic. He enlarged the festival of Dionysus, a god of nature and wine, and the Panathenaic Festival, held eight days every July to celebrate the unification of Attica. The latter festival featured dramatic contests as well as the usual athletic games, poetry competitions, and recitals of Homer. Pisistratus gave prestige to the new art form of drama and made it available to the poor. He sponsored a definitive edition of Homer's poems. He maintained the political institutions of Solon, though subordinating them to his will.

Pisistratus's son Hippias succeeded him as dictator of Athens in 527 B.C. Unfortunately for Hippias, he never learned the wisdom that Dionysius, the *tyrant* (dictator) of Syracuse, attempted to impart to his own son. Once when Dionysius rebuked his son for being insolent to a citizen, saying, "I never behave like that," the son replied, "Ah, but you didn't have a tyrant for a father"—to which Dionysius retorted, "No, and if you behave like that, you won't have a tyrant for a son." In 514 B.C., Hippias's brother Hipparchus was assassinated at the Panathenaic Festival by a man Hipparchus was pressuring into a love affair. Considering the murder a political assassination aimed at himself, Hippias became oppressive. Combined with an economic recession, Hippias's oppression produced a popular revolt, which forced him to flee to Persia in 510 B.C.

The Spartans, who had helped the Athenians drive Hippias and his friends out of Athens, attempted to impose an oligarchy of 300 Athenian aristocrats on the city. Two years of civil war ensued.

In 508 B.C., Cleisthenes and the democratic party of Athens expelled the Spartan king Cleomenes and a small contingent of Spartan soldiers. The Athenians then defeated the armies of Sparta's allies, Chalcis and the Boeotian League, in two separate battles. Sparta was not sufficiently intent on imposing an oligarchy on Athens, which was not a Peloponnesian polis, to press the matter.

It was at this time, following the overthrow of Hippias, that "tyrant" became a pejorative term in Athens. This antidictatorial strain would later culminate in the writings of Aristotle, who portrayed tyrants as enemies of free speech and assembly, employers of spies, builders of distrust, impoverishers of the people, and initiators of war.

Like Solon before him, Cleisthenes was made sole archon for one year in order to revise the laws of Athens. Cleisthenes established the first major democracy in world history. He reduced the power of the Areopagus and made the Ecclesia, the assembly of all citizens (adult males twenty and older, except for slaves and resident foreigners) the supreme legislative body of Athens. The Ecclesia passed all laws, and its decisions could not be appealed. The Ecclesia assembled to vote on legislation every ten days; the average attendance was 5,000. The new Council of 500 prepared the assembly's agenda, executed its laws, handled public finances, and received foreign envoys. The Council of 500 was completely responsible to the Ecclesia. Since council members were chosen by lot, and citizens could not serve more than twice in a lifetime, each citizen was likely to sit on the council at least once during his lifetime. Cleisthenes abolished the four-tribe organization, based on bloodlines, through which Athenians elected their local leaders, since it gave the aristocrats too much power and divided the polis by clan and by region. He replaced the system with ten new tribes. Each tribe consisted of *demes*, subdivisions containing citizens from each part of Athens and from different clans. The new system forced Athenians of all persuasions to cooperate, thereby increasing unity. All Athenians came to see the city of Athens as their own, since the city was the logical meeting place of the new multiregional tribes. Each tribe elected a *strategos* (general). The only elected leaders in Athens, the strategoi soon became the most influential leaders of the polis, gradually taking over the responsibilities of the archons. Cleisthenes also instituted the practice of ostracism, though it was not successfully applied until 487 B.C. Every spring, Athenian citizens voted for the banishment of the Athenian they considered "most dangerous" to the polis. Provided that at least 6,000 votes were cast, the man who received the largest number of votes would be exiled for ten years to a place more than three days' journey from the polis. Each citizen wrote his choice on an *ostrakon* (a shard of pottery). (A few citizens added expletives and caricatures.) Although ostracism was often abused by influential popular leaders called *demagogues* (leaders of the people), who had their rivals banished, it was intended as a way of neutralizing overly ambitious aristocrats, who might otherwise subvert the democracy.

The reforms of Cleisthenes completed the transformation of Athens from a backwater polis, torn by economic and political strife, into a flourishing city-state with a new sense of purpose, a new self-confidence, and the first major democracy in world history. This transformation proved vital to the defense of Greece against a massive Persian invasion.

BACKGROUND: GREEK UNITY AND DISUNITY

Although the Greeks were divided into a multitude of poleis, they coalesced well enough to defeat the most powerful army in the world. Aside from the fear of enslavement to Persia, four cultural bonds united the Greeks. First, they shared a common language, though it was divided into the Doric, Ionic, Aeolic, and other dialects. Second, they shared a love of Homer's poems.

Third, the Greeks shared a common religion. They worshipped twelve primary gods, immortal beings who inhabited Mount Olympus, the tallest mountain in Greece. These gods included Zeus (the king of the gods), his wife and sister Hera (goddess of women), his brothers Poseidon (god of the sea) and Hades (or Pluto; god of the underworld), his sister Hestia (goddess of the hearth), and his children Athena (goddess of wisdom, who had sprouted full-grown from the head of Zeus), Apollo (god of truth, music, and archery), Hermes (god of trade and messenger for Zeus), Aphrodite (goddess of love), Hephaestus (god of crafts), Ares (god of war), and Artemis (goddess of the hunt). The Greeks often named their children in honor of the gods (e.g., Herodotus meant "given by Hera"). Despite the gods' often unethical behavior, they fascinated most ordinary Greeks, just as modern film stars fascinate ordinary Americans, in spite of, or even because of, their ethical lapses. The average Greek might live vicariously through his gods, who could behave as he generally could not.

Beneath the twelve principal gods were countless demigods, the most popular of whom were Demeter (Zeus's sister and goddess of grain), Dionysus (god of wine), and Asclepius (god of healing). According to Greek mythology, after Hades had kidnapped Demeter's daughter Persephone and had taken her to the underworld, Demeter had been too distraught to continue her essential work of making crops grow. As a result, many humans had starved. Zeus had then settled the dispute with a compromise: Persephone would stay with Hades only one-quarter of the year. This myth explained the winter months, when crops would not grow. A series of "mysteries," secret religious rites, sprouted up around Demeter and Dionysus. Some of Dionysus's female followers (the *maenads*), when possessed by the god, ascended Mount Parnassus, tore wild animals to pieces with their bare hands, and ate the raw meat. One myth alleged that the Titans, a collection of thoroughly depraved deities, had eaten Dionysus when he was a boy. After striking down the Titans with one of his thunderbolts, Zeus had repaired the demigod. According to this myth, the smoldering remains of the Titans became the human race. Hence humans were wicked but retained a trace of the divine through Dionysus, since the Titans had digested him. The festivals of both Demeter and Dionysus often featured obscene jokes, gestures, and objects, such as giant phalluses. The Greeks made pilgrimages to the many shrines of Asclepius, especially to his original shrine at Epidaurus, hoping for cures. Although Asclepius was generally thought to heal the visitors who slept in his temples by appearing in their dreams and instructing them on the proper cure, his priests at Cos and Pergamum also relied on such natural healing techniques as diet, exercise, and herbs. The Greeks also made pilgrimages to the principal Panhellenic shrines at Dodona and Delos.

The Greeks, along with some foreigners, also turned to the oracle of Delphi for advice. The Greeks considered sacred Delphi the center of the universe, partly because of its location in central Greece. There a series of virgin priestesses, who always bore the title "Pythia," sat in a dark and eery sanctuary. Engraved on the pediment above the entrance to the sanctuary were the Greek maxims "Know thyself" and "Nothing to excess." According to legend, after the visitor addressed his question to a male functionary, and the functionary presented it to Pythia, the prophetess inhaled the vapor emanating from a chasm. Intoxicated by the vapor, the oracle lapsed into a trance and uttered wild cries, which represented the voice of Apollo speaking through her. The functionary then interpreted the often incoherent shrieks and reworded them in hexameters. However suspect these colorful details—especially the chasm and the vapor, which are entirely absent from early accounts—it is clear that the oracles became wealthy and powerful through gifts and bribes and through their considerable influence on the actions of their visitors. For instance, the enemies of a particular polis might pay handsomely to know what advice Pythia had given that city-state's emissaries, since they were likely to follow it. Others might pay the oracle to give a certain party the advice they wished them to hear. For instance, Cleisthenes and other Athenian enemies of the tyrant Hippias bribed Pythia to begin every prophecy for the Spartans, no matter what their question, with the phrase "Athens must be liberated!" (The Spartans finally did aid the Athenian dissidents in expelling the tyrant, though probably for more practical reasons than sheer exasperation with the oracle's harassment. The Spartans vainly hoped that Athens would join the Peloponnesian League.) The oracles were able to establish a respectable record of accuracy, primarily because their prophecies were often vague, but also because their steady stream of visitors from all over the Mediterranean world provided them with the large body of information necessary to make accurate predictions.

Except for the oracle of Delphi and a few other seers, most Greek priests wielded little power. Not expected to be uncommonly wise or virtuous, these caretakers of temples and shrines generally required and received no special training. There was no institutional framework to unite priests as a clergy, to teach ethics, or to formulate doctrine. Like most other religions of the day, Greek religion was concerned with outward ritual, not inner belief. Greeks never prayed without offering sacrifice, expecting help from the gods in return for their gifts. Nevertheless, they believed that the gods rejected the sacrifices of oath-breakers and other ne'er-do-wells. Bliss and punishment in the afterlife were generally believed to be reserved for a few select heroes and villains, the mass of humankind coming to an end in Hades, a shadowy place that was neither heaven nor quite hell. And even these vague conceptions were only half-believed; most Greeks remained agnostic concerning the afterlife.

Finally, the Greeks shared common athletic games. The most famous and significant of these were the Olympic Games, held for five days every fourth summer at Olympia, "for the greater glory of Zeus." As many as 50,000 Greeks attended these games, which allegedly began in 776 B.C. Olympic winners were awarded olive wreaths taken from a sacred tree. Wars were temporarily postponed for the games. The first day of the festival was devoted to sacrificing 100 oxen on the altar of Zeus, which consisted of a mound of ashes that had accumulated over previous centuries. The second day was allotted to foot races. Subsequent days were apportioned to boxing, wrestling, the pancratium (a combination of boxing and wrestling), the pentathlon, horse races, and chariot races. Initially, boxers wound straps of soft leather over their fingers as a sort of primitive boxing glove, but in later times switched to harder leather, sometimes even weighted with metal. Wrestlers, who performed nude (for better holds?), had to throw their opponents to the ground three times to win. The pancratium continued until a participant acknowledged defeat. The pentathlon consisted of sprinting, long jumping, javelin throwing, discus hurling, and wrestling. The most popular contest was the chariot race. Around 248 B.C., a Macedonian named Belistiche became the only woman to win this contest. The closing event of the games was a race run in full armor. Boys' competitions in boxing and running and women's foot races were added in later years.

Olympic winners were treated as heroes by their home poleis, which generally gave them houses, land, or free meals for the rest of their lives. The resultant incentive to win led to occasional cheating. In a few instances, beginning in 388 B.C., athletes were caught bribing rivals. In such a case, the athlete was stripped of his award and made to pay a fine, which was used to fashion a bronze statue of Zeus featuring an inscription against cheating. Only full-blooded Greeks could participate in the Olympic Games, since the games were a Greek religious event.

Other games, begun after 600 B.C., included the Pythian Games (held every four years at Delphi in honor of Apollo; winners received laurel wreaths), the Isthmian Games (held every two years at Corinth in honor of Poseidon; winners received pine needles), and the Nemean Games (held every two years in Argolis in honor of Zeus; winners received parsley). Unlike the Olympics, these games included contests in music, drama, and poetry, as well as athletic competitions.

Yet, despite the cultural bonds that united the Greeks, it should be noted that many poleis, considering themselves unable to resist the awesome power of the Persian army, refused to help their fellow Greeks, or even joined with the Persians. Thessaly, Thebes, Argos, Crete, Corcyra, Syracuse, other Italian city-states, and various Ionian poleis either remained neutral or collaborated with the Persians. Some opposed the Greek alliance against Persia out of long-standing animosities toward other poleis. Argos was a traditional enemy of Sparta and Thebes of Athens (Athens had aided tiny Plataea in a land dispute against the more powerful Thebans). Powerful Syracuse refused to aid the Greek alliance unless given command of Greek armed forces. (Carthage soon attacked Syracuse, making Syracusan help impossible, in any case. Carthage, a powerful former colony of Phoenicia, which was now a subject nation within the Persian Empire, probably synchronized its attack on Syracuse with the Persian invasion of Greece in 480 B.C.) The number of Greeks who remained neutral or collaborated with Persia was so large that postwar Greece witnessed a level of finger-pointing and recrimination unmatched anywhere until post–World War II France.

BACKGROUND: THE PERSIANS

The Medes of western Iran had taken control of most of the Near East after 612 B.C., when they had joined with the Chaldeans to overthrow the Assyrian empire. But around 550 B.C., Cyrus the Great, the king of Persia (central Iran), wrested control of most of the Near East from the Medes. The Persians were related to the Medes, another Indo-European people. Indeed, the Greeks often mistakenly used the word "Mede" interchangeably with "Persian."

In 546 B.C., Cyrus added the Lydian empire, located in what is now central Turkey, to his possessions. Croesus, the king of Lydia, had made the fatal blunder of attacking Persia. When Croesus had asked the oracle of Delphi, "What will happen if I attack the Persians?" she had replied, "A great empire will fall." On the assumption that the oracle meant the Persian Empire, Croesus had attacked Persia. But the oracle had really meant Croesus's own empire—or so it was assumed later, after his kingdom had been conquered. In any case, having conquered the Lydian empire, Cyrus hardly paused before swallowing the undisciplined poleis of Ionia, which had already come under the informal control of Lydia, as well as the rest of western Asia Minor. Cyrus imposed puppet dictators on the Ionians. The Persian conquest of Lydia and Ionia placed the empire's massive forces on the doorstep of Greece. The same Cyrus who had freed the Hebrew prophets from their Babylonian captivity now threatened Greek liberty.

In 529 B.C., Cyrus died fighting the Scythians, the savage nomads of southern Russia, who decapitated him. Using camel caravans to maintain his water supply, Cyrus's son Cambyses II extended Persian rule to Egypt and to the Greek colony of Cyrene in what is now eastern Libya in 525 B.C. In emulation of the Egyptian pharaohs, Cambyses then married his own sister and began acting like a god. Going completely mad after failing to conquer Nubia due to water supply problems, Cambyses committed suicide in 522 B.C.

The following year, Cambyses' distant cousin Darius I succeeded him. Darius quickly expanded the Persian Empire eastward to the doorstep of India. In 513 B.C., he conquered eastern Thrace, but failed to push north beyond the Danube. Darius constructed the famous "royal road" from Sardis to Susa, thereby converting a three-month, 1,500-mile journey into a three-day trip when using swift horses. He also increased government efficiency by reorganizing the empire and by dispatching investigators to each of the provinces. The Persians established their chief administrative centers at Susa, Ecbatana, Persepolis, and Sardis. The first three cities were located in what is now western Iran, Sardis on the western frontier in Asia Minor. At its height, the Persian Empire consisted of one million square miles containing nearly seventy million people.

The Persians were capable and relatively mild rulers, as long as subject peoples paid their tribute. The growth of a new ethical religion, built on the teachings of the Persian philosopher Zoroaster, moderated Persian rule. Since honesty was the most important requirement of the religion, Zoroastrians like Cyrus were shocked at the immorality of the Greek marketplace (the *agora*), claiming that the Greeks maintained "a special place, marked out, where they meet to cheat one another."

Yet, the Persian emperors were also absolute monarchs who considered themselves the earthly regents of the supreme god Ahura Mazda. Even their satraps were termed "slaves" of the emperor.

THE FIRST PHASE OF THE PERSIAN WARS, 499–490 B.C.

The Ionian Rebellion

In 499 B.C., disgruntled with Persian taxes and puppet dictators, the Ionians rebelled against Persia. The Ionians succeeded in expelling most of the dictators and the small Persian garrisons that kept them in power. Most of the Ionian poleis then replaced the dictatorships with democratic governments. Sympathetic to the Ionian cause for cultural and ideological reasons, and concerned that Persian control of the Hellespont might disrupt vital grain shipments from the north, Athens dispatched twenty warships to the aid of the Ionians. The polis of Eretria, located north of Athens on the island of Euboea, contributed an additional five ships. By contrast, the Spartans refused to send an army to Ionia, fearing that while their army was so far from home, Argos would attack Sparta and incite a helot revolt. In the following year, the Ionians, with Athenian and Eretrian help, burned Sardis. In 494 B.C., Darius put down the Ionian revolt and burned Miletus in revenge. The surviving men of Miletus were deported to Mesopotamia and the city's women and children were enslaved. Nevertheless, in an attempt to mollify the other Ionians, Darius allowed them to maintain their democratic systems, though they still had to follow the orders of the satraps in matters important to the empire.

In 492 B.C., Darius, who had already shown signs of interest in adding Greece to his empire, dispatched a Persian fleet to attack Athens and Eretria in retribution for their aid to the Ionians. The fleet was destroyed by Aegean storms, which drove the Persian ships onto the sharp rocks of Mount Athos. Nevertheless, Mardonius, the fleet's commander, completed the conquest of Thrace and persuaded Macedon to form an alliance with Persia, thereby extending Persian influence into northern Greece.

PHASE TWO, 490–480 B.C.

Still determined to gain revenge against the Greeks as well as to add Greece to the Persian Empire, Darius sent a second fleet across the Aegean Sea to attack Eretria and Athens in 490 B.C. The Persians captured and burned Eretria and enslaved its citizens through the treachery of some of the city's dissident factions, who opened one of the gates to the enemy. The Eretrians were deported to Persia, where they were held in the village of Ardericca. Their despair was captured on a tombstone: "We who once left behind the loud-roaring swells of the Aegean lie here in the midst of Ecbatana's plain. Farewell famous Eretria, our lost fatherland; farewell Athens, bordering on Euboea; farewell beloved sea. We are Eretrians from Euboea by birth, but we lie here, near Susa—alas!—so far from our country."

The Battle of Marathon (490 B.C.)

After sacking Eretria, the Persians executed a flawless landing at Marathon, twenty-five miles northeast of Athens. Persian commanders Datis and Artaphernes selected Marathon as the landing site on the advice of Athens's former dictator Hippias, because it possessed a protected beach and level ground for the Persian cavalry. Hippias also hoped that the Persians might gather aid from his former supporters as they marched toward Athens. (Darius had agreed to make Hippias satrap of Athens once it was conquered.) But the Athenians had no intention of allowing the Persians to march on Athens. They quickly dispatched a force under the command of Miltiades. The Persians were astonished when the outnumbered but more heavily armored Athenians charged their illustrious army. By keeping his center weak, Miltiades fooled the Persians into attacking it, breaking through it, and surging forward. The Persians then found themselves surrounded, after the right and left wings of the Athenians defeated the Persians' weak wings, composed of Ionian subjects, and closed in around them. The Persians fled in a wild panic, leaving behind 6,400 dead, out of a total force of 30,000, while the Athenians lost only 192 out of 10,000 soldiers. The Spartans arrived late from an important religious festival, grunted their approval at the Athenian victory, and returned home.

After the battle, Miltiades ordered Phidipides, who had trained as a long-distance runner, to run from Marathon to Athens and proclaim the victory. According to legend, Phidipides ran the twenty-five miles to Athens, cried, "We have been victorious!", collapsed, and died. In honor of this exploit, the modern Olympic Games instituted the "marathon race."

The Athenians' stunning victory at Marathon punctured the Persian aura of invincibility and gave the Athenians a tremendous sense of self-confidence. The victory convinced the Athenians that their radical experiment in democracy might actually succeed.

The revolt of Egypt against Persia (487–485 B.C.) and the death of Darius (486 B.C.) combined to delay the next, and by far the largest, Persian invasion of Greece. Darius had become so single-minded in his quest for revenge that he had instructed a slave to whisper in his ear three times every night while serving dinner: "Master, remember the Athenians!"

Xerxes I, his successor, initially cared little about vengeance, until his brother-in-law Mardonius, who wished to be satrap of all of Greece, began provoking him to rage over the humiliating defeat at Marathon.

Themistocles (c. 524–459 B.C.)

Meanwhile, Themistocles, strategos and leader of Athens, made two vital contributions to the Greek victory in the Persian Wars. First, he persuaded the Athenians to allocate new funds for the expansion of the Athenian fleet from 70 to 200 ships. After the mines at Laurium, south of Athens, yielded an unusually large quantity of silver in 483–482 B.C., some Athenian leaders proposed dividing the money among the citizens, since few expected the Persians to return. Themistocles was able to convince the Athenian people to support his alternative proposal to expand the fleet by playing on popular fears of Athens's traditional enemy, Aegina, and by persuading them to accept his interpretation of an important prophecy. When an Athenian delegation had asked the oracle of Delphi for advice on the Persian threat, she had shrieked that they should "flee to the ends of the earth"—by which she had meant that they should leave Greece to the Persians and establish a colony in the western Mediterranean, the ends of the known world. But the stubborn Athenians had refused to leave until Pythia gave them "some better oracle about our country." Pythia had then replied that Athens would be destroyed. But she had added: "Safe shall the wooden wall continue for you and your children. . . . Holy Salamis, you shall destroy the offspring of men." While some Athenians interpreted this prophecy as advising them to huddle behind the "wooden wall" of the Acropolis, Themistocles persuaded most Athenians that the "wooden wall" represented the fleet, an interpretation bolstered by the mention of Salamis, one of Athens's island possessions. Since the priestess had used the term "Holy Salamis," instead of "Cruel Salamis," Themistocles argued that the Athenians were destined to win a major victory there. Themistocles had probably known for a long time that the narrow strait between Salamis and Attica was the ideal location for a battle with the Persian navy. He may even have included a reference to Salamis in his question in order to coax the priestess into answering as he desired. At any rate, the construction of so large a fleet meant that the new Athenian ships had to be manned, in large part, by rowers paid by the state. The lower classes had never before played so large a role in Greek warfare. It was the Athenian fleet, expanded between 483 and 480 B.C., that proved the crucial factor in the Greek victory over the Persians.

Second, Themistocles played a leading role in reconciling many of the quarrelsome cities of Greece and forging them into a confederacy against Persia. In 481–480 B.C., representatives from thirty-one Greek poleis met at

Corinth to formulate defensive plans. The Athenians agreed to grant Sparta command of the confederacy's army and the navy, though Athens was contributing more than half of the Greek fleet. Themistocles understood that this concession was necessary to avoid dangerous squabbling. But Athens and many other poleis strongly objected to the Spartan proposal to station the entire Greek army at the Peloponnesian isthmus, a plan that would have surrendered all of northern and central Greece to the Persians. The Spartans argued that the Persian army so outnumbered the Greek infantry that the Greeks' only hope of victory was to make their stand at a narrow point like the isthmus. But since the other Greeks were unwilling to surrender their homes to the Persians, the Spartans were forced to agree to a compromise plan, which involved keeping most of the army at the isthmus, but stationing a Greek detachment at a mountain pass in northern Greece called Thermopylae.

PHASE THREE, 480–479 B.C.

The Persian invasion force was the largest ever fielded in Greece, consisting of approximately 200,000 men and 1,000 ships. The empire's motley army consisted of Persians and numerous subject peoples and mercenaries, including Ethiopians, who carried stone weapons and painted themselves red and white before battle, an Arab camel corps, and Iranian horsemen with lassoes. Though Xerxes knew that these subject peoples were less loyal to him than his own Persians were, he considered them useful because they were more expendable and because their outlandish dress and behavior might frighten the enemy. The Greek army was much smaller than the Persian army and the Greek fleet consisted of only about 450 ships.

Starting from Sardis in May 480 B.C., the Persian army marched to the Hellespont. The Persians crossed the turbulent Turkish Straits by lashing ships together to form a bridge. The army had to raise walls on either side of the bridge so that the expedition's animals would not be alarmed at the sight of the sea surrounding them as they crossed. In June, the Persians marched through Thrace, clearing forests to fashion a road for their huge army. In July and August, they crossed Macedon and Thessaly. Meanwhile, Persian emissaries were collecting enough bowls of earth and water from terrified Greeks to hold a mud wrestling contest. Persian custom required a surrendering nation to present a bowl of earth and a bowl of water to the imperial messenger to symbolize Persian control of the surrendering nation's land and water. Every polis except Athens and Sparta obliged the Persians in this manner. The Athenians threw their messenger into a pit and told him to collect his own earth; the Spartans threw theirs into a well and told him to collect his own water.

The Battle of Thermopylae

At its narrowest, the mountain pass at Thermopylae is only fifty feet wide, making it a perfect defensive position for a small number of men. The Persians would not be able to use their overwhelming numerical superiority to advantage by surrounding the Greeks, since they could only fit a certain number onto the battlefield at a given time. Nor would so small an area allow the Persians to take advantage of their superiority in cavalry and archery. (According to Herodotus, Persians were taught only "to ride, to shoot, and to tell the truth.") A mere 7,000 Greeks, led by King Leonidas I and his 300 Spartans, awaited the massive Persian army in the August heat. Leonidas had ascended one of the two Spartan thrones after his half-brother King Cleomenes had lost his mind and begun beating respected aristocrats with his walking stick. (While imprisoned for his insanity, Cleomenes had died a mysterious death, which the Spartans called suicide.) Leonidas's army at Thermopylae was supposed to have been larger than it was, but most of his troops arrived late from the Olympics.

When Xerxes' scouts reported that the Spartan soldiers were lounging around and combing their hair, the Persian king laughed at their effeminacy. But Demaratus, a former Spartan king who had been deposed through the conspiracy of his colleague Cleomenes and had taken refuge in Persia, told Xerxes that he should not laugh. The Spartans always took care to groom themselves before a battle because they were prepared to die and wished to look good when they did so. Xerxes was hardly impressed. He could not believe that anyone would dare to oppose his massive army, particularly the Greeks, who lacked kings to instill a proper fear and obedience in their soldiers. But Demaratus shrewdly identified the source of Greek power and discipline: "They are free, but not completely free; for law is their master, and they fear it more than your men fear you. They do whatever it commands, and it always commands the same thing: they must never flee from battle, no matter how many are their enemies; they are to hold their ground, and there they are required either to conquer or die." Indeed, there was not a single major battle in which a defeated Greek general survived. When a Spartan soldier reported the rumor that the Persians were so numerous their arrows blocked out the sun, Leonidas remarked: "How pleasant then, if we're going to fight them in the shade."

Amazed that so small a detachment would dare to resist his massive army, Xerxes ordered his men to *capture* the Greek army. But the Spartans, fighting at the front of the Greek line, repelled three charges, sending the Persian lines crashing backwards each time. Jumping up and down in frustration, Xerxes then called on his elite corps, "the Immortals," to attack the Greek line. Handicapped by the shorter length of their spears, most of the Immortals died. On the third day of the battle, however, a

Greek named Ephialtes showed the Persians a secret pass that led behind the Greek army. Once a Persian detachment had gotten behind him, Leonidas realized that his army would be encircled and slaughtered. He ordered all but his 300 Spartans to retreat. Seven hundred Thespians remained with the Spartans, refusing to leave. Leonidas instructed the remaining 1,000 Greeks to eat breakfast in expectation of dinner in Hades.

Although the Spartans and Thespians fought well, driving some of the Persians into the sea and killing two of Xerxes' younger brothers, all but two of the Spartans and most of the Thespians were slain. The two surviving Spartans were so disgraced they later committed suicide. One of them, who was blind, was called a coward for requesting and receiving permission to retreat because of his disability. The Spartans claimed that a soldier did not require sight where the fighting was close and the enemy provided so many targets. At any rate, the infuriated Persians decapitated Leonidas's corpse and placed his head on a stake.

Why did Leonidas choose to die at Thermopylae? First, someone had to cover the retreat of the rest of the army. Second, the oracle of Delphi had prophesied that the Persians would either destroy Sparta or kill a Spartan king. Knowing this, Leonidas was prepared to sacrifice his life for his city. Fully conscious of the perilous nature of his assignment, he had brought with him to Thermopylae only those Spartans who possessed living sons, so that their family lines would continue if they died. After the war, a monument honoring the Spartan dead was erected at Thermopylae. On that monument was inscribed the famous epitaph: "O stranger, go and tell the Spartans that we lie here, obedient to their commands."

The Persians lost 20,000 men to the Greeks' 4,000 in the Battle of Thermopylae. Xerxes' clumsy attempt to hide this fact from his own men—by having 19,000 of the Persian casualties secretly buried in a poorly camouflaged pit—fooled no one. Persian morale was badly damaged, and Xerxes grew suspicious of his contingent of Ionians. Hoping to encourage such suspicion, Themistocles had scrawled Greek messages to them on the rocks. The Battle of Thermopylae inspired the Greeks and became an enduring symbol of courage in a seemingly hopeless cause. To cite just one example, Texans at the Alamo remembered Thermopylae. The battle also provided the Greeks with the time required to inflict a serious naval defeat on the Persians at Artemisium, which, in turn, made possible the crucial victory at Salamis.

The Battle of Artemisium

At roughly the same time as the Battle of Thermopylae, the Greek fleet, under the Spartan Eurybiades, waged a fierce battle against the Persian fleet nearby at Artemisium. The Persians had already lost 200 of their 1,000 ships merely advancing across the notoriously stormy Aegean Sea. According to Herodotus, a Greek named Ameinocles acquired great wealth from the Persian goblets that washed up on his beachfront property.

Many Greeks wanted to leave Artemisium, so as not to risk the 271 ships stationed there against the remaining 800 Persian ships. But Themistocles bribed Eurybiades and another leading general to insist that the fleet stand and fight. The Persians then made a fatal error. They were so certain of victory that they detached 100 ships from the fleet for the sole purpose of capturing any Greek ships that attempted to escape. Learning of this tactic, the Greeks decided on a surprise attack on the main Persian fleet. The battle itself, fought intermittently for three days, was indecisive: both the Greeks and the Persians lost 100 ships. But the Persian detachment of 100 ships whose task was to prevent a Greek escape was utterly destroyed by a storm. Nevertheless, the defeat of the army at Thermopylae forced the Greek fleet to retreat southward to Salamis.

The Destruction of Athens

The Persian army then marched into southern Greece. Xerxes' soldiers found few people in Athens, which had been largely evacuated. The women and children had fled to Troezen in the Peloponnesus, and nearly all of the men had joined the fleet at Salamis. The rest of the men refused to leave the city, still insisting that Pythia's "wooden wall" was the wall that encircled the Acropolis. Unfortunately, that wooden wall became a blazing wall after the Persians pounded it with flaming arrows. Still, the feisty Athenians refused to surrender. They extinguished the fires and rolled boulders down on the Persians. But when the Persians found a temple outside of the Acropolis close enough to allow a steep climb over the wall, the situation became hopeless for the Athenians. Some committed suicide, while others were killed. Reveling in their revenge, the Persians burned Athens to the ground. Xerxes dispatched a messenger to Persia to announce the long-sought victory. The Athenians later buried the remnants of these temples, now considered defiled, and rebuilt from scratch. Happily for historians, burial preserved a great deal of early Athenian architecture and sculpture.

The Battle of Salamis (480 B.C.)

The Greek naval commanders at Salamis voted to sail for the isthmus to support the army, which was building a wall across it in preparation for the Persians. But Themistocles realized that if the commanders were allowed to sail away, each would make a panic-stricken dash for his own polis, and Greece would be enslaved. Even if the commanders sailed for the isthmus, they would find themselves fighting the Persians in the open sea, where the Persians could exploit their greater numbers and maneuverability. Therefore, Themistocles persuaded Eurybiades, this time without a bribe, to call a second council meeting. There, Themistocles noted the wisdom of facing the Persians in the narrow strait of Salamis. When Adeimantus of Corinth rebuked Themistocles for speaking, since he no longer had a polis to represent now that Athens lay in ruins, Themistocles retorted that Athens had a greater polis than Corinth, since, with its ships and soldiers, it could take any polis it desired. Finally, Themistocles warned that if the Greek fleet did not remain and fight at Salamis, the Athenians would immigrate to Siris in Italy. Without the Athenian fleet, Greece would surely fall to the Persians. Themistocles' threat persuaded the other captains to remain at Salamis for a while.

But soon the Peloponnesian captains, fearful of being cut off from their homes, began to agitate for a third council meeting. In fact, it appeared that these captains might even sail away without permission. To prevent their flight, Themistocles dispatched a trusted slave to tell Xerxes that he wished to defect to the Persian side and that the Persians should encircle Salamis to keep the Greek fleet from escaping. His message also exaggerated the degree of disunity within the Greek camp, implying an easy Persian victory.

Xerxes swallowed the bait. When the news that Xerxes had surrounded Salamis reached the Greek captains, they were left with no choice but to stand and fight.

Although outnumbered by 600 to 370 ships, the Greeks possessed two significant advantages that help explain their victory in the Battle of Salamis. First, the narrowness of the strait, only one mile in width, prevented the Persians from using their greater numbers and maneuverability to surround the Greeks and allowed the Greeks to use their battering rams to great effect. Second, the Greeks were more highly motivated than the Persians. While the Greeks were fighting for their families, their poleis, and their liberty, the conscripted Phoenician, Egyptian, and Ionian sailors who formed the bulk of the Persian navy would benefit little from the conquest of Greece. This is what Herodotus meant when he wrote, "Free men fight better than slaves."

The battle proceeded disastrously for the Persians. On the frequent occasions when the Persian captains were forced to retreat, they found it impossible, since the waters behind them were crowded with other Persian ships. Trapped, the Persian vessels were rammed by the Greek triremes. The Persian ships sank, and their crews, floundering in long robes, generally drowned. In one instance, the brilliant Queen Artemisia of Caria (south of Ionia), in a desperate attempt to escape an Athenian battering ram, bore down on a Persian ship blocking her retreat and sank it. This act of "friendly fire" by the queen, who commanded five ships in the battle, actually redounded to her benefit, since none of the crew of the ill-fated ship survived. Assuming that Artemisia had defected from the Persians, the captain of the Athenian ship who had been chasing her broke off his pursuit, and Xerxes, who assumed that the ship she had sunk must have been Athenian, heaped praise on her. In fact, overwhelmed by frustration and anger at the looming disaster, Xerxes, who was watching the battle from a throne erected on an Attic hill, declared: "My men have behaved like women, my women like men!" Later, the Athenians, who were among the most chauvinistic of Greeks, offered a 10,000 drachma reward for Artemisia's capture, since, as Herodotus put it, "there was great indignation felt that a woman should appear in arms against Athens."

Because the Battle of Salamis determined the outcome of the Persian Wars, which determined the fate of Western civilization, it must rank as one of the most significant battles in history. The Greeks sank more than 200 Persian ships, killing as many as 40,000 Persians, including another of Xerxes' brothers, while the Greeks lost only 40 ships. Essential to furnishing the massive Persian army with food and other vital supplies and to maintaining communications with the Persian Empire, the Persian fleet had been routed. Xerxes issued a frantic order for his remaining ships to retreat to Persia.

Mardonius's Final Offensive

Fearful of what might happen to him, since he had been the one who had urged Xerxes to invade Greece, Mardonius begged Xerxes to allow him to remain in Greece with a large detachment. Xerxes agreed. After wintering in Thessaly, Mardonius prepared to resume hostilities in the spring of 479 B.C.

Mardonius dispatched the king of Macedon, an old friend of Athens, to persuade the Athenians to form an alliance with the Persians. Alarmed, the Spartans sent their own envoys to Athens to convince the Athenians to reject the Persian offer. The Macedonian king reported that Xerxes would give the Athenians whatever land in Greece they desired and would rebuild their city if the Athenians joined him. On the other hand, if the Athenians did not form an alliance with the Persians, they could expect the Persians to single them out for further reprisals. The Spartans then appealed to the Athenians' reputation as a freedom-loving people and to the common bonds of Greek culture. Finally, the Spartans offered to help feed Athens, since Xerxes had destroyed the harvest, and even promised to give the Athenians a new home in the Peloponnesus, which could be better defended against future Persian attacks.

According to Herodotus, the Athenians replied to the Macedonian king:

> We know as well as you that the power of the Mede is many times greater than our own. We did not need to have *that* cast in our teeth. Nevertheless,

we cling so to freedom that we shall offer what resistance we may. Tell Mardonius this: "So long as the sun keeps his present course, we will never join alliance with Xerxes." Nay, we shall oppose him unceasingly, trusting in the aid of those gods and heroes whom he has lightly esteemed, whose houses and whose images he has burnt with fire. And come not again to us with words like these; nor, thinking to do us a service, persuade us to unholy actions. You are the guest and friend of our nation; we would not have you receive hurt at our hands.

To the Spartans, the Athenians replied:

It was natural no doubt that the Lacedaemonians should be afraid that we might make terms with the barbarians. But, nonetheless, it was a base fear in men who knew so well of what temper and spirit we are. Not all the gold that the whole earth contains, not the fairest and most fertile lands, would bribe us to take part with the Medes and help them to enslave Greece. Even could we have brought ourselves to do such a thing, there are many very powerful motives that would now make it impossible. The first and chief of these is the burning and destruction of our temples and the images of our gods. . . . Again, there is our common brotherhood with the Greeks, our common ancestry and language, the altars and sacrifices of which we all partake, the common character we bear. . . . Know then . . . that while one Athenian remains alive we will never join alliance with Xerxes. We thank you, however, for your forethought on our behalf and for your wish to give our families sustenance, now that ruin has befallen us . . . but, for ourselves, we will endure as we may, and not be burdensome to you.

In the spring of 479 B.C., Mardonius again occupied and destroyed Athens. Still, the Athenians refused an offer of alliance, even killing one of their own councilors who dared propose its consideration.

The Battles of Plataea and Mycale (479 B.C.)

The Athenian rejection of Xerxes' offer of alliance made another battle inevitable. This final battle was fought at Plataea, on the spurs of Mount Cithaeron, where the ground was impassable for the Persian cavalry. Under the leadership of the Spartan Pausanias, Leonidas's nephew, a large Greek army faced off against an even larger Persian army. Each Greek soldier swore an oath before the battle: "I shall fight to the death, and I shall not count my life more valuable than freedom." After withstanding a fierce assault by Persian archers, the Spartans charged the Persian center. Mardonius was killed, along with 50,000 of his troops. The Persians fled in panic, nearly all of them slaughtered in their retreat from Greece. Pausanias then ordered that the lavish dinner the Persians had prepared beforehand be served to his own staff, exclaiming: "By the gods, with food like this what greedy characters the Persians were to chase after our barley-bread!" The same day a Greek fleet of 110 ships, under Latychidas of Sparta and Xanthippus of Athens, attacked remnants of the Persian fleet beached at Mycale off the coast of Asia Minor. Fighting off the Persian marines, the Greeks torched the fleet.

The poet Simonides composed two of the greatest epitaphs in history for those who died in defense of Greek liberty at Plataea. For the Athenian dead he wrote: "Hastening to ensure the freedom of Greece, we lie here, enjoying ageless glory." And for the Spartan dead: "Though they have died, they have not died, for their courage raises them in glory from the rooms of Hades."

Exile and Death

But Themistocles was not able to enjoy the glory of his victory for long. In 471 B.C., his rivals succeeded in having him ostracized. Themistocles complained that the Athenians treated him like a plane-tree: when it was stormy they ran under his branches for shelter, but as soon as the storm cleared, they plucked his leaves and lopped off his branches. On another occasion he used a more pungent analogy to convey the fickleness of the Athenian people toward himself, saying, "I do not admire the sort of men who use the same vessel as a wine pitcher and a chamber pot."

Themistocles lived in Argos for several years, until called back to Athens to stand trial on the ridiculous charge of plotting treason against Athens with Persia. The accusation was not only the work of Themistocles' rivals in Athens, but also of the Spartans, who may have feared his presence in Argos, Sparta's traditional enemy. The Spartans pressed Athens to force Themistocles to stand trial before a general Greek congress, which the Spartans dominated, rather than before an Athenian jury.

Realizing that he could not prevail in such a trial, Themistocles made his way to Persia, ironically the only secure place of refuge from his Greek enemies. The shrewd Athenian learned the Persian language within a year and acquired influence at the court of Artaxerxes, Xerxes' son, who had assumed the throne following his father's assassination in 465 B.C. Thrilled to have in his custody the Athenian who had inflicted so great a defeat on Persia, Artaxerxes gave Themistocles three cities in Asia Minor, including Magnesia, where Themistocles died around 459 B.C.

The Legacy of Themistocles

Unquestionably, Themistocles was arrogant, unscrupulous, and greedy. After the war, he attempted to enrich himself by using the threat of the Athenian fleet to extort money from various poleis. Nevertheless, it is equally certain that Themistocles contributed more than anyone else to the Greek victory in the Persian Wars. When all of the Greek commanders met after the war to determine who had contributed the most to victory, each commander voted for himself first and Themistocles second.

The victories of the Persian Wars gave the Athenians a strong sense of pride and confidence. In the eyes of the Athenians, Athens had given up its rightful command of the Greek fleet, had rejected the tempting offer of a Persian alliance, and had twice suffered the terrible vengeance of Xerxes, all for the sake of Greek freedom. Athens's participatory democracy had weathered great storms, and by demanding much of its citizens, had produced great men. Interpreting the outcome of the Persian Wars as the victory of democracy over monarchy, Athenians began to perceive their system of government as the source of their strength and became determined to expand the power of the majority even further.

The victory of the tiny Greek republics over the seemingly invincible Persian Empire inspired countless republicans across the centuries—most notably American revolutionaries over two millennia later, when they too took up a seemingly hopeless struggle against the greatest empire of their day. The Founding Fathers read with admiration Herodotus's *Histories* and Plutarch's life of Themistocles. They accepted without reservation Herodotus's conclusion as to the source of the Greek victory over the Persians: "Free men fight better than slaves." This insight inspired the founders to believe that they could defeat the British and secure American independence at a time when few objective observers shared that opinion. After the Coercive (or Intolerable) Acts were passed in 1774, John Adams expressed a common view: "The Grecian Commonwealths were the most heroic Confederacy that ever existed. . . . The Period of their glory was from the Defeat of Xerxes to the Rise of Alexander. Let Us not be enslaved, my dear Friend, Either by Xerxes or Alexander." When Thomas Jefferson wished to compliment Adams, a staunch supporter of a strong American navy, he compared Adams with Themistocles, whose success in building the Athenian fleet had secured victory for Greece in the Persian Wars.

4

✛

Pericles: Democratic Reformer

Under the leadership of Pericles, Athenian democracy reached its apex. Athens became a true democracy, in which common citizens possessed an unprecedented degree of power. Athens assumed the leadership of a confederacy centered in the Aegean, an empire that prevented further incursions by Persia into Greece. Among the products of Periclean Athens were art and architecture that remain the wonders of the world, the three greatest tragedians of ancient Greece, the most famous philosopher of the ancient world, and the first historians. The classicist C. E. Robinson once wrote: "Athens' heyday lasted less than eighty years, and the number of her adult male citizens scarcely exceeded fifty thousand. Yet this handful of men attempted more and achieved more in a wider variety of fields than any nation great or small has ever attempted or achieved in a similar space of time." Fifth-century Athens constituted both the culmination of Greece's Archaic period and the birthplace of Western civilization.

THE DELIAN LEAGUE

Once the Persians had been driven from Greece, Sparta, a land power, had neither the motivation nor the ability to free Ionia and to end the Persian naval threat. In order to accomplish these goals, in 478 B.C. a large number of poleis bordering on the Aegean Sea formed the Delian League, headquartered on the sacred island of Delos. The league agreed to maintain a 200-ship fleet. The confederation was funded by the contributions of member poleis and by money seized from those city-states that had collaborated with the Persians during the war. Each member polis was required to contribute either a specific number of manned ships or their equivalent in money, based on its degree of wealth. Since nearly all of the other poleis chose to contribute money, Athens provided almost all of the league's ships.

It was the duty of the Athenian leader "Aristides the Just," one of the founders of the Delian League, to assess the wealth of each polis and determine its contribution. No assessment of his was ever challenged. Many poleis were assessed at only one ship.

Legends concerning the virtue of Aristides became part of Greek lore. One such story claimed that during a vote for ostracism, an illiterate man whom Aristides did not know asked the statesman to write the name "Aristides" on his potsherd for him. Startled, Aristides asked the man, "Has this Aristides injured you in some way?" The man replied that he did not even know Aristides, but was just sick and tired of hearing all of this praise of "Aristides the Just." Shaking his head sadly, honest Aristides wrote his own name on the man's potsherd. (Indeed, Aristides was banished that year, 483 B.C., at the instigation of his rival Themistocles, though he was later recalled when the Persians invaded Greece, and he distinguished himself leading the Athenians at Plataea. Athens was fortunate that Aristides had been banished in 483 B.C., since he had been one of the leading opponents of Themistocles' naval construction program. Virtue and wisdom do not always go together.) On another occasion, when Aristides was prosecuting an opponent, and the jury refused to listen to the defendant's case, Aristides jumped to his feet and demanded they do so. At another time, when Aristides acted as an arbitrator in a dispute, one party reminded him that the other party had once injured Aristides. Aristides replied: "Do not tell me about that. Tell me what he has done to you. I am here to judge your case, not mine." Before the Battle of Marathon, Aristides gave up his turn at command to Miltiades and persuaded the other generals to do so as well, since Miltiades was the best of the generals. After the battle, when Aristides was placed in charge of guarding the enemy's spoils, he did not help himself to any. Despite the numerous opportunities for the acceptance of bribes that his tenure as the league's assessor afforded him, Aristides left the post poorer than when he had assumed it. Indeed, since he did not even leave behind enough money to pay for his own funeral, the state paid for it and for his daughters' dowries.

The turning point in the history of the Delian League came in 465 B.C., when Thasos, a polis rich in precious metals, decided to leave the confederacy. Although Ionia had been liberated and the Persian threat had been considerably reduced, Athens treated the secession of Thasos as a revolt and crushed it. The Athenians not only reimposed the polis's assessment, but also tore down the city's walls and seized a gold mine from it. Athens then forced some Aegean poleis that had not joined the league to do so, a policy that raised the number of member states to approximately 140. The Athenians explained that if they were forced to reduce the fleet through lack of funds, Persia would again threaten Greece. Why shouldn't all of the Aegean poleis that benefited from Athenian naval protection pay what all agreed was a fair price for it? The poleis that refused were taking advantage of their neighbors.

Athens established and maintained democratic governments in those member poleis that revolted. The Athenians explained that the imposition of democracy on league members was merely designed to ensure their future loyalty to democratic Athens and to protect their citizens from greedy and powerful aristocrats. (Indeed, many poleis that did not belong to the Delian League, such as Argos and Syracuse, established democratic systems without the slightest pressure from Athens.) The Athenians considered it a dangerous policy to allow foreign aristocrats who had proved themselves disloyal to Athens to continue to rule their poleis. They noted that Sparta had long since installed oligarchies in the poleis of the Peloponnesian League.

In 454 B.C., after losing a whole army and two fleets helping Egypt launch an ill-fated rebellion against Persia, the Athenians moved the treasury of the Delian League from Delos to Athens in order to better protect it from a resurgent Persian navy. In 445 B.C., the Athenians required that disputes between league members—even those between Athens and its allies—be settled in Athenian courts. The Athenians explained that settling disputes in the relatively fair Athenian courts was better than settling them through internal warfare, which would destroy the league. Most imperial powers of the day did not use courts at all. As the Athenians told the Spartans, the attitude of most powerful cities was that "where force can be used, courts of law are unnecessary." Indeed, most of the league members' complaints did not concern the fairness of Athenian courts, but regarded the expense of staying in Athens while awaiting a hearing, a need exploited by the city's greedy innkeepers. Finally, the Athenians offered the right of appeal to Athenian courts for any allied citizen facing the death penalty or the deprival of citizenship in his own polis. To some citizens of member poleis, especially to aristocrats already angry with Athens for robbing them of their power, these actions constituted clear evidence that Athens had become a tyrannical power and that the "Delian League" had become the Athenian empire.

Indeed, the Athenians did effect an air of imperialism. Aristides' successors increased league members' assessments. The Athenians expropriated land from their "allies" to build their own settlements, which were often little more than garrisons to watch over the allies. The Athenians also used the league fleet to establish colonies elsewhere. They used their control of the Hellespont to levy a 10 percent tax on grain exported through the Turkish Straits anywhere but to Athens. They mandated the use of Athenian coinage throughout the league, though this policy was partly due to the desire to substitute a standardized, silver currency for the heterogeneous coinage of the allies, which varied considerably in substance and weight. Finally, they demanded that each ally send a cow and a panoply of arms as an offering at the city's Panathenaic Festival. Athens had become the political, military, economic, and cultural center of the Aegean.

CIMON

The most powerful political leaders in Athens were the ten strategoi, the only elected officials. One of the strategoi usually led the prodemocratic faction, another the proaristocratic faction. Since common men could vote in the Ecclesia, Athens's legislature, the leader of the prodemocratic faction sometimes possessed such power that he was able to have his rival banished. But the leader's military power, like that of the other strategoi, rested on his annual election, and his political power was based solely on his ability to persuade. In other words, all of the leader's power was dependent on the continuous support of the people.

Cimon, a son of Miltiades who had distinguished himself at Salamis, succeeded Themistocles as the leader of Athens. Though not particularly eloquent, Cimon was brave and just, refusing all bribes. It was Cimon who greatly reduced the Persian threat to Greece by defeating them and capturing two hundred Persian ships in a naval battle near the Eurymedon River on the western coast of Asia Minor in 466 B.C. On the same day, he defeated Persian land forces, thereby freeing parts of Asia Minor. Cimon also led the Delian League in clearing the Aegean Sea of pirates. He ordered the construction of sturdy walls from the city to Piraeus, Athens's best harbor. These walls would allow Athens to resist sieges by continuing to import food via the sea. Although Cimon's aristocratic sympathies inclined him to maintain friendly relations with the Spartans, even naming his own sons after them, the Spartans remained deeply suspicious of the new Delian League. (As early as 479 B.C. an anxious Sparta had suggested that all poleis outside the Peloponnesus destroy their own walls, since they might be useful to the Persians in the event of another invasion, and rely on the Spartan army for protection instead. Most poleis had simply ignored the suggestion. Themistocles, on the other hand, had quietly accelerated work on the reconstruction of Athens's walls, had presented Sparta with the fait accompli, and had warned that thenceforth Sparta must consider Athens capable of defending itself.)

Although Cimon won popularity for a while by giving his own money, food, and clothes to the poor, his aristocratic leanings and pro-Spartan policies finally led to his ostracism in 461 B.C. After the helots, with help from some of the perioikoi, had taken the opportunity to revolt afforded by a devastating earthquake, an embarrassed Sparta had requested Athens's assistance in crushing the revolt. Cimon had persuaded the reluctant Athenians to dispatch 4,000 soldiers to Sparta, asking, "Will you look on Greece lamed and Athens without her yoke-fellow?" But alarmed by the democratic spirit of the Athenian soldiers and worried that these soldiers might go over to the helots' side, the Spartans had changed their minds about Athenian aid. The Spartans had told the Athenians that their services were no longer needed and that they should go home. The Athenians blamed Cimon for this humiliation, since they had not wanted to aid the Spartans in the first place.

Following his decade of exile, Cimon returned to Athens and died fighting against the Persians on Cyprus. Plutarch later offered Cimon the backhanded compliment that his accomplishments were especially impressive considering that he was exceptionally lazy and drunk most of the time.

DEMOCRATIC REFORMS

Ephialtes

Ephialtes, Cimon's successor, led Athens less than one year before a Boeotian assassin hired by Athenian aristocrats killed him. While in office, Ephialtes persuaded the Ecclesia to transfer all judicial power from the aristocratic Areopagus, except for its ancient authority to hear homicide cases, to the democratic heliaea. First created by Solon but given little power, the heliaea was a body of 6,000 jurors chosen by lot annually from among citizens thirty years and older. Between 101 and 2,501 jurors (usually 501) were selected by lot out of the 6,000 to serve on each particular jury. Due to the large size of the juries, a majority vote, cast by secret ballot, was sufficient for a decision. A chairman presided over the trial. There were no lawyers. The defendant had to plead his own case, though he might hire a speechwriter to assist him. Whoever brought forth the charge acted as prosecutor. Each side argued its case in six minutes, or in some multiple of six minutes, as measured by water dripping from a special jar. Whenever a jury found a defendant guilty of a crime for which there was no specific penalty, the jurors then decided between the penalties proposed by the defendant and the prosecutor. Whenever a plaintiff brought forth a case so dubious he was unable to win at least one-sixth of the jury vote, he was punished. (Like modern Britain's "English rule," which states that if a plaintiff loses a civil suit he must pay the defendant's court costs, this policy was designed to discourage frivolous litigation.) Significantly, Ephialtes also pushed through the Ecclesia a measure authorizing the payment of jurors, thereby making it possible for the poor to serve on juries.

Pericles

Pericles, the son of Xanthippus (the hero of Mycale) and protégé of Ephialtes, led Athens from 454, when he was about thirty-six, until his death in 429 B.C. Pericles forced all outgoing members of the Council of 500 to submit to the assembly an "audit," an account of their official acts. Until a council member did so, he could not leave Athens or sell property. Under Pericles, the polis used "surplus funds" from the Delian League to pay members of the Council of 500 one drachma per day, thereby allowing the poor to participate in the council. He also used league funds to rebuild the temples of the Acropolis and to fill them with some of the greatest art ever produced. These public works programs provided employment, especially for rowers put out of work by peace, and increased Athens's beauty and fame. One critic, who was later ostracized by the people, questioned the propriety of using league funds in such a manner and added that Pericles was dressing Athens "like a vain woman with precious stones and statues and thousand-talent temples." Pericles retorted that since Athens had lost her temples fighting the same Persians the league had been created to oppose, it was only just that the league reimburse Athens for its losses. He also deflected criticism by offering to spend his own money on some of the works, if the people considered his public spending excessive. The people refused his offer. Pericles created prestigious offices (the *litourgoi*), held by the wealthy, that required the officeholder to pay for ships, plays, statues, and other public services, which would be dedicated to himself. In this way, Pericles made the wealthy vie with one another for the honor of strengthening, educating, and beautifying Athens.

Pericles was the kind of man who was equally comfortable discussing the finer points of poetry and charging into battle. A man of immovable dignity, Pericles once ignored the taunts of a heckler for an entire day while conducting business in the agora. The heckler even followed Pericles home at the end of the day, still spouting insults. By then it was dark, so Pericles dispatched a servant with a torch to lead the man home. Pericles never attended parties, saving all of his energy for state affairs. He was very frugal, to the distress of his daughters-in-law. He was a man of great eloquence. Comics depicted him wielding a thunderbolt in his tongue, and a political rival who was fond of wrestling used this analogy concerning Pericles' rhetorical ability: "Whenever I throw him in wrestling, he beats me by arguing that he was never down, and he can even make the spectators believe it." Yet Pericles spoke only about important subjects, leaving his friends to speak on minor matters, so that the people would not tire of him.

Despite his numerous accomplishments, Pericles adopted a harsh stance toward Sparta that ultimately proved fatal to Athens. Athenian and Spartan forces, joined by some of their allies, fought a series of battles in Boeotia between 460 and 446 B.C., leading some historians to call the conflict the "First Peloponnesian War."

Pericles was willing to use bribery to promote Athenian interests whenever necessary. In 446 B.C., a huge Spartan army poised to attack Athens retreated for no apparent reason. That year, when Pericles submitted his audit to the assembly, there was one item in his account concerning which he refused to speak: ten talents "for necessary purposes." Since everyone knew what had happened earlier in the year, and since everyone knew that Pericles would not steal money (he cared so little about wealth he allowed his own estate to decay), no one questioned the expenditure. The furious Spartans executed the royal advisor whom Pericles had bribed into persuading King Pleistoanax to retreat, and they imposed so large a fine on the king himself he was forced to flee Sparta. The words "for necessary purposes" remained good for a laugh on Athens's comic stage for another generation.

WAS ATHENS A DEMOCRACY?

Some modern critics have questioned Athens's claim to the title of first major democracy. The Athenians granted citizenship to 50,000 adult males at most, out of a total population of about 250,000. The Athenians excluded women, children, *metics* (resident foreigners—*metoikoi*, "those who live with" us), and slaves from the franchise.

But no society enfranchises children or resident foreigners. True, after 451 B.C., when the Ecclesia passed Pericles' law making Athenian descent on both sides of one's family a requirement for citizenship, an act perhaps motivated by a large influx of metics, it became virtually impossible for metics to become citizens. But such restrictions were typical among the ancient Greeks, who considered the polis an extended family. More remarkable is the unprecedented laxity of Athens's naturalization laws from the days of Solon (594 B.C.) until 451 B.C. While it is also true that a metic could not own land, speak in court, or marry a citizen, a person walking through the streets of Athens who came across a prosperous shield or leather factory had no way of knowing whether its owner was a citizen or a metic. Prosperous and loyal to Athens, metics socialized freely with Athenian citizens. By the time of the outbreak of the Peloponnesian War in 431 B.C., the population of Athens included 30,000 metics, most of whom were engaged in trade at the port of Piraeus.

At the same time, Athens possessed about 120,000 slaves. Every ancient society owned slaves. Most slaves were prisoners of war, whether acquired directly in military campaigns or through slave traders. Small farmers who owned a few slaves worked beside them. Nearly all masters lived in the same house with their slaves. Wealthy Athenians often used their slaves as domestic servants or hired them out to others or to the polis. Indeed, the polis itself owned some slaves, who were employed as road builders, coin minters, secretaries, executioners, heralds, and even policemen. Scythian slaves were employed as policemen so that no Athenian citizen would ever have to lay violent hands on another. When it was time for the assembly to meet, the policemen went out into the agora and herded citizens to the meeting by walking behind them with outstretched ropes dipped in red paint. Some slaves learned and practiced a trade, purchased their freedom with the profits (they received one-sixth of their earnings), and established their own businesses; a few who belonged to merchants became the stewards of their masters' overseas ventures. Indeed, it was often impossible to tell a slave from his master. As the Athenian orator Demosthenes once noted: "One may see many a servant in Athens speaking his mind with greater liberty than is granted to citizens in some other states." Contrary to popular myth, the leisure time that Athenians and other Greeks utilized to revolutionize philosophy, science, art, and literature was not chiefly the product of slavery, but of a frugal lifestyle. Most harshly treated were the mine slaves, who lived much of their lives hundreds of feet below ground. In fact, many slaves were sent to the mines as punishment for some offense.

Although there was never a genuine abolitionist movement in Athens, or anywhere else in the ancient world, some fifth- and fourth-century Athenians did criticize slavery. Euripides referred to slavery as "that thing of evil, by its nature evil, forcing submission from a man to what no man should yield to." Plato wrote, "A slave is an embarrassing possession." The Stoics denounced slavery as an intolerable violation of natural law.

It is also true that the status of women in Athenian society, like that of women in most other Greek societies, was unenviable. Few women were educated, since their sole functions were to bear children and to manage the household. Custom forced women to stay in their own quarters in the back of the house when their husbands entertained guests. By necessity, lower-class Athenian women worked as spinners, weavers, and vendors, but upper-class women were not allowed to work outside the home. Women were allowed to attend plays but sat apart in the back rows. Athenian women possessed few legal rights. They could own only clothes, jewelry, and slaves. They could not enter into any business transaction involving more than a small amount of money. Wealthier men generally kept an educated, foreign-born mistress called a *hetaira* (companion). The hetairai sometimes owned businesses and often moved about the city more freely than the sequestered wives, sisters, and daughters of many citizens, who could only leave the house during festivals or on other special occasions. In Sophocles' *Tereus,* Procne, while preparing to kill her own son in revenge for her husband's seduction of her sister, declares: "We [women] are nothing. When we reach puberty and understanding, we are thrust out. . . . Some go to strangers' homes, others to foreigners', some to joyless houses, some to hostile. And all this, once the first night has yoked us to our husbands, we are forced to praise and to say that all is well."

Yet it would be wrong to assume that all Athenian women were docile. Socrates' wife, Xanthippe, was notoriously harsh toward her husband— justifiably so, since his philosophical dialogues did not bring in any money with which to feed the family. Xanthippe once even assaulted Socrates in the agora, tearing the cloak off his back. When Socrates' friends advised him to strike back, he refused to take the bait, replying: "Yes, by Zeus, in order that, while we are sparring, each of you may join in with, 'Well done, Socrates!', 'Good punch, Xanthippe!'" When Xanthippe scolded Socrates and drenched him with water, he said, "Did I not say that Xanthippe's thunder would end in rain?" When one of their three sons complained bitterly to his father about his mother's nagging, Socrates urged the young man to be patient with her, reminding him of the aggravations and troubles Xanthippe had endured on his behalf when he was a baby. Socrates said of his wife's scolding: "I have gotten used to it, as to the continued rattle of a windlass." When asked why in the world he had married her, he replied that one of his chief goals in life was to get along well with people, and he figured that if he could get along with her he could get along with anyone. Despite these good-natured jests, theirs was hardly a loveless marriage. Xanthippe wept profusely at his execution.

Legend has it that Pericles' mistress, Aspasia, played a large role in his public decisions. Pericles had divorced his wife, by mutual consent, years before he took Aspasia as his mistress in 445 B.C. At the time he was about forty-five, and Aspasia about twenty-five. Plutarch later claimed that Aspasia was responsible for an Athenian decision to aid her home polis of Miletus against its traditional enemy, Samos. Politically adept, Aspasia had once been a diplomat of sorts for the king of Persia. Socrates and other Athenian philosophers visited her frequently, and she tutored numerous would-be politicians in the art of public speaking. Socrates called Aspasia "the admirable mistress I have in the art of speaking—she who has made so many good speakers, one of whom was the best among all the Greeks—Pericles." When Pericles' enemies tried her for impiety in the 430s B.C. (the real purpose of the trial was political), Pericles had to weep and plead for her until the jurors, always gratified to see their leaders cut down to size, voted for acquittal.

Of course, women were not guaranteed the right to vote by the U.S. Constitution until 1920 and did not begin to approach social equality until the 1960s. Indeed, modern criticism of Athens as "undemocratic" highlights the ambiguity of the word "democracy." If democracy means the political participation, however indirect, of all adults, then democracy is a twentieth-century invention. If, on the other hand, it means the direct political participation of all citizens, however narrowly the citizenry is defined, then democracy was a purely ancient phenomenon, since every modern democracy is representative, not participatory.

Whatever its faults as perceived through the subjective lens of modern values, the participatory nature of Athenian democracy prevented the rise of an inefficient and haughty bureaucracy and produced citizens who were excellent soldiers, sailors, legislators, administrators, and judges. Athens demanded so much talent from its citizens and gave them so much freedom to express their talent the city produced an incredible array of geniuses. To an Athenian, public service was as much a duty to oneself as an obligation to the polis.

ATHENIAN ART AND ARCHITECTURE IN THE AGE OF PERICLES

Pericles appointed Phidias to supervise the colossal project of reconstructing the Acropolis temples the Persians had destroyed, granting him a huge budget of 5,000 talents. The speed with which the Acropolis was transformed—all of the work was nearly finished in a decade—was astonishing considering the genius of its works. Many observers expected that the project would take generations to complete. Even Plutarch, who could be critical of Athenian democracy, later marveled at the grace, beauty, and durability of the temples. He noted that "they were created in so short a span, and yet for all time" and that they possessed "a youthful vigor which makes them appear to this day as if they were newly built." "This day" was over five centuries later.

The most famous and impressive of the temples, designed by Ictinus and constructed by the master-builder Callicrates, was the Parthenon, the temple dedicated to Athena Parthenos (Athena the Maiden), built between 447 and 432 B.C. The largest Doric-style temple in Greece, the building is 228 feet long and 101 feet wide. A photograph cannot capture the beauty of the Parthenon. It possesses a grandeur beyond its size. Ictinus calculated the spacing, height, and curvature of the marble columns with remarkable precision. He included a host of subliminal features in the structure that account for much of its emotional impact. Aware that a perfectly symmetrical building appears asymmetrical from a distance, he achieved the appearance of perfect symmetry by tilting the front of the building inward less than one degree (about two inches) and by increasing the circumference of the corner columns about two inches. He also sloped the temple's platform more than four inches from the center to the corners. He placed eight columns in the front and rear, instead of the usual six, and seventeen columns on each side. He used Ionic columns for the internal colonnade, thereby relieving the grandeur of the Doric temple with a touch of elegance.

The centerpiece of the Parthenon was Phidias's forty-one foot, ten-inch statue of Athena, armed with spear and shield and wearing her helmet and magical goatskin cloak. He fashioned Athena's face and hands from ivory and her draperies from gold that weighed more than a metric ton. The total cost of the statue was 750 talents, the equivalent of the annual income of 12,750 workers. As a worshiper entered the dark temple, he would see nothing. Then, as his pupils began to dilate, he would find himself in the presence of the enormous, exquisite Athena, whose image was reflected in a shallow pool that stood before her. The pool also helped preserve the ivory by humidifying the atmosphere. Unfortunately, the statue was destroyed in a fire in the fifth century A.D.

The Parthenon was further adorned with ninety-two external metopes, various pedimental groups, and a long, internal frieze—in all, the most substantial body of first-class sculpture that any Greek temple has left us. A small army of sculptors from different parts of Greece descended on the Acropolis, moving from project to project under the supervision of Phidias. They observed one another's work, exchanged ideas, and competed for glory. The artistic climate must have been similar to that of Renaissance Florence. In just a few years, these sculptors set the standards by which Western art—including that of Renaissance Florence—would be judged for centuries.

Sculpted by many different artists from 442 to 438 B.C., the metopes depicted battle scenes between the gods and the giants and between the Greeks and the Amazons. One exquisite metope featured a mourning Athena, wearing her helmet and the thick woolen dress of an Athenian noblewoman, leaning heavily on her spear, head bowed, reading a casualty list on a stele below. The common theme of the metopes was the victory of civilization over barbarism, reason over irrationality. It was no easy victory; in some of the reliefs the heroes are losing.

The pedimental groups were equally impressive. The western group portrayed the battle between Athena and Poseidon for dominion over Athens, the eastern her birth from the head of Zeus, cloven free by the ax of Hephaestus.

A continuous frieze circumscribed the wall inside the colonnade. A band 3 feet, 5 inches in height and 524 feet in length, this frieze depicted the Panathenaic procession. The procession begins at the west or rear door, proceeds around the sides, and culminates over the east door, where priests, elders, and the family of gods—from elderly Zeus to little Eros (Cupid), sheltered under his mother Aphrodite's parasol—await the worshipers. The speed and vigor of the horses is contrasted with the Olympian calm of their riders. Each figure is interesting in its own right, yet each relates to the whole, the triumphant combination of the unique and the universal that is the essence of great art.

The Parthenon was Athena's temple for nine centuries, a Christian church for ten, a mosque for nearly four, and a tourist attraction for more than a century now. It was fairly well preserved until 1687, when it was badly damaged by Venetian artillery, which struck a gunpowder magazine the Turks had stored in the temple, in the belief that no one would dare fire on the Parthenon. In 1800, Lord Elgin, the British ambassador to Turkey, which then controlled Greece, secured permission from the Turks to remove some of the Parthenon's pedimental sculptures and reliefs to London, where they are still housed in the British Museum. This was an act of imperialism, to be sure, but one that saved the reliefs from the storms and air pollution that defaced much that remained on the Acropolis in Athens.

Opposite the Parthenon stood the Erectheum, a temple dedicated to Athena, Poseidon, and the mythical king Erectheus, constructed between 421 and 405 B.C. While Ionic porticoes fronted its eastern and northern sides, its southern side featured the famed Porch of the Maidens. The columns of this portico were six maidens (the *caryatids*) who appeared to support that side of the temple on their heads. In addition to an olive tree planted by Apollo and a salt spring created by Poseidon, the temple housed an olive-wood statue of Athena, embellished by gilt, which the Athenians had unearthed and which they believed had fallen from heaven. (It was actually a statue fashioned by other Athenians centuries earlier. Fifth-century Athenians did not know that their ancestors had sculpted wood.) Each year, during the Panathenaic Festival, the people brought the decayed statue a new robe, woven and embroidered by the girls and women of Athens, which took almost nine months to fashion. Every four years there was a Greater Panathenaia, in which a much larger robe was woven for Athena by professional, male weavers who had won a contest.

Yet another temple located on the Acropolis was that of Athena Nike (Athena Victory), constructed in the 420s B.C. The elegant, well-proportioned little structure housed winged female figures, dressed in windblown, tight-clinging draperies, who represented victory in battle.

First accused of stealing gold, a false charge soon refuted, and then of insinuating his own image and that of Pericles among the warriors on the shield of his giant statue of Athena, Phidias left Athens and moved to Olympia. There, he fashioned a famous colossal statue of Zeus, also made of ivory and gold. The statue was so large Greeks claimed that Zeus sat by necessity, since if he stood, he would take the roof off the giant temple in which he was housed. One of the Seven Wonders of the Ancient World, the majestic statue presented the greatest of gods with so sublime and gentle an expression, it was said that the statue could console the deepest of sorrows. (The figure was later used as the model for a colossal statue of George Washington. The sight of an enormous Washington draped in classical robes amused many observers. One fan of Washington protested that the general had been too careful of his health to wander around half-naked in such a fashion. A prankster climbed the huge statue and shoved a large "plantation cigar" in Washington's mouth.)

The constraints placed on Greek architects and sculptors by the existence of only three types of columns and by limited space for metopes paralleled the human struggle to achieve greatness despite the limitations and shortness of life. The essential elements of Greek culture, the emphasis on restraint, dignity, and proportion, are all present in fifth-century Athenian art.

DRAMA IN THE AGE OF PERICLES

The Athenians developed drama, the source of many modern forms of entertainment, from the religious rites of the cult of Dionysus. In these rites, a chorus of men sang and danced. Although Athenian drama eventually moved beyond the few stories concerning Dionysus, even in later days a statue of Dionysus was carried in procession from a temple outside the city to the theater, so that he could watch the plays performed in his honor.

Around 534 B.C., Thespis introduced an "answerer," who conversed with the chorus—the beginning of dramatic dialogue (hence the term "thespian" for actor). By wearing different masks, the answerer could play a different character each time he took the stage. Masks were also more clearly visible than an actor's face in a large theater with only natural lighting, and they contained megaphone-like devices that projected the actor's voice. Unfortunately, masks also hampered emotional expression, since the actor had to wear the same facial expression throughout the scene. As a result, characters often had to talk about feelings that might otherwise have been expressed facially.

Not every Athenian was a fan of drama. One statesman was reputed to have prophesied: "If we allow ourselves to praise and honor make-believe like this, the next thing will be to find it creeping into our serious business."

The fifth century B.C. witnessed the perfection of the two types of drama, tragedy and comedy, both of which were staged at the new Theater of Dionysus beneath the Acropolis. (Plays had formerly been staged around a cart in the agora.) Tragedies were performed in tetralogies, three tragedies followed by a shorter comedy known as a "satyr play," the chorus of which consisted of satyrs—the drunken, oversexed, cowardly, buffoonish, horse-tailed, and goat-eared companions of Dionysus. What made the tragedies so remarkable was their disciplined portrayal of intense emotion. While violence formed an important element of tragedy, it was always enacted offstage. Though characters alluded to past events, all of the action within the play took place within a twenty-four hour period. As on the Shakespearean stage two millennia later, male actors portrayed female characters. Unfortunately, the music and dances of the chorus (the "choreography") that originally accompanied the dialogue were not recorded for posterity.

At the height of Athenian drama as many as 30,000 people gathered to see a performance. Attendance was not restricted on the basis of age, gender, or citizenship. The state provided funds for the payment and costuming of three actors in each play. As in the days of Shakespeare, playwrights often acted in their own plays, as well as directed and produced them. Since drama was considered a craft, sons often succeeded fathers as playwrights. Competitions typically pitted three tetralogies, or five comedies, against one another.

Aeschylus

The three greatest Athenian tragedians were Aeschylus, Sophocles, and Euripides. Aeschylus introduced a second actor, who came on and off the stage, playing different parts, while the *protagonist* remained onstage. Aeschylus also introduced costumes and painted scenery to the Greek stage. Scene-painting greatly influenced the wall paintings in aristocratic homes for centuries. Aeschylus wrote ninety plays, only seven of which survive. Graced by simple but vivid dialogue that steadily built emotion, his tetralogies won thirteen competitions.

Having fought at Marathon, where his brother had died, Aeschylus composed the *Persians* (472 B.C.), a dramatic account of the Greek victory in the Persian Wars. Some historians believe that Aeschylus wrote the play in the hope of restoring wartime unity in Athens and in order to remind Athenians of the immense services of Themistocles, who was under severe political attack. (Pericles, a young supporter of Themistocles at the time, financed the play's production.) But, if this is so, Aeschylus failed; as we have seen, Themistocles was ostracized. An associated purpose was the glorification of Athenian democracy. When the Persian queen Atossa inquires concerning the Athenians, "Who stands over them as shepherd? Who is master of the host?", the chorus replies proudly: "Of no single master are they called the subjects or the slaves." Nevertheless, Aeschylus imbues the Persians with tragic grandeur, depicting the ghost of Darius as great and wise.

Aeschylus's *Prometheus Bound* recounts the traditional story of the god Prometheus, punished by Zeus for foiling his plan to eliminate the human race. Prometheus had given humans fire, a gift that ensured their survival. In the play, Prometheus refuses to speak the word of submission that will free him. His last words are, "Behold me, I am wronged," his fortitude proving him greater than the universe that wrongs him. Aeschylus envisioned fate as a worthy adversary one must fight. His heroes are always bloodied but never bowed.

Aeschylus began the practice of forming the three tragedies of the tetralogy into a single unit. In Aeschylus's most famous trilogy, the *Oresteia* (458 B.C.), Agamemnon's wife, Clytemnestra, murders him in the bathtub, in part to seize the throne of Argos in combination with her lover, Agamemnon's cousin Aegisthus, and in part to avenge her daughter Iphigenia, whom Agamemnon had sacrificed to Artemis so that the winds would allow the Greek expedition to reach Troy. (The Greeks viewed the practice of human sacrifice with horror.) Clytemnestra then compounds her crime by abusing her daughter Electra for mourning her father and by seeking to kill her son Orestes, whose vengeance she fears. At the command of Apollo, Orestes then murders his mother to avenge his father (as well as to free Electra from her enslavement and to gain the throne). Orestes gains admission to his mother to do the dark deed by pretending to be the bearer of the news of his own death, news at which she rejoices. (Legend has it that an ancient "method actor," playing Electra in the scene in which she holds the urn that is supposed to contain the remains of her dead brother, carried the ashes of his own dead son to induce the required emotions.) Despite Clytemnestra's cruelty, it is not easy for Orestes to kill his own mother; he must steel himself, as when he first sacrificed a trembling animal on an altar. He hesitates. His mother pleads. Electra shrieks at him to strike. He does—with Aegisthus's sword, the very one his mother had used to kill his father. When Aegisthus arrives, the disguised Orestes tells him that the covered body he sees is Orestes. A joyous Aegisthus pulls back the covers to find Clytemnestra. A sword fight ensues, ending in the death of Aegisthus by the same sword. Orestes remarks: "I am borne along by a runaway horse." An elder summarizes: "Crime begets crime and slayers are slain." The Furies, a group of vengeful goddesses, then pursue Orestes for killing his mother. Athena finally steps in, establishing the Areopagus, the Athenian law court for homicide cases, in order to promote justice through law. The Furies prosecute Orestes, while Apollo defends him. Athena breaks the tie vote of the Areopagus in Orestes' favor. Athena appeases the Furies by telling them that they will have a shrine in Athens and will be worshipped forever as the now transformed Eumenides (the Kindly Ones). The play ends with a twilight procession, as the Eumenides are led to their sacred grotto.

Aeschylus's trilogy possessed two themes. First, although sin produced misery, misery produced wisdom. Aeschylus wrote: "Wisdom comes through bitter pain. . . . Against our will comes wisdom to us by the awful grace of God." Second, while every crime must be punished, or it would destroy society, it must be punished by law. The polis was the only proper tool of justice; private vengeance had no place in society. This was a powerful message, coming in the wake of Ephialtes' assassination. The play's condemnation of civil strife and exaltation of the Areopagus's role in homicide cases, the role to which it had just been reduced by Ephialtes' reforms, was a timely effort at conciliation and pacification.

Nevertheless, the assassination of Ephialtes may have played a role in Aeschylus's decision to leave Athens for Sicily, where he died in 456 B.C. (A more critical account claims he left in distress after losing a prize in competition with Sophocles.) After Aeschylus's death, the Ecclesia voted to grant a chorus to any citizen who proposed to revive one of his plays.

Sophocles

Sophocles was perhaps the most revered of the Athenian tragedians. Twenty-four of Sophocles' forty-one tetralogies won first prize, including a prize won in competition against Aeschylus when Sophocles was only twenty-seven. Sophocles never finished lower than second place in any dramatic competition. Unlike Aeschylus, Sophocles did not form the three tragedies of his tetralogy into a single unit, but presented each as a separate play. Although each play lasted only about an hour, there was no sense of haste, since the play concentrated on the climax of a traditional tale. Sophocles introduced a third actor, thereby allowing for the presentation of more complex situations. His style was direct, lucid, and simple.

Sophocles' two greatest plays were *Antigone* (441 B.C.) and *Oedipus the King* (after 429 B.C.). *Antigone* pits duty to conscience and family against duty to law and country. The play commences after Polynices has attempted to seize the Theban throne from his brother Eteocles. Both brothers have been killed in combat and their uncle Creon has taken the throne. The stern Creon has refused to allow the rebel Polynices a proper burial, leaving his body exposed to wild animals. Creon has even declared that anyone attempting to bury Polynices will be put to death. The opening of the play reveals this edict, which creates a crisis for Polynices' sister Antigone. While it is her sisterly duty to bury her brother, since his spirit cannot rest without a proper burial, it is also her duty to obey the laws of the polis. The passionate and determined woman buries her brother, risking the wrath of the king. Antigone makes an argument for what philosophers will later term natural law: "No edict can override the unwritten laws of the gods. For they are not of today or yesterday, but live forever." Infuriated, Creon sentences Antigone to death by entombment in a cave. He explains: "He whom the city places in power must be obeyed in things both small and great, just and unjust. . . . There is no greater evil than anarchy. It is anarchy that destroys cities, ruins homes, and breaks the ranks of allies, throwing spearmen into retreat." Creon's son Haemon, fiancée to his cousin Antigone, retorts: "One man does not make a city. . . . It is the soul of vanity to consider oneself alone wise." But stubbornly unwilling to reverse his decision, Creon declares: "Even if one must fall from power, it is better to be ruined by a man and so escape the name of one worsted by a woman." Nor will Creon's pride allow him to submit to his son or to popular opinion: "Are men of my age to be schooled by children? . . . Shall the city tell *me* what I should do?" The seer Tiresias issues a final rebuke to Creon: "You have thrust a living soul into the grave and denied a grave to a corpse." Tiresias's prophecy of doom finally causes Creon to relent, but it is too late. Antigone hangs herself by her girdle in the cave, prompting the suicides of both Haemon and Eurydice, Creon's wife. Sophocles' message seems to be that although obedience to legitimate law is a citizen's most sacred duty, the citizen is not obliged to obey illegitimate and unjust laws, imposed by the fiat of a dictator, against the voice of his or her own conscience.

Sophocles rarely presented characters plagued by inner tensions. Rather, Sophocles preferred to present moral dilemmas through the dialogue of characters with competing views (e.g., Antigone's argument for conscience versus her sister Ismene's argument for obedience). Sophocles captured both the grandeur and the tragedy of human life: "Many are the wonders of the world, and none so wonderful as man. . . . Language, wind-swift thought . . . these he taught himself, and how to find shelter from the storm's fierce darts of ice and rain. He strides into the future, powerless against nothing. From death alone he finds no escape, though he has devised remedies for diseases once incurable. Clever, ingenious man, with skill beyond imagining, he makes his way, now to evil, now to good."

In *Oedipus the King*, a play Aristotle later called the perfect tragedy because of its controlled passion, it is prophesied to King Laius of Thebes that a son of his will one day kill his father and marry his mother, Queen Jocasta. Terrified, Laius orders a herdsman to expose Laius's infant son Oedipus in the mountains. Pitying the poor child, the herdsman entrusts him to a family in Corinth. When full grown, Oedipus leaves Corinth due to an oracle that tells him that he will one day kill his father and marry his mother. Oedipus does not know that his parents in Corinth are not his biological parents. At a crossroads Oedipus accidentally kills his real father, Laius, in self-defense. Years later he migrates to Thebes, where he marries Jocasta and becomes a beloved and revered king. Ironically, the very steps that Laius and Oedipus take to forestall their respective fates actually bring them about. The ubiquitous seer Tiresias warns Oedipus of "the awful web from which you cannot escape." Yet all might still be well if not for Oedipus's tragic flaw, his need to search relentlessly for truth, which eventually leads him to discover that he has suffered the wretched fate predicted for him. Oedipus laments not only his own fate, but that of his daughter-sisters: "Shunned at every festival, they will come home in tears. And when they are ripe for marriage, what man will have them?" Overwhelmed by horror and anguish, Oedipus blinds himself and his mother-wife Jocasta commits suicide.

Oedipus the King has two themes. First, in the most complex and seemingly accidental combination of events there is a design, though humans do not understand it. Second, humans can triumph over despair, despite the most terrible suffering. While they cannot change fate, they can ally themselves with the good and suffer and die nobly. Despite his suffering, Oedipus's relentless and heroic pursuit of truth—even as he begins to glimpse its horror—bestows on him a tragic grandeur. Oedipus has all the markings of a Greek tragic hero; in the words of H. R. Joliffe, he is "high enough to fall, good enough to win our sympathy, hurt enough to frighten us, and treated unjustly enough to stir our pity." At the beginning of the sequel, *Oedipus at Colonus*, Sophocles presents Oedipus in all his tragic greatness: "So Oedipus in the course of his years stood firm and bleak as a darkened, windswept northern cape lashed by waves from every side, a sea of troubles breaking on his shores—rejected by men, but dearer to the gods."

While writing plays, Sophocles also served as treasurer of the Delian League and strategos of Athens. When Sophocles was ninety, his eldest son sued him. Tired of waiting for Sophocles to die and leave him his estate, the sixty-year old son sued for control of the property on the grounds of his father's senility. To refute his son's claim Sophocles brought a recent sample of his poetry to the trial. Impressed by these lines from *Oedipus at Colonus,* the jury dismissed the case and fined the son for filing a frivolous suit. Yet, by then, Sophocles was himself a tragic figure, having written: "Youth lusts for life. Age longs for rest. And none but a fool would seek too long a span of winter years when joys are few and griefs are many."

Euripides

Composed in the latter part of the fifth century B.C., the plays of Euripides, the last of the three great Athenian tragedians, foreshadowed the new drama that revolutionized Greek theater in the fourth century B.C. Euripides worked in a secluded cave fitted up as a study on the island of Salamis. The author of ninety-two plays, Euripides won only five prizes because his plays purposely left people disturbed and dissatisfied, though his clever, realistic dialogue and music were highly popular. Sophocles claimed: "I portray men as they ought to be. Euripides portrays them as they are."

Euripides' plays emphasized the individual over the polis. He reduced the role of the chorus, which often represented society, and expanded the role of the individual character. Indeed, Euripides himself avoided a role in Athenian public life, in sharp contrast to Aeschylus, who had fought at the Battle of Marathon, and Sophocles, who had served as strategos. Rather than dealing with matters of society or the polis, Euripides centered his action around tragic, unique, even abnormal characters. Euripides added more suspense, action, and complicated plots, in contrast to the simplicity of most fifth-century tragedy. His passionate plays lacked the usual Greek restraint and the common emphasis on the universals of the human condition. They were about specific humans, not humankind.

Euripides has been called "the poet of the world's grief." One of his characters asks: "Since life began, has there in God's eye stood one happy man?" Unlike the other tragedians, Euripides did not grant sorrow any redemptive power.

Euripides joined the growing chorus of intellectuals who condemned the irrationality of traditional Greek religion. He wrote: "Say not there are adulterers in heaven. Long since my heart has known it false. God if he be God lacks nothing. All these are dead, unhappy tales. . . . If gods do evil, then they are not gods." Euripides virtually banished the gods from the body of his plays, saving them for the final scene, when a divinity often appeared to tie up loose ends in the plot. One of Euripides' characters, Bellerophon, even declares: "Does someone say that there are gods in the heavens? There are not, there are not—unless one chooses to follow old tradition like a fool. Look for yourselves—do not accept my words—but hear what I say. Tyrants kill men and rob them of their goods, and break their oaths, and lay whole cities waste; and still they prosper more than the pious and gentle do. And I know little cities, honoring gods, subject to greater ones, not so devout, held down by superior force of arms."

Another aspect of Euripides that set him apart from most previous playwrights was his great sympathy for women. In *Alcestis* (438 B.C.), the earliest surviving play of Euripides, King Admetus of Thessaly learns from the Fates, goddesses responsible for determining the life span of each individual, that his time has expired. But the Fates allow the king the opportunity to find a substitute who will die in his place. Only his wife, Alcestis, who loves him more than life itself, agrees to serve as the substitute. She explains, "I could not bear to have you torn from me and see our children fatherless." Alcestis's courage contrasts sharply with her husband's shameful cowardice. Euripides even has Admetus and his father, Pheres, disrupt Alcestis's funeral with a comical argument about which of the two men is the greater coward for not offering to die, to the great embarrassment of the onlookers. (Pheres: "I know of no law in Greece that fathers must die for their sons. . . . Death is long and bitter; life is short and sweet. You love the light of day. Do you think your father does not love it, too?" Admetus: "You old men are liars when you complain of age and pray for death. For just let Death come near you, and you refuse to go. Suddenly old age is no burden at all." Pheres: "Me a coward? Look who says so! Oh, you have hit on a clever scheme to live forever. Just keep persuading your wives to die for you.") Admetus realizes too late his folly in sacrificing so noble a wife. He tells her, as she lays dying: "There shall be no pleasures when you are gone. . . . Only those without wives and children are happy. For Death can only strike them once." But *Alcestis* has a happy ending: Heracles wrestles Death for possession of Alcestis and wins her back.

In *Medea* (431 B.C.), Euripides shows compassionate understanding of the violence to which women could be driven by social constraints. Medea has saved the life of Jason of Iolcus (in Thessaly) and has helped him capture the Golden Fleece. Her passionate love for him has even led her to leave her own father and to kill her own brother. Medea has then returned with Jason to Greece and has borne him two sons. An ungrateful snob, Jason then plans to violate his vows to Medea by abandoning her and marrying Creusa, the daughter of Creon, the king of Corinth. Learning of the plan, Medea groans: "The one who was all the world to me has proved the vilest of men." Engulfed by an ever-growing rage, she plans her revenge, though aware of her own increasing madness. She poisons Creusa and Creon and kills her own two sons with a sword, declaring, "I, who gave them their life, will take it away." Medea is then carried away on a fiery, dragon-propelled chariot dispatched by her grandfather He-lios, the sun god, so that the furious Jason cannot get his hands on her. (According to myth, Jason then wandered about, forlorn, before taking up residence in his famous but now dilapidated ship, the *Argo*, until a rotting beam fell on his head and killed him.)

Transformed by a harrowing internal conflict into a bloodthirsty de-mon, Medea expresses the rage, frustration, hopelessness, and loneliness of a foreign woman in a Greek city:

> We women are the most unfortunate creatures. First, with an excess of wealth it is required for us to buy a husband [a reference to the dowry] and to take for our bodies a master; for not to take one is even worse. And now the ques-tion is serious whether we take a good one or bad one; for there is no easy es-cape for a woman, nor can she say no to her marriage. She arrives among new modes of behavior and manners, and needs prophetic power, until she has learned at home how best to manage him who shares the bed with her. And if we work out all this well and carefully, and the husband lives with us and lightly bears his yoke, then life is enviable. If not, I'd rather die. A man, when he's tired of the company in his home, goes out of the house and puts an end to his boredom and turns to a friend or mistress of his own age. But we are forced to keep our eyes on one alone. What they say of us is that we have a peaceful time, living at home while they do the fighting in war. How wrong they are! I would very much rather stand three times in the front of battle than bear one child. . . . I am alone in an alien land, scorned by my husband, a help-less captive, without a mother or brother or kinsman to turn to. . . . O Zeus, why do men not carry some outward sign of their worth like coins? Then we could recognize the villainous soul in time.

But Medea's rage transforms her from a victim into an avenger, and she at last declares: "Never think of me as a poor, weak, defenseless wife, for I am a different breed of woman—kind to my friends, but a vengeful fury to those who wrong me. Only such a woman is worthy of glory." These lines were quite subversive for their day. Though now regarded as one of the classics of Greek literature, *Medea* placed last in its competition.

Trojan Women (415 B.C.), produced just after the Athenian massacre of Melos during the Peloponnesian War, highlighted the horrors of war by portraying the Greek destruction of Troy through the eyes of the Trojan women, who were raped, enslaved, and forced to watch their children sac-rificed over Achilles' grave or hurled from the walls of the city. The pres-sure of war had eliminated all considerations of decency. Yet Hecuba, the Trojan queen, remains a wise and heroic figure. She declares of her fallen city: "Had God not turned in his hand and cast to earth our greatness, we would have passed away giving nothing to men. They would have found no theme for song in us nor made great poems from our sorrows."

In *Iphigenia in Aulis* (410 B.C.), Iphigenia, daughter of Agamemnon, bravely offers herself as a sacrifice to Artemis so that the goddess will subdue the winds that prevent the Greeks from sailing to Troy. Iphigenia declares: "All Greece depends upon me now. I alone have the power . . . to free the daughters of Hellas forever from barbarian lust. . . . This body is mine to give to whom I will. I give it to Greece. . . . Greece must never bow down to barbarians." She marches boldly, head held high, to the altar to be sacrificed.

King Archelaus of Macedon attracted Euripides to his court shortly before Euripides' death in 406 B.C. One legend has it that Euripides was torn to pieces by dogs. At any rate, on learning of Euripides' death, Sophocles appeared in mourning at the Festival of Dionysus.

COMEDY AND THE PERICLEAN LEGACY OF FREE SPEECH

Perhaps an even more impressive tribute to the Periclean legacy of free speech than Athens's great tragedies was its continued tolerance, even after Pericles' death, of raucous, uninhibited comedy, plays that often included the merciless ridicule of political leaders. There is no record of Pericles ever taking offense at the comic playwrights of Athens, though they often poked fun at him. His tolerance of even the most personal abuse on the comic stage set a precedent of free speech that even Pericles' less tolerant successors were unable to reverse.

Aristophanes

Though Pericles did not live to see the comedies of Aristophanes, Athens's greatest comic playwright, his plays stand as a testimony to the remarkable breadth of free speech in the society that Pericles' leadership had helped to create. Aristophanes satirized everyone—other playwrights, public officials, philosophers, generals, wars, and the people themselves. His plays combined poetry, fantasy, buffoonery, indecency, puns, and parody. They traversed a remarkable range, from the most sophisticated humor to the most scatological brand of comedy. His actors wore ludicrous masks and padded clothes, the male characters often displaying exaggerated leather penises. The masks were sometimes caricatures of the famous people he lampooned. Yet his plays often included beautiful and serious verse. While *The Babylonians* (426 B.C.) depicted the cities of the Delian League as slaves grinding at Athens's mill, *Knights* (424 B.C.) portrayed the Athenian demagogue Cleon as the slave of the fickle *Demos* (the people).

The Clouds (423 B.C.), which won third prize at a festival, so ridiculed Socrates that the philosopher later complained at his trial that the play had prejudiced the people against him. (Nevertheless, according to Plato, the playwright and the philosopher remained friends years after the play was produced.) In the play, Strepsiades sends his son Pheidipides to Socrates' "thinking shop" to learn how "to win any case, however bad," so that Strepsiades can avoid paying his debts if taken to court. An eccentric Socrates sits suspended in a basket so that he can have "lofty thoughts." He declares that thunder is not caused by the gods, but by the collision of dense clouds—which he compares with the flatulence of a man who has just eaten a large meal. He scoffs at those who believe in the gods. But Strepsiades' plan backfires. Pheidipides learns at Socrates' school that it is acceptable to strike his father. Now shameless, Pheidipides tells his horrified father: "It's delightful to be acquainted with the wisdom of today, and to be able to look down on convention. . . . What is law, anyway? It must have been made at some time, and made by a man just like you and me." Furious, Strepsiades burns down Socrates' thinking shop. Aristophanes slandered Socrates in this play, attributing to him the atheism and moral relativism of the more extreme Sophists. Aristophanes chose Socrates to represent the sophistry he detested due to Socrates' fame as a philosopher—all Athenians would recognize the name—and either did not bother to learn Socrates' actual beliefs or did not care to present them accurately.

The Wasps (422 B.C.) satirized the epidemic of litigation in Athenian society. The chorus consisted of old, idiotic jurors who carried skewers as their stingers. One character, a son, has to shut his father up in the house, guarded by slaves, to keep him out of the law courts.

Women were as often the butt of Aristophanes' jokes as men, though Aristophanes displayed an uncommon belief in the intelligence of at least some women. In *Lysistrata* (411 B.C.), the women of Greece take an oath to withhold sex from their husbands until the men agree to end the Peloponnesian War. After the male leader of the chorus coins a famous phrase, "We can't live with you, and we can't live without you," Lysistrata, the leader of the striking women, asks the men, "Is it right that we shall not be allowed to make the least little suggestion to you, no matter how much you mismanage the City's affairs? . . . I am a woman, but I am not brainless." The wise Lysistrata soon has the Athenian and Spartan ambassadors compromising—marking out the geographical territory they want, using a nude female as their map, and singing songs about the Persian Wars, when Athenians and Spartans had fought together to save Greece. *Thesmophoriazusae* (411 B.C.) concerns women who hatch a plot against Euripides because of his alleged misogyny, a vehicle that allows Aristophanes to ridicule the tragedian.

Indeed, even death could not shield Euripides from Aristophanes' barbs. In *The Frogs* (405 B.C.), the god Dionysus, patron of drama, descends into Hades determined to set Athenian theater back on track by returning with whomever he determines to be the greatest tragedian. Sophocles is too peaceable to participate in a contest, so Aeschylus and Euripides are left to vie with each other for the honor by ridiculing each other's lines. Aeschylus wins the contest.

In the whimsical *Assemblywomen* (393 B.C.), the Athenians decide to turn the government over to women, who institute socialism. In *Wealth* (388 B.C.), Wealth is blind and gives his benefits to the wrong people. As a result, Chremylus consults the oracle at Delphi to learn how he can turn his son into "a scoundrel, wicked, rotten through and through," so that the poor youth can be a success in Athens. Apollo then shows Wealth that Asclepius can cure blindness. When Wealth regains his eyesight, a rich woman loses her gigolo, who now has his own wealth. Wealth is then enthroned in his home of the good old days, the Athenian treasury.

Combining a love of solid, old-fashioned country people with a remarkable energy and exuberance, Aristophanes displayed a rare humanity and an irresistible charm. At a party Plato discussed in his *Symposium*, Aristophanes explained the origin of romantic love with the following fable. There once were creatures of a single gender that had two heads, four arms, and four legs. The gods feared them but wanted their sacrifices, so Zeus cleaved them in two with bolts of lightning. Aristophanes explained: "When the original body was cut through, each half wanted the other and hugged it; they threw their arms around each other, desiring to grow together in the embrace. . . . So you see how ancient is the mutual love implanted in mankind, bringing together the parts of the original body, and trying to make one out of two, and to heal the natural structure of man. . . . Each one seeks his other half. . . . The way to make our race happy is to make love perfect, and each to get his very own beloved and go back to our original nature."

Fortunately for Aristophanes, there were no libel laws in Athens. Enraged when *The Babylonians* was performed before an audience containing foreign dignitaries, Cleon prosecuted the young playwright for slandering the city in the presence of foreigners. But no one could touch the clown prince of Athens. The next year he returned with an even harsher attack on Cleon (in *The Acharnians*), calling him "a coward" and "a cheat," whose lips "spewed out a torrent of sewage." Though Aristophanes wisely penned the play under a pseudonym, the identity of the author must have been obvious. Referring to the absence of foreigners in the audience on that occasion, a character in the play slyly remarks, "Now we are by ourselves."

Fearless, Aristophanes lampooned everyone from the gods to the audience itself. Even in the midst of the Peloponnesian War, a struggle to the death against Athens's hated enemy, Sparta, Aristophanes repeatedly produced plays attacking both the war itself and the Athenian people's general penchant for war. He even made a character who clearly represented the playwright himself declare that the Spartans "have a good many legitimate grievances against us."

The leader of the chorus in Aristophanes' *The Acharnians*, though speaking tongue-in-cheek, spoke truly when he instructed the audience regarding the playwright: "Hold on to him. He'll carry on impeaching every abuse he sees, and give you much valuable teaching, making you wiser, happier men. . . . Nor will you drown in fulsome praises, such as all the rest bestow on you. He thinks his job is to teach you what is best."

HISTORICAL WRITING IN THE AGE OF PERICLES

Herodotus

Although he was not an Athenian, Herodotus of Halicarnassus (in Caria), spent four, life-transforming years in Athens (447–443 B.C.), where the city's great minds influenced him deeply. Justly called the "Father of History," it was Herodotus who first used the term *historia* (meaning research or inquiry) to refer to study of the past.

Herodotus differed from the mythologists of previous eras in several ways. First, although Herodotus did not banish the supernatural completely from his *Histories,* an account of the Persian Wars, he attributed most past events to natural causes. He portrayed human action as the prime determinant of history. Herodotus's belief that the wisdom of Themistocles and the courage of free men had won the Persian Wars contrasted sharply with the constant meddling of the gods in Homer's *Iliad* and in the other Greek poems. Herodotus even discussed those occasions when prophecies of the oracle of Delphi had proved inaccurate or when the oracle had been bribed to favor a side in a dispute.

Second, unlike the mythologists, Herodotus based his history on real research. Herodotus did a remarkable job of gathering evidence throughout the eastern Mediterranean world and weaving it together into a plausible narrative. His accuracy was astonishing, considering that some of the events he related had occurred centuries before his time and that he had to rely mostly on oral sources even for more recent events. While he did exaggerate the size of the Persian army, that error was due partly to the unreliability of his Persian sources.

Third, unlike the mythologists, Herodotus always identified his sources, even when he doubted their veracity. He wrote: "For myself, my duty is to report all that is said; but I am not obliged to believe it all alike—a remark which may be understood to apply to my whole history."

Indeed, after Herodotus related the popular story of a diver who swam eleven miles underwater without ascending for air, he deadpanned: "My own opinion is that on this occasion he took a boat."

Fourth, the difference between history and mythology was further expressed in the decision of Herodotus and his successors to write prose, not poetry—significantly, the same decision previously made by many of the Ionian scientists. Though his work was highly amusing, Herodotus's principal purpose was to inform, only secondarily to entertain.

Exiled from Halicarnassus in 457 B.C. for his alleged opposition to Persian rule, Herodotus traveled through much of the known world—Egypt, Cyrene, Tyre, Mesopotamia, Arabia, the Black Sea, and the north Aegean—gathering material for a geographical work. He then landed at Athens, where Pericles and Sophocles befriended him. The city itself, as well as Athenian stories of the Persian Wars, so impressed Herodotus that he decided to change his topic of study. The first part of Herodotus's *Histories* concerned the rise of the Persian Empire, the second part the resulting wars with Greece.

Herodotus was not only the first historian, but also one of the most entertaining historians who has ever written. His hilarious digressions on Near Eastern cultures, the products of a passionate curiosity and love of life, represent a gold mine of anthropological research. Indeed, Herodotus has also been called the first anthropologist, sociologist, and archaeologist. No subject was too small or inconsequential to evoke Herodotus's interest, none too dull for his fertile imagination to enliven. A typical example was Herodotus's discussion of the theory that Egyptian skulls were harder than Persian skulls. A true empiricist, Herodotus felt compelled to test the hypothesis. So he journeyed to a battlefield where the Egyptians and Persians had recently fought and began smashing corpses over the head with rocks. He found that while Egyptian skulls could barely be cracked with huge stones, Persian skulls could be crushed using small rocks. Having validated the hypothesis, Herodotus then developed a typically imaginative theory to explain the phenomenon. Because Egyptians shaved their heads and walked about without any head covering, while the Persians wore their hair long and wrapped in a turban, the Egyptians required thicker skulls to withstand the heat of the sun. This was almost a theory of natural selection.

Another tale typical of Herodotus is that of Darius I's accession to the Persian throne. When Cambyses, the previous emperor, died without an heir, the seven leading noblemen of Persia met to determine who should replace him. The seven decided to allow the gods to decide. (Ancient peoples often employed what we would call "games of chance" to allow the gods to participate in important decisions.) The seven Persian aristocrats decided to ride their favorite horses to a certain spot before dawn the next day. The owner of the first horse to neigh after sunrise would become the new emperor. Darius's lowly groomsman found a way to fix the contest. Before dawn, he rubbed the genitalia of the favorite mare of his master's horse, then stuffed his hands in his cloak to preserve the smell. Then, as the sun rose at the designated location, the groomsman pretended to fasten the horse's bit. The horse smelled his hands and neighed. That is how Darius became emperor of Persia, the most powerful man in the world. This story is typical of Herodotus, because it demystifies an important event, attributing its outcome to a clever human, rather than to the gods. (In reality, it was not quite as easy as all that; Darius had to win a brief but bloody civil war to secure his throne.) Herodotus is like a favorite uncle—brilliant, endearingly eccentric, and, above all, always fun.

Unfortunately, Herodotus died at the Athenian colony of Thuria in 425 B.C. before he had completed the *Histories*. Ironically, the very man who immortalized Athens at the height of its glory was barred from becoming an Athenian citizen by his friend Pericles' recent restrictions on naturalization.

Thucydides

Thucydides, an Athenian of aristocratic lineage whose family owned rich mines, has been called the "first scientific historian." By this it is meant that he was the first to remove supernatural causation from history altogether. He also began the association of "history" with political and military affairs, an equation that dominated Western historiography until the 1960s, when Herodotean "social history" was resurrected—though even Herodotus had felt compelled to justify his lengthy, anthropological digressions on the dubious grounds of establishing the background for his central concern, the Persian Wars. For millennia the association of "history" with political and military affairs made it the exclusive study of adult male aristocrats, leaving little place for a discussion of the lives of lower-class males, women, children, and slaves.

Thucydides began his *History of the Peloponnesian War* by remarking that although his work would not be as entertaining as that of some unnamed but obvious predecessor, he hoped it would be "a possession for all time." Thucydides succeeded. A masterpiece of concision and precision, Thucydides' history is filled with insights that are so universal in application it continues to be read and cited by the best historians, political scientists, and military strategists. Thucydides' distinction between the underlying and immediate causes of war still dominates that field of inquiry. His grave and intense language effectively conveys the drama of history.

Thucydides believed that history was cyclical. If one selected an important set of events that included many variables and closely investigated that historical sequence, one would find a pattern that could be used to predict future events. Although Thucydides believed that human development proceeded in cycles, his belief in the utility of history implied that knowledge of the past might allow humans to break these cycles.

The Peloponnesian War began when Thucydides was thirty years old. He believed that historians should write only about recent events, since he doubted the accuracy of oral accounts of the distant past. Because of this, some have called Thucydides a journalist rather than a historian, though in several instances he did recount the events of past centuries—largely to show that past wars had been inferior to the Peloponnesian War in size and significance.

Like Herodotus and most subsequent Greek and Roman historians, Thucydides had a habit of creating fictitious speeches for historical figures as a means of conveying their personalities and ideas. But Thucydides assured the reader that in such cases he did his best to faithfully reflect the content, if not always the wording, of what had actually been said.

In 424 B.C., while strategos, Thucydides was ostracized for arriving too late to defend the Athenian colony of Amphipolis against a Spartan attack. Located in Thrace, Amphipolis, the "city surrounded" by the looping Strymon River, was a vital source of metals and timber and an essential base for protecting grain shipments from the Black Sea region.

Thucydides' period of exile, much of it spent in the Peloponnesus, left him with plenty of time to write a history. His banishment probably increased his bitterness toward Athenian democracy, which he portrayed, at least in the later stages of the war, as the severest form of mob rule. Indeed, Thucydides' writings bolstered an antidemocratic tradition that dominated Western literature until the rise of representative democracy in the nineteenth century. Even Thucydides' reverential treatment of Pericles was perhaps a way of contrasting him with the demagogues who succeeded him, one of whom (Cleon) had played a leading role in Thucydides' ostracism.

Yet, Thucydides retained an obvious love for his former polis and displayed great pity at its suffering. Furthermore, however colored by his own experience, much of what Thucydides wrote was probably true. Some modern critics have been so infuriated that any historian would dare to highlight the negative aspects of democracy that they have missed the opportunity to use Thucydides to learn more about the weaknesses of democracy—knowledge that is essential to its survival and improvement. Fortunately, most historians still acknowledge and seek to emulate the rare degree of balance in Thucydides' narrative. Although he fell short of his impossible goal of complete objectivity, Thucydides was perhaps the greatest of all the ancient historians.

Thucydides returned to Athens after the war ended in 404 B.C., but died about four years later, before he could complete his *History of the Peloponnesian War*. It ends in midsentence in the year 411 B.C.

CAUSES OF THE PELOPONNESIAN WAR

The three underlying causes of the Peloponnesian War were fear, pride, and fatalism. The Spartans had been suspicious and fearful of Athens's Delian League from the time of its establishment and now felt threatened by the polis's newfound power and by its democratic system.

Relations between the two poleis were worsened by a long-standing commercial rivalry between Athens and Corinth, Sparta's principal ally in the Peloponnesian League. In 434–433 B.C., Corinth waged war against Corcyra (Corfu), a neutral Greek island in the Adriatic Sea, due to a dispute over Epidamnus in what is now Albania, a colony that the two poleis had founded jointly. In 433 B.C., alarmed by a Corinthian naval construction program, Corcyra abandoned its traditional policy of neutrality and asked Athens for aid.

Athens decided to aid Corcyra in its conflict with Corinth for three reasons. First, the Athenians feared the results of a Corcyraean defeat. At the time, the three greatest naval powers in Greece were Athens (300 ships), Corcyra (120 ships), and Corinth (100 ships). If the Corcyraean navy fell into Corinthian hands, the Peloponnesian League, already superior to the Delian League in land power, would approach it in naval power. Second, the Athenians were dazzled by the Corcyraeans' offer to join the Delian League if the Athenians aided them in their war against Corinth. Such an alliance between Athens and Corcyra would give the Delian League complete naval supremacy. Third, fatalism contributed to Athens's decision. Many Athenians considered war with Sparta inevitable and sought to increase Athenian power in preparation for that conflict. According to Thucydides, the Corcyraeans encouraged Athenian fatalism, saying: "If any of you imagine that war is far off, he is grievously mistaken, and is blind to the fact that Lacedaemon [Sparta] regards you with jealousy and desires war." Pericles shared this perspective since he doubted that Greece could remain half democratic and half oligarchic. Territorial disputes might be settled by negotiation, but ideological differences could not be compromised.

Although Athens dispatched only thirty ships to defend Corcyra, Corinth was forced to retreat in humiliation, rather than risk war with Athens. Nevertheless, fearful of Corinthian machinations in Potidaea, which was both a Corinthian colony and a member of the Delian League, Athens ordered the Potidaeans to expel their Corinthian ambassadors and to raze their walls on the seaward side. The Athenians also increased Potidaea's assessment to the League from six to fifteen talents. When Potidaea revolted, the Athenians surrounded the city, trapping Corinthian envoys inside.

Corinth, now infuriated enough to desire war, called a meeting of the Peloponnesian League at Sparta (432 B.C.). There, again according to Thucydides, the Corinthians played on Spartan pride and fear: "The world used to say that you were to be depended upon. . . . If our present enemy, Athens, has not again and again annihilated us, we owe more to her blunders than to your protection. Indeed, expectations from you have before now been the ruin of some whose faith induced them to omit preparation. . . . Do not sacrifice friends and kindred to the bitterest enemies, and drive the rest of us in despair to some other alliance." The Corinthians' threat was unmistakable.

Megara, another Spartan ally, complained about Pericles' harsh decree prohibiting Athenian allies from trading with the Megarians. The Athenians were still angry with the Megarians for breaking away from Athens, and massacring an Athenian garrison in the process, in 446 B.C. More recently, the Athenians believed the Megarians had killed an Athenian herald.

The able Spartan king Archidamos warned against the devastation war would bring to Greece, noting that young men often romanticized war because they had no experience of it. But Archidamos's rivals portrayed his wisdom as cowardice, and Sparta declared war on Athens.

THE PELOPONNESIAN WAR

The Spartan Invasion of Attica

Nine months later, the Spartan army invaded Athenian territory (431 B.C.), forcing the country people to retreat behind the walls of the city. But though the Spartans destroyed the Athenians' crops, the Athenians could still supply themselves with food and other essential supplies as long as they controlled the seas. Athens and its allies possessed 600 ships to the 150 ships of Sparta and its allies. Better yet, while the Athenians possessed 6,000 talents, the Spartan treasury was virtually empty.

The Speech

It was the Athenian custom to honor all of the city's fallen soldiers with a public funeral each year. Each of the polis's ten tribes carried a giant cypress coffin containing the remains of its casualties in a procession leading to the public cemetery outside the city. The coffins were carried on biers, with an empty eleventh bier representing those missing in action. The public funeral featured an oration, delivered by the most distinguished and respected citizen of Athens. In 430 B.C. that man was Pericles, and he delivered one of the greatest speeches in Western history.

Pericles began his speech (recounted by Thucydides) by denying his ability to honor Athens's fallen heroes. Rather, through their supreme sacrifice, the soldiers had bestowed honor on him and on all other Athenians. Pericles then glorified the individualistic, democratic way of life the heroes had died defending, contrasting it with the totalitarian, oligarchic system of Sparta:

> Our constitution does not copy the laws of neighboring states; we are a pattern to others rather than imitators ourselves. Its administration favors the many rather than the few; this is why it is called a democracy. If we look to the laws, they afford equal justice to all in their private differences . . . class conditions not being allowed to interfere with merit; nor again does poverty bar the way—if a man is able to serve the state, he is not hindered by the obscurity of his condition. . . . We do not feel called upon to be angry with our neighbor for doing what he likes. . . . But all this ease in our private relations does not make us lawless as citizens. Against this, fear is our chief safeguard, teaching us to obey the magistrates and the laws, particularly such as regard the protection of the injured. . . . We throw open our city to the world and never exclude foreigners from any opportunity of learning or observing. Although the eyes of an enemy may occasionally profit by our openness, we trust less in system and policy than in the native spirit of our citizens; while in education, where our rivals from their very cradles by a painful discipline seek after manliness, we live exactly as we please, and yet are just as ready to encounter every legitimate danger. . . . We cultivate refinement without stinting and knowledge without effeminacy; wealth we employ more for use than for show, and place the real disgrace of poverty not in owning to the fact, but in declining to struggle against it. . . . Again, in our enterprises we present the singular spectacle of daring and deliberation, each carried to its highest point. . . . In short, I say that as a city we are the school of Hellas; and I doubt if the world can produce a man who . . . is equal to so many emergencies, and graced by so happy a versatility, as the Athenian.

In this speech, Pericles transformed the traditional heroic ethic, the quest for immortality through fame and glory, by applying it to a city rather than to an individual hero. The new heroes of his day, he proclaimed, fought not for their own individual glory, like Achilles, but for the immortal fame of their city. Pericles' funeral oration is similar in argument, if not in style, to Abraham Lincoln's Gettysburg Address. But, in stark contrast to Lincoln, Pericles never mentioned the gods, though the occasion was perfectly suited to such a reference. It is unclear whether this glaring omission was due to Pericles' irreligiosity or to Thucydides'.

The Plague

Unfortunately, the overcrowding caused by the migration of the country people into Athens created the perfect breeding ground for a plague that devastated Athens in 430–429 B.C. and again in 427–426 B.C. The plague (perhaps bubonic), carried from Egypt to Athens by a trading vessel, ravaged parts of the Persian Empire as well. Thucydides, who contracted and survived the plague and nursed many sick friends, described the plague's symptoms:

> It [the internal body] burned so that the patient could not bear to have on him clothing or linen even of the very lightest description. . . . What they would have liked best would have been to throw themselves into cold water; as indeed was done by some of the neglected sick, who plunged into the rain tanks in their agonies of unquenchable thirst . . . though it made no difference whether they drank little or much. Besides this, the miserable feeling of not being able to rest or sleep never ceased to torment them.

Physicians were among the first to die, since they contracted the disease from its earliest victims. Some men managed to escape death by severing infected extremities. Even predatory birds avoided the unburied bodies, or died after eating them. Thucydides continued: "No remedy was found that could be used as a specific; for what did good in one case did harm in another. Strong and weak constitutions proved equally incapable of resistance, all alike being swept away, although nursed with utmost precaution." Those who became ill were filled with despair. Athenians avoided each other but perished anyway. Thucydides concluded:

> The bodies of dying men lay one upon another, and half-dead creatures reeled about the streets and gathered round all the fountains in their longing for water. The sacred places also in which they [the country people] had quartered themselves were full of corpses . . . for as the disaster passed all bounds, men, not knowing what was to become of them, became utterly careless of everything. . . . All burial rites before in use were entirely upset, and they buried the bodies as best they could. . . . [Wood, used for pyres, became scarce.] Sometimes getting the start of those who raised a pile, they threw their own dead body upon the stranger's pyre and ignited it. . . . Present enjoyment, and all that contributed to it, was considered both honorable and useful. Fear of gods or law there was none to restrain them. . . . No one expected to be brought to trial for his offenses, but each felt that a far severer sentence had been already passed upon them all.

One-quarter of the Athenian population died at this time, including Pericles himself. Pericles had been elected strategos almost thirty times, holding the office thirteen straight years before the people had ousted him and fined him in 430 B.C. In their rage, the people had blamed the plague on Pericles' strategy of retreating within the city. But, of course, Pericles had had no alternative to that strategy, since it would have been suicidal to engage the larger and better-trained Spartan infantry. Overcome with remorse, the people had reinstated Pericles in 429 B.C. By then, Pericles' two sons by his first wife, his sisters, some of his other relatives, some of his friends, and his assistants had all died of the plague, and he himself had contracted it. Although Pericles survived the disease itself, he died of a resultant exhaustion, at the age of about sixty, later that year. Shortly before Pericles' death, the assembly exempted his son by Aspasia from Pericles' own naturalization restrictions, so that his family line might continue among the citizenry of Athens. But Pericles' political successors, lesser men who lacked the courage to oppose the people when they were wrong, would lead Athens to ruin.

Defeat

Alcibiades, one of those successors, persuaded Athens to launch a massive invasion of Sicily in 415 B.C. The Athenians lost 4,500 of their own men, 40,000 allies, and 200 ships—one-third of their army and most of their navy—in Sicily. The Sicilian disaster produced revolts among Athens's allies and even inspired a coup that produced a brief period of oligarchic rule in Athens itself (411 B.C.). More importantly, sensing a golden opportunity to gain the vengeance against Athens that had so long eluded them, the Persians began financing the construction of a large Spartan fleet and the payment of its crews. The destruction of the Athenian fleet in the Sicilian campaign, when combined with the construction of a new Spartan fleet, proved the turning point in the war, threatening Athenian control of the seas.

Nevertheless, the Athenian leader Cleophon refused to accept a generous Spartan peace offer that would have preserved the status quo. Although the Athenians won a naval victory at Arginusae in 406 B.C., victory soon turned to defeat, when the short-tempered Athenian assembly executed the six victorious generals for failing to rescue drowning rowers in stormy seas. Five thousand men had drowned in the great confusion of that stormy evening. The Greeks believed that the souls of such men, denied a proper burial, could not enter Hades, but must wander the earth as shades. The generals, one of whom was the son of Pericles and Aspasia, were denied a proper trial. The generals insisted that they instructed a captain to rescue men clinging to the wreckage; for obvious reasons, the captain denied that the order had been issued.

Ever optimistic (or stubborn), the Athenians again rejected a Spartan peace overture that would have left them part of their former empire. In

405 B.C., largely through the incompetence of Athenian generals (their best generals had just been executed), the brilliant Spartan general Lysander caught the remaining Athenian navy by surprise on the beach at Aegospotami at the Hellespont. Not only had the Athenian generals chosen a poor location on an exposed beach, but they had allowed the rowers to roam about at will, and had even failed to post a watch. When Alcibiades, who had been banished from Athens, left his nearby retirement villa to warn the Athenian generals against these mistakes, one of them snapped: "It is we who are in command here, not you." The Spartans destroyed or captured all but 9 of the 170 remaining ships in the Athenian fleet. They also captured 3,000 rowers, all of whom they put to death. By then, neither side had the slightest claim to the moral high ground. The Spartans had massacred the prodemocratic leaders of Miletus, and Athens had decreed that the right thumbs of all prisoners be severed, so that they could not hold a spear again.

The Spartans controlled both land and sea for the first time. They used it to prevent Athens from importing food and collecting money from allies. Meanwhile, the Spartan troops stationed on Athenian soil prevented the Athenians from cultivating a crop of their own and from using the silver mines at Laurium. As a result, the Athenians had to melt down sacred statues for gold and to replace their famous silver coins with silver-coated copper coins. Athenian slaves used the opportunity to flee (only to be enslaved by others). To worsen the city's food shortages, Lysander returned all prisoners to Athens and decreed that any Athenian caught outside the city would be killed.

By 404 B.C., Athens had been starved into submission. Legend has it that in Lysander's excitement at the end of this twenty-seven year war, he wrote home to the ephors, "Athens is taken," to which the ephors, irritated by Lysander's un-Spartan verbosity, replied, "'Taken' would have been enough."

One of Sparta's allies (by one account Thebes, by another Corinth) proposed that Athens be razed and that the entire Athenian population be sold into slavery—just as the sleepless Athenians expected. But after a man from Phocis sang a few lines from Euripides' *Electra,* the allies decided that it would be an outrage to destroy a city that had produced such a poet. Instead, the Spartans dismantled Athens's walls, as well as the "long walls" connecting the city with Piraeus, and demolished all but a few of Athens's ships. They also replaced Athenian democracy with the rule of the "Thirty Tyrants," a group of ruthless Athenian aristocrats, and maintained a garrison on the Acropolis.

Ironically, through Greek disunity the Persians had managed to secure the revenge against Athens that they had failed to gain by their own efforts in the Persian Wars. The lesson would not be lost on Macedon and Rome.

THE LEGACY OF PERICLES

Periclean Athens not only exerted an enormous influence over much of the art, architecture, and literature subsequently produced by the Western world, but also inspired democratic experiments throughout history. Although most political theorists before, during, and after the Periclean Age considered the Athenian political system too democratic and unstable, that judgment began to change in the nineteenth century. Hellenism, and in particular a love for Athens, began to sweep the Western world, as democracy became increasingly popular and property qualifications for voting were reduced or eliminated. Though still subordinate to Latin in Western pedagogy, the Greek language, in the form of the Attic dialect, began to assume a more prominent position within the educational system. Histories of the ancient world began to depict the Periclean Age as a golden age in human history. Although this new adulation of Athens's political system, like the excoriation of previous centuries, sometimes went too far, Athens's importance as the first major democracy in history cannot be doubted.

5

✝

Plato: Founder of Western Philosophy

Before Plato, Greek "philosophers" were mostly scientists who studied the laws of the physical universe. It was Plato who began a sophisticated inquiry into such matters as metaphysics, epistemology, ethics, and the other issues that have come to define what we now term "philosophy." Not only has Platonism exerted a considerable influence throughout Western history, but every opposing philosophy was either formed in opposition to it or, at the very least, was compelled to come to grips with Plato's arguments. It was Plato, more than any other philosopher, who set the terms for philosophical discourse up to this very day. Alfred Lord Whitehead's famous exaggeration, "All of western civilization is but a series of footnotes to Plato," becomes more accurate if one but substitutes "philosophy" for "civilization."

SOCRATES (c. 470–399 B.C.)

So much of what we know of Socrates' philosophical beliefs comes from dialogues written by Plato, his most brilliant student, that many intellectual historians question whether we can rightly speak of a Socratic philosophy independent of Platonism. How many of the opinions that Plato ascribed to Socrates in the dialogues were really Socratic, and how many were merely Plato's own views? Regardless of one's position on this question, it seems certain that Plato studied under a charismatic man named Socrates and that Socrates' life, death, and beliefs exerted a profound influence on Plato.

A pronouncement of the oracle of Delphi first led Socrates, the son of a sculptor and a midwife, on a search for philosophical truth. When asked by one of Socrates' friends if Socrates was the wisest man in the world, the oracle had replied, "Wise is Sophocles, wiser is Euripides, but wisest of all is Socrates." This declaration had astonished Socrates. He could not believe that he was the wisest man in the world, since he did not think he knew anything at all. But surely Apollo would not lie. Socrates began to question all Athenians reputed to be wise—politicians, playwrights, and craftsmen—to discover if any were wiser than he. Employing the "Socratic method," an intense line of questioning aimed at defining objects and ideas and refining propositions by examining their logical consequences, Socrates revealed numerous inconsistencies in the arguments of these "wise men." Socrates finally concluded that the oracle's statement was "a kind of joke": Socrates was the wisest man because he alone recognized his own ignorance.

By making fools of the leading men of Athens, to the delight of the city's youth, who began to idolize and emulate Socrates (they also admired his fearlessness in combat and his ability to drink immense amounts of wine without any visible effect), Socrates helped bring about his own death. Socrates created other enemies in the city by finding fault with democracy, by speaking well of the dreaded enemy, Sparta, and by criticizing the traditional portrayal of the gods. He believed, contrary to the stories recited by the poets, that the gods were completely virtuous and that they did not honor the sacrifices of the wicked. Still other critics of Socrates noted that both the traitor Alcibiades and the bloodthirsty tyrant Critias had been his students. Some Athenians recalled that Critias had written a poem claiming that the gods were the invention of an ingenious ruler, who had hoped to make evildoers fearful of an all-seeing eye. Although nothing could have been further from Socrates' beliefs, and though Socrates had once risked his own life by defying Critias's order that he arrest one of Critias's political opponents, many Athenians assumed that Socrates was responsible for Critias's cynicism. Finally, Anytus, one of the most powerful men in Athens (one of the two men who had led a successful revolution against Critias and the Thirty Tyrants), was angry with Socrates for turning his son against him by filling his head with philosophy. When Anytus ordered his son to devote his time to the family tannery rather than pursuing Socratic philosophy, the young man became a bitter drunkard.

In 399 B.C., Socrates was arrested for impiety and for corrupting the youth. Socrates was convicted by a jury vote of 281 to 220, a relatively close margin. Even then Socrates could have avoided death by offering exile as his punishment. Instead, he proposed a fine of 3,000 drachmas, to be paid by his friends, since he himself possessed only 100 drachmas. Even this penalty he offered only belatedly and with great reluctance. His first suggestion had been that *the city should pay him* for his essential service as a "gadfly" who stung the citizens out of their lethargy. Indeed, he had declared: "Being convinced that I have wronged no man, I certainly will not wrong myself; I will not give a sentence against myself and say that I am worthy of something bad." Outraged by his insolence, the jury chose the death penalty (the prosecutors' alternative) by a larger margin than that which had convicted him.

Socrates' final address to the jury, as recorded in Plato's *Apology of Socrates* ("apology" meant an explanation or defense; Socrates never apologized for anything), remains one of the most powerful speeches in Western history. Socrates declared: "It is not death which is difficult to escape, gentlemen; no, it is far more difficult to escape wickedness, which pursues us more swiftly." He warned those who had convicted him not to rejoice too quickly:

> You have done this thing to me in the hope that you might thus avoid having to give an account of your lives, but I tell you that the result will be just the opposite of what you expected. For now there will be many who will call you to account, men whom I have held back, though you were not aware of it. They are young men, and so they will be more severe with you, and you will be even angrier and more upset than you are now. You are mistaken if you think that by putting men to death you will prevent anyone from chastising you for not living as you should.

To those who had voted for his acquittal, Socrates concluded affectionately:

> And you also, judges, must regard death hopefully and must remember this one truth: that no evil can come to a good man, either in life or after death, and the gods do not neglect him. . . . When my sons are grown, I would ask you, my friends, to punish them, and I would have you trouble them, as I have troubled you, if they seem to care about money, or anything else, more than virtue; or if they pretend to be something when they are really nothing, then reprove them, as I have reproved you, for not caring about that which they ought to care, and for thinking that they are something when they are really nothing. And if you do this, both I and my sons will have received justice at your hands. And now is the hour to depart, I to die, and you to live. Whichever of these fates is the better one is by no means clear to anyone, except to the gods.

Socrates then rejected an informal arrangement that would have allowed him to escape Athens. He told his friend Crito, who urged him to flee, that he did not wish to live in another polis, to dislocate his sons, and to put his friends' lives and property in peril. But, more importantly, he noted, in a quintessentially Greek fashion, that the "Law," which had given him life (his mother and father had been married through it) and nourishment, was even more worthy of respect than one's parents, since it was the lifeblood of the entire polis. By remaining in Athens when he had come of age, he had consented to be governed by its laws. Should he now break this solemn covenant in order to gain a few more years of life? (He was seventy years old.) And what kind of life would it be? One without self-respect or the respect of others. For it was not the Law itself, but a mere jury of men, that had injured him. If he were to raise his hand against the Law, he would place himself in the wrong, destroy his whole life's work, and make a mockery of his own teachings concerning virtue. How could he be trusted in any other decent polis if he showed contempt for the laws of his own? Would he not validate the unjust decision against him; would it not appear likely that a corrupter of laws might also have been a corrupter of youth? Socrates asked: "Shall I not obey the laws, which have protected me until now? I stood my ground in the army, where my generals posted me; shall I not stay at my post now, where the gods have placed me?"

Socrates was executed with a cup of hemlock. He went to his death serenely, saying that he was looking forward to meeting *and questioning* all of the great figures of history. He assumed that they would not evict him from Hades for asking questions. He assured his weeping friends that only his body, which was but a meaningless shell, would die. The real "Socrates" was the soul, not the body, and the soul was immortal. Complete truth could be acquired by the soul only after death, since "so long as we have the body with us in our inquiry, and our soul is mixed up with so great an evil, we shall never attain sufficiently what we desire, and that, we say, is truth." Hence, of all people, philosophers should most welcome death: "If you see a man fretting because he is to die, he is not really a philosopher but a philosoma—not a wisdom-lover but a body-lover." Socrates hinted that only philosophers enjoyed a blessed state of complete wisdom, as companions of the gods, in the afterlife. Like the Pythagoreans, but far less dogmatically, Socrates intimated the possibility of reincarnation for other souls: souls virtuous by "habit and custom without philosophy" entered into new human bodies, while impure souls entered into animal bodies or became shadowy apparitions wandering the earth. When one of Socrates' students offered him a beautiful garment in which to die, Socrates said: "What, is my own good enough to live in but not to die in?" Socrates' last words were: "Crito, we owe a cock to Asclepius. Pay it, and don't forget now." Most historians believe that Socrates was referring to a severe illness from which Plato had just recovered: those who recovered from an illness were expected to donate a chicken to the priests of Asclepius, the god of healing. But there is another, more intriguing possibility—that the cock was for himself, that Socrates was equating his own passage from this miserable world into a better existence with the healing of an illness. At any rate, Socrates' execution transformed him into a martyr for philosophy, virtue, and free speech, an enduring inspiration to countless people for 2,400 years.

Drawing on the Pythagoreans, Socrates had argued for the existence of natural law, a universal code of ethics, divine in origin, that remained the same at all times and in all societies and that could be discerned by human intuition. He claimed that there were "unwritten laws" that had been formulated by the gods and that were "uniformly observed in every country." The duty to revere the gods and one's parents were two such laws. He argued that humans were innately good. The understanding of good and evil was imbedded in human nature and accessible through intuition, rather than through reason (logic) acting on sensory experience. Socrates explained that the body was an "obstacle" to knowledge. He contended: "And the best sort of thinking occurs when the soul is not disturbed by any of these things—not by hearing, or sight, or pain, or pleasure—when she leaves the body and is alone and, doing her best to avoid any form of contact with it, reaches out to grasp what is truly real."

Partly as a result of this emphasis on intuition over the senses, Socrates led a fairly ascetic life. He pitied those who devoted their lives to insignificant things like making money. He declared: "A life without examination is not worth living." (Significantly, he did not say, "The unexamined life is not worth living," as he is frequently mistranslated. It was as important to examine others as to examine oneself. Had Socrates merely examined himself, he never would have gotten into trouble.) He once said that other men seemed to live only that they might eat, while he ate only that he might live. Once, when Socrates invited some rich men over to his humble abode and his wife, Xanthippe, was ashamed of the dinner, he told her: "Never mind, for if they are reasonable they will put up with it, and if they are worthless, we shall not trouble ourselves about them." When walking through the marketplace, Socrates once exclaimed: "How many things there are that I can do without!"

But Socratic (and Platonic) claims that sensory experience was an obstacle to knowledge were inconsistent with Socrates' equally prominent statements on the importance of education. Socrates (and Plato) often suggested that education (ethical training, which employs reason and the senses) was essential to perfecting the innate goodness of humans, an insight that later formed the core of Stoicism.

Socrates' equation of virtue with wisdom also left out the vital element of willpower. Socrates claimed: "Justice and every other form of Virtue is Wisdom. . . . He who knows the beautiful and good will never choose anything else." This formulation denied the possibility that one could know the good in a rational sense yet be unable to achieve it because of the sensual lure of evil. Indeed, in Plato's touching *Symposium*, an emotional and thoroughly intoxicated Alcibiades tells Socrates that he knows he should be virtuous, and tries, but is rarely able. Plato seemed not to note that the anecdote revealed a flaw in Socratic and Platonic theory—a flaw that is hardly surprising, since Greek tradition lacked the Judaic concept of original sin.

PLATO (c. 428–347 B.C.)

At the very least, Plato systematized and expanded Socratic philosophy. A champion wrestler, Plato (his real name was Androcles; "Plato" was a nickname referring to either his "wide" body or "broad" forehead) had become a student of Socrates at the age of twenty. In the wake of Socrates' execution, Plato left Athens and traveled to southern Italy and Sicily. From the Pythagoreans there, especially Archytas of Tarentum, he learned the importance of mathematics. He then returned to Athens, where he established the Academy in 387 B.C. Located in the groves one mile west of Athens, near the shrine of the local hero Academus, the Academy was a school of higher education that taught philosophy, astronomy, biology, mathematics, and political theory. It operated for nearly a millennium before the Byzantine emperor Justinian closed it in A.D. 524.

Platonism combined the insights of Heraclitus with those of Pythagoras. Plato argued, as had Heraclitus, that the world of the senses was an imperfect world that remained in a constant state of flux. Thus, human knowledge of the material world was limited not only by the imperfection of the senses, but also by the fluctuating nature of matter itself. But Plato also believed, as had Pythagoras, in another, perfect world, the "world of the forms," in which ideas like beauty and justice lived a real and eternal existence. The world of the senses was but a shadow, a pale imitation of the real world, the world of the forms. All human ideas, whether of material objects or of concepts, were intuitive representations of immaterial forms existing on another plane. Dispersed throughout the universe, the divine soul continually acted on matter in an effort to replicate the forms within the world of the senses. But matter, by its inherently disorderly nature, passively resisted the order that the divine soul sought to impose on it, so that the material world that resulted, while the best of all possible material worlds, did not conform perfectly to the world of the forms. The human soul, eternal like the divine soul, the forms, and matter, was a dismembered portion of the divine soul that temporarily occupied a body composed of matter.

Plato's theory of ethics proved as influential as his metaphysics. He identified the four cardinal virtues as prudence, temperance, justice, and courage, a list that would be repeated not only by Platonists but by other philosophical schools for centuries thereafter.

Disillusioned with the democratic government of Athens even before it had executed his mentor, Plato wrote *The Republic* in 374 B.C. In this dialogue, Plato presented his ideal polis, a city ruled by an aristocracy of thoroughly educated "guardians" led by a "philosopher-king." Since these wise guardians would be able to distinguish the true good (truth, justice, and virtue, which were accessible only through philosophical understanding) from the false good (wealth, power, and prestige), they would consider their governing function an obligation rather than a source of loot. Plato wrote: "The city where those who are to rule are least anxious to be rulers is of necessity the best managed." The guardians would govern in the best interests of the people, who would be divided into warriors and workers. (Plato believed that war was a fact of human life, writing: "Only the dead have seen the end of war." Indeed, if later writers can be believed, Plato himself had fought valiantly in the Athenian army.) The three groups in Plato's republic corresponded to the three parts of the soul (mind), in descending order of importance: wisdom, love of honor, and love of pleasure. Plato's Spartan-style system made the citizen a specialist, contrary to the traditional Greek emphasis on versatility.

The guardians would control all aspects of life, including marriage. To prevent selfishness among the guardians, all of their property would be held in common, and their children would be taken from them at birth and raised communally by all of the adults, so that none would even know which was his own child. Once women were past the child-bearing age, they could mate with whomever they wished. All illegitimate children and those "born defective" would be killed at birth. The guardians would make a careful determination of each individual's proper place in society. Those able to grasp the nature of the forms and to apply them to practical situations—that is, the virtuous and the wise—would be placed on the guardian track. They would be taught mathematics and logic, which employed "pure reason" to comprehend the changeless Idea of the Good, and would undergo physical training, to prevent softness. They would be prohibited from studying "anything that is not perfect"—meaning anything associated with the flawed, ever-changing material world. They would be prohibited from drunkenness or idleness. Those who failed the numerous intellectual and physical tests administered to them throughout their lifetimes would be demoted as unfit to share in the rule. Those who passed these tests would participate in the government of the city after age thirty-five. They would be allowed to retire from day-to-day administration at age fifty. The strong and courageous would be placed on the warrior track. Warriors would have no private property and eat in common mess halls, like the Spartans. They would not be permitted to enslave other Greeks or to burn their property while at war. The rest of the people would be trained in various trades, according to their differing aptitudes.

All citizens, including females, would begin on the same plane and would be educated to the limit of their ability. Plato argued that men and women "differ only in one thing, that the male begets and the female bears the child." He added: "No practice or calling in the life of the city belongs to woman as woman, or man as man, but the various aptitudes are dispersed among both sexes alike." Indeed, Plato himself had admitted a few women of exceptional ability into his Academy.

The guardians would control all artistic expression, since art appealed to the irrational element in the soul, so as to prevent the spread of immorality. While emotion was not in itself bad, it must be shaped and utilized to promote virtue and not vice. To that end, the gods must be portrayed as honest, peace-loving, virtuous, and changeless. Children must always be taught that virtue led to happiness, and vice to unhappiness. To make guardians and warriors brave, they must be taught that the afterlife was good. Among musical instruments only the simple lyre and harp would be allowed, among songs and poems only hymns to the gods and praise of the good. Painters, architects, and even furniture makers must be monitored so that their works projected a spirit of beauty and harmony. Plato declared: "To hate what one ought to hate and to love what one ought to love: this is true education."

Plato intended his republic to represent the form of polis. By their very nature, forms could only be approximated in the imperfect world of the senses. Nevertheless, they were essential as models. The role of the statesman, then, was to use the form or ideal of the polis as a painter used his object, as a goal of emulation, though it could never be reproduced completely in the material world. To even approximate his ideal, the statesman, like the painter, must be acutely aware of his materials, including their limitations, and how to use them. Thus, while Plato understood that his ideal republic could not be fully replicated in the world of the senses, he was confident that a wise statesman, blessed with auspicious circumstances, could at least approximate it. Indeed, Plato ended the *Republic* with this significant conclusion concerning the prospects of creating a republic similar to that which he had just described: "Difficult it is indeed, but possible somehow." Plato explained that a polis similar to his republic could be inaugurated by removing children from their parents at an early age, taking them out to the countryside, and training them in the proper way.

At the urging of friends, Plato accepted the invitation of Dionysius I, dictator of Syracuse, to serve as a tutor to his son Dionysius II in 367 B.C. Either because he grew weary of Plato's rebukes concerning the gluttony and sexual promiscuity of the Syracusan court or for political reasons, the dictator sold Plato into slavery. A friend bought the philosopher's freedom, and he returned home.

Plato then composed a series of practical treatises on politics, in the process introducing the influential theory of mixed government. In the *Laws*, a work in which Plato suggested a legal code for a small city to be established in Crete, Plato stated that there were three simple forms of government: monarchy (rule by the one), aristocracy (rule by the few), and democracy (rule by the many). But each of these forms degenerated over time. Monarchy degenerated into tyranny, aristocracy into oligarchy, and democracy into ochlocracy (mob rule). Plato then suggested that perhaps the best government would be a mixed government, one that balanced the power of the one, the few, and the many. Plato's mixed government theory became one of the most significant theories in Western history.

Nevertheless, though the *Laws* departed from the *Republic* in advocating a mixed government rather than an oligarchy of guardians, the *Laws* retained much of the rigidity of the *Republic*. Citizens under forty would be prohibited from traveling for fear they would be corrupted by foreign luxury. The sole exception would be Olympic athletes, since their exertions would bring glory to their city. No atheism or ritualistic religion would be permitted; religion would be based solely on belief in the gods and in virtue. While those dissidents amenable to learning would be reformed, the adamant would be imprisoned or killed.

Plato's eloquence was so astonishing his prose was often compared with Homer's poetry, which was, indeed, his object of emulation. His graceful and versatile style ranged from lighthearted to solemn, often utilizing poetic allegories to convey otherwise inexpressible profundities. His praise for the moral life ("If it should be necessary for me to either do wrong or be wronged, I would choose for myself to be wronged") earned him a central place in Western philosophy. Plato's pupil Aristotle wrote of him: "He was the only man, or at least the first, who showed, through his words and through his life, how a man can become both good and happy at the same time." Cicero later added that if God ever chose to speak in human words, he would write like Plato. Plato was buried in a garden at his beloved Academy.

PLATO'S OPPONENTS AMONG THE GREEKS

All philosophers who followed Plato were forced to come to grips with his ideas. Some adopted them, some modified them, and some rejected them, but none could ignore them. Indeed, all of the other influential philosophies developed in the effort to refute Plato.

Aristotle (384–322 B.C.)

Aristotle, Plato's most brilliant student, moved to Athens from Stagira (in Chalcidice) at the age of seventeen. Aristotle's father had served as physician to Philip II, the king of Macedon. Aristotle taught at the Academy until Plato died and the Academy passed to Plato's nephew Speusippus. (Some historians believe Aristotle left Athens even before Plato's death due to anti-Macedonian sentiment there.) In 335 B.C., Aristotle returned to Athens and opened the Lyceum, a rival school located in the sacred grove of Apollo Lyceius.

Aristotle presented his philosophy in two great works, the *Metaphysics* and the *Nicomachean Ethics*. Edited by his son Nicomachus, the latter work was the first treatise on ethics ever written. Aristotle envisioned the Prime Mover, or first cause, as a perfect, immortal, immutable unity but not one who intervened in natural processes. He argued that all knowledge was learned: "There is nothing in the intellect that was not first in the senses." He denied the existence of intuition and innate goodness, suggesting that virtue was a product of rational training and habit. Aristotle claimed: "We are not made good or bad by nature."

Aristotle generally defined virtue as the "Golden Mean," the most rational point between behavioral extremes (e.g., the mean between cowardice and rashness, abstinence and indulgence, and self-deprecation and vanity), though he noted that some emotions (like envy) and some actions (like adultery) were always wrong. Sometimes the "mean" was actually closer to one extreme; for instance, the virtue of courage was closer to rashness than to cowardice. Aristotle conceded: "It is no easy task to find the middle. . . . Wherefore, goodness is rare and laudable and noble."

According to Aristotle, virtue did not generally consist in the rigid application of those absolute moral laws for which Socrates and Plato searched, but in a difficult daily struggle to discern the probable effects of one's behavior in a given context. An act that might be moral in one instance might be immoral in another. But, though Aristotle was a contextualist, he was not an extreme relativist: He believed that while ethics varied with context, it was still possible to deduce from experience the appropriate behavior for each particular situation. He would not have agreed with the extreme relativist position that one act was as moral or immoral as another.

Aristotle agreed with Socrates and Plato that the reward for virtue was earthly happiness through self-respect and the respect of others, as surely as the penalty for vice was unhappiness. Aristotle claimed: "Bad men are full of regrets." While Aristotle expressed no opinion on the existence of an afterlife, he clearly viewed earthly happiness as the ultimate prize.

If earthly happiness depended on virtue, and if virtue depended on rational training and habit, as Aristotle contended, it followed that the proper role of both the polis and the friend must be to help the individual in his quest to become virtuous by encouraging him to adopt the appropriate habits. Reflecting centuries of Greek tradition, Aristotle wrote: "Legislators make the citizens good by forming habits in them . . . and it is in this that a good constitution differs from a bad one." Since the attainment of virtue was as difficult as it was essential, it could be achieved only through mutual aid. The polis in which one lived and the company that one kept were crucial to one's chances of becoming virtuous and, hence, happy. This logic explains why ancient political theorists focused so much attention on prohibiting immoral behavior. Immorality was like a cancer that would grow until it corrupted all of society, thereby making it almost impossible for the individual to lead a moral life. It was absurd to pretend that individual immorality had no effect on social virtue, or visa versa. No man was an island. Aristotle claimed: "Man is a social animal and one whose nature is to live with others." Society preceded the individual. The polis was a body, each individual a limb. Virtuous friends were "the greatest of external goods" because they helped one achieve virtue. Aristotle wrote: "If a friend becomes wicked, it is necessary to lead him back into goodness. For it is a better and more loving act to aid him in acquiring character than to aid him in acquiring wealth." Friends were bound together by the closest ties. When asked, "What is a friend?" Aristotle replied, "One soul dwelling in two bodies."

Aristotle's *Politics* immortalized Plato's theory of mixed government. In the process of analyzing the governments of 158 poleis, Aristotle cited numerous examples of actual mixed systems in the ancient world. One of the "mixed governments" Aristotle cited was that of Sparta. Yet, Sparta's status as a mixed government is questionable, as the power of the Spartan kings and of the Spartan majority seems to have been too weak to effectively check the power of the council of elders. Indeed, Aristotle himself seemed to have understood this at times, remarking regarding the elders, "The lack of accountability for their acts and the life tenure of their office are greater privileges than they deserve." He added: "The fact that the people who are not participants in the office remain quiet is no proof of the goodness of this practice."

Aristotle's famous elaboration of Plato's mixed government theory contributed greatly to the establishment of a mixed government in the United States under the U.S. Constitution. At the Constitutional Convention, Alexander Hamilton and other Founding Fathers cited Aristotle on the need to establish a mixed government. Thus, the founders balanced the power of the federal government between the one (the president), the representatives of the few (the Senate), and the representatives of the many (the House of Representatives).

Aristotle also became the first political theorist to argue that a large middle class was essential to republican government. He claimed that those who possessed a golden mean of income lacked the arrogance of the rich and the envy of the poor. Furthermore, having "neither so much property that they are able to enjoy a leisure free from all business cares, nor so little that they depend on the city for support," they would "ask that the law should rule for them" rather than constantly overturning the laws. They were "least prone either to refuse office or to seek it, both of which tendencies are dangerous to poleis." But Aristotle made it clear that the middle class he favored was one composed of farmers, not one formed from the merchants and traders, a class Aristotle despised for their obsession with profit.

Unfortunately, Aristotle's *Politics* also included an influential defense of slavery. Aristotle argued that some were born to lead and others to follow: "The element which is able, by virtue of its intelligence, to exercise forethought is naturally a ruling and master element; the element which is able, by virtue of its bodily power, to do the physical work, is a ruled element, which is naturally in a state of slavery." Just as the mind should rule the body, so those with better minds should rule those with better bodies. Aristotle connected slavery with the universal rule of humans over animals, adults over children, and males over females, power relationships he considered equally natural—though he argued that the rule of male over female should be closer to that of a statesman over fellow citizens than to that of a monarch over his subjects. Slavery was both natural and beneficial to the slave: "Those whose function is to use the body and from whom physical labor is the most that can be expected are by nature slaves, and it is best for them, as it is for all inferior things I have already mentioned, to be ruled." The master was distinguished from his slave not only by his greater intelligence—though Aristotle conceded that in actual practice the slave was sometimes more intelligent than his master—but also by his greater love of liberty. At one point, Aristotle implied that anyone who would allow himself to be enslaved, rather than taking his own life, did not possess the passion for liberty requisite for a citizen in a republic: "For he is by nature a slave who is capable of belonging to another and therefore does belong to another." Aristotle sometimes seemed to suggest, as had Plato, that while it was wrong to enslave fellow Greeks, it was appropriate to enslave "barbarians," who were "natural slaves"—a doctrine useful to Alexander, Aristotle's pupil, in his conquest of the Persian Empire. Slaveholders wielded Aristotle's defense of slavery as a powerful weapon throughout Western history.

Perhaps the most versatile philosopher in human history, Aristotle single-handedly created the Western curriculum, defining its various fields of study. His obsession with, and immense talent for, categorization stemmed from his belief in the divinely ordained order of the universe and its accessibility to human reason. His *Organon* (Instrument or Tool) and his *Rhetoric* became the standard textbooks for the respective studies of logic and oratory for over two millennia. The "Father of Zoology," he analyzed the anatomies, breeding habits, and migrations of 540 animals. He correctly rejected the popular view that acquired characteristics (e.g., large muscles gained through exertion) were inheritable by offspring. He was the first biologist to dissect animals extensively. He wrote concerning mathematics, astronomy, physics, meteorology, geology, chemistry, anatomy, history, and literary criticism. His *Poetics* was the first systematic treatment of aesthetics.

If Aristotle's style is sometimes dry and convoluted, it is partly because most of his surviving works exist in the form of lecture notes. The works that he wrote for the public, his poems and plays, did not survive. His convoluted style also stems from his supreme dedication to truth, which caused him to prefer the inconclusive discussion of problems to artificial conclusions. He always clarified issues while doing justice to their complexity, the scholar's most difficult task.

There was hardly a field of study Aristotle did not influence. One ancient commentator reckoned the number of his works at 400, another at 1,000, though only 47 survive. Medieval theologians like Thomas Aquinas called Aristotle "the Philosopher" and "the master of those who know." Indeed, by the Middle Ages Aristotle's influence had become too great, so that the quest for truth, to which he had devoted his entire life, had become impeded by the fanatical manner in which his followers clung to his errors in astronomy and physics. (He argued that the earth lay at the center of the universe, that motion required a continuous force, and that heavier objects fell faster than lighter ones.) In contrast to some of his followers, Aristotle himself remained ever humble, writing: "While individually we contribute little or nothing to truth, by the union of all a considerable amount is amassed."

In arguing that the material world was less real than the world of the forms, Platonism had emphasized contemplation over observation. In embracing the material world as the ultimate reality, an evolutionary but orderly place whose principles of operation human reason could discover and discern, Aristotle restored the significance of empirical knowledge. Ralph Waldo Emerson once wrote that every man was a follower of either Plato or Aristotle. Both contributed greatly to modern science—Plato to its emphasis on mathematics, and Aristotle to its emphasis on empirical observation.

Stoicism

Zeno, a tall, gaunt Phoenician from Citium in Cyprus who had been shipwrecked in Athens while on a trading expedition in 310 B.C., established the philosophy of Stoicism. The Stoics were so named because Zeno lectured at the city's Stoa Poikile (Painted Porch), a public colonnade.

The Stoics believed that all reality was material. But while basic matter was passive, the Logos or World Soul, a finer sort of matter, was the active, animating portion of the universe. Drawing from Plato, Stoics held that human souls were fragments of this common World Soul, a consciousness that diffused itself through space to create and sustain the universe. The World Soul had been called many names over the centuries, including "God," "Fate," and "Zeus." The names of the gods merely represented the World Soul's different attributes. The individual soul, which had an intuitive comprehension of the eternal truths of the World Soul, could be fully reintegrated into the World Soul after death if it had been well cared for in life. The World Soul created and destroyed the universe in an eternal cycle; at intervals, the universe was consumed by fire, and an identical universe was formed in which the same events were repeated.

The Stoics believed in the spiritual equality of all humans. While most contemporary religions and philosophies were hierarchical in nature, the Stoics considered women and slaves spiritually equal to free men.

The Stoics were also fatalists. They believed that the universe was an endless chain of causation, like a river destined to flow in a certain direction. Since it was futile to battle the inexorable current of the universe, the Stoics emphasized the need to endure such hardships as pain, sorrow, and death patiently.

The Stoics believed that earthly happiness was the reward of virtue. An individual who put himself at odds with the natural flow of the universe, through wicked acts, could not truly be at peace with himself and with others. The fruits of virtue were self-respect and the respect of others, both of which were necessary to human happiness.

Building on the work of Pythagoras, Socrates, and Plato, the Stoics were the first to fully develop and emphasize the concept of natural law. Cleanthes of Assus (c. 331–232 B.C.), a disciple of Zeno and a former boxer who made his living watering gardens and milling grain at night, taught that virtue lay in "living agreeably to nature in the exercise of right reason."

The Stoics took a middle position between Plato and Aristotle concerning the mechanics of natural law. Although the Stoics agreed with Plato that humans possessed an innate predisposition to virtue, they denied that natural law could be grasped solely through intuition, which required the help of reason acting on sensory information. As Maryanne Cline Horowitz once aptly summarized this aspect of Stoic philosophy: "They believed that the mind is born predisposed to certain ideas which are not yet consciously held. These ideas are evoked and developed through the stimulus of sense impressions and the development of reason." Zeno portrayed the human soul as a spark from the "Great Flame" (the World Soul), which could be extinguished by a bad upbringing. Stoicism exerted a great influence on the Romans and on the Founding Fathers of the United States, whose Bill of Rights was the product of a long tradition traceable to the Stoic concept of natural law.

Epicureanism

Born of Athenian parents, Epicurus (341–270 B.C.) moved to Athens from Samos around 307 B.C. He agreed with the guiding principle of the Platonic, Aristotelian, and Stoic philosophies: that earthly happiness was the reward of virtue. In one of his three surviving essays, written in the form of a letter, he declared: "The virtues go hand in hand with pleasant living, and the good life cannot be divorced from them. . . . The just man enjoys the greatest peace of mind, while the unjust is full of the utmost disquietude."

But like Democritus, who influenced him greatly, Epicurus denied the existence of anything other than matter and void. The universe was eternal, though it possessed numerous perishable worlds, some of which were hospitable to life and some of which were not. Epicurus believed that the gods were material beings, though consisting of a type of matter superior to that which composed humans, and that they did not interfere in the affairs of humans. He claimed: "What is happy and indestructible neither is troubled itself nor causes trouble to others." Furthermore, there was no such thing as intuition, spirit, or soul. Epicurus wrote: "It is upon sensation that reason must rely when it attempts to infer the unknown from the known." Humans must use reason, acting on information provided by the senses, to deduce from nature those moral laws essential to earthly happiness and must test them through experience.

Epicurus's emphasis on testing moral principles to determine their consequences did not lead him to moral relativism. Since the universe was orderly, Epicurus assumed that human experience naturally favored some moral codes over others. Hence, through reason and experience (trial and error), humans would inevitably be led in the same direction—toward the four cardinal virtues Plato had identified, in fact.

Epicurus agreed with the Stoics that happiness could be attained through an untroubled state neither agitated by excessive pleasure nor subject to avoidable discomfort and pain, a state he termed "ataraxia." Ataraxia, in turn, could be achieved only by freeing the body from pain, through a moderate lifestyle, and by freeing the mind from fear of the supernatural and of death. While the Stoics sought to diminish the fear of death by focusing on its inevitability (why worry about something one could do nothing about?) and on its benevolence (death simply involved reintegration into the World Soul), Epicurus sought to achieve the same objective by preaching that death was nothingness and, hence, not to be feared: "Death, [considered] the most horrible of all evils, is nothing to us; for when we are alive it doesn't exist for us, and when it is present we no longer exist."

The Epicureans also preached withdrawal from moneymaking, politics, and romantic love, each of which was likely to trouble the mind. Epicurus wrote: "You must free yourself from the prison of politics." (Although equally concerned with preserving serenity, the Stoics doubted that it could be preserved by flouting one's responsibility to participate in public affairs.) Like the Stoics, the Epicureans also denounced luxury, since dependence on it would lead to unhappiness if misfortune took it away, and espoused a belief in moral equality.

Unlike the Stoics, the Epicureans believed in free will. All was not planned; there was an element of chance in the universe. Atoms sometimes deviated slightly from their normal trajectories without cause.

Critics of Epicureanism managed to stigmatize it as mere "hedonism," the advocacy of sensual pleasure. Although nothing could have been further from Epicurus's meaning, his use of the word "hedone," which could mean either "happiness" or "pleasure," gave fodder to his slanderers. Epicurus himself complained of this calumny:

When we say, then, that pleasure is the greatest good, we are not referring to the pleasure of debauchery or those that consist of sensual gratification, as some people claim because of their ignorance, disagreement with our views, or deliberate falsification of our teachings; what we mean, rather, is the freedom of the body from pain [through moderate living] and the mind from torment. It is not a string of drinking-bouts and revelries, not sexual love, not the enjoyment of the fish and other delicacies of a luxurious table, which produce a pleasant life; it is sober reasoning, searching out the grounds of every choice and avoidance, and banishing those beliefs through which the greatest tumults take possession of the soul. . . . It is not possible to live pleasurably without living sensibly and nobly and justly.

Thomas Jefferson, John Stuart Mill, and numerous others throughout Western history have embraced various forms of Epicureanism.

Skepticism

Though differing on various issues concerning human nature and the nature of the gods, the philosophies of Plato, Aristotle, the Stoics, and Epicurus all shared an optimism concerning the ability of humans to understand natural law and, through such an understanding, to become virtuous and to achieve earthly happiness. But a minority of Greek philosophers, called skeptics, argued that humans could never find truth, moral or otherwise. Intuition did not exist, human reason was fatally flawed, and the senses were often deceptive. Since the universe was in a constant state of flux, and humans were an integral part of the flux, rather than objective observers of it, it was impossible for them to learn the true nature of the universe. Humans were like swimmers being swept downstream by rapids, all the while flattering themselves that they could accurately envision what the whole river must look like from above.

Skepticism was first advanced as a philosophy by the Sophists of the fifth century B.C. The Sophists were itinerant professors who taught for a fee. Socrates, who never accepted money for teaching, called them "prostituters of wisdom." They shunned "useless speculation" about the universe and the gods, teaching such "practical" subjects as rhetoric, logic, and statesmanship. They were much in demand by the rising middle class, who were conscious of their lack of education.

The Sophists were moral relativists. Protagoras of Abdera in Thrace, one of their leading philosophers, declared, "Each man is the measure of all things," a clear declaration of moral relativism and rejection of natural law. (Plato later responded, "To us, God is the measure of all things.") Protagoras was a friend of Pericles, who selected him to draft the laws for the colony of Thuria. Protagoras's statement, "I know nothing about the gods, either that they are or they are not or what are their shapes," contributed to his banishment from Athens and to the burning of his works in the agora. But, again, the motive was largely political; Pericles' political opponents exiled nearly all of his friends because this was the only way they could get at him. Protagoras denied the existence of Platonic intuition, arguing that all knowledge came through reason and the senses, both of which were flawed.

Other Sophists taught that human laws were arbitrary and worthy of little respect, a radical break with the Greek reverence for law. Gorgias of Leontini argued, first, that there is nothing, second, that even if there were something humans could not understand it, and, third, that even if they could understand it they could not communicate it. He taught rhetoric and laughed at those who claimed to teach virtue. Antiphon, another Sophist, seemed to take such relativism to its logical, proto-Machiavellian conclusion when he allegedly declared: "It is very useful to behave justly when there are witnesses to one's conduct, but when there is no chance of being found out, there is no need to be just."

Diogenes the Cynic (c. 412–323 B.C.), the most famous skeptic, was the son of a rich banker from Sinope in the Crimea who moved to Athens after he was exiled with his father for "altering the currency." It was Diogenes who first uttered the famous statement, "The love of money is the source [mother-city] of all evil." (The apostle Paul later paraphrased this as, "The love of money is the root of all evil" in 1 Tim. 6:10.)

Diogenes opposed popular customs and values and lived in a large, clay pottery jar, an idea he derived from the self-sufficient snail. Indeed, the name "cynic" came from *kuon*, meaning "dog," since it was noted that Diogenes lived much like a dog. Once, when Diogenes saw a child drinking from cupped hands, he threw away his cup. When told that he should pursue his runaway slave—who probably ran away because he was tired of living like a dog with Diogenes—Diogenes replied, "It would be absurd if Manes can live without Diogenes, but Diogenes cannot live without Manes." He also advocated free love and opposed marriage.

Diogenes possessed a dark view of human nature. He often wandered the streets with a lit lantern, even in the daytime, claiming that he was looking for an honest man. When someone asked him why people gave money to beggars, but not to philosophers, he replied, "Because they fear that they may become lame or blind one day, but they never expect to become philosophers." Seeing the son of a prostitute throwing rocks at the self-righteous mob goading him, Diogenes said, "Careful now, don't hit your father."

Diogenes expressed disdain for Greek religion. When temple officials arrested a man for stealing a bowl from a temple, Diogenes declared, "The great thieves are leading away the little thief."

Diogenes was equally skeptical concerning the power of human reason. He called Plato's *diatribe* (lecture) a *katatribe* (waste of time). He said that whenever he saw a steersman or physician at work, he believed that humans were the most intelligent of animals, but when he encountered interpreters of dreams, seers, and conceited and wealthy people, he considered humanity the most foolish species.

Few men impressed Diogenes. When Alexander the Great visited Corinth, where Diogenes was staying at the time, the general went in search of the philosopher and finally found him sunbathing. Standing over the philosopher with his entourage, Alexander formally introduced himself, but Diogenes remained silent. Alexander then asked if there were anything he could do for the philosopher. Diogenes raised himself up on one elbow, glared at the conqueror of Greece, and replied, "Yes, you can stand aside and stop blocking my sun." Alexander went away, shaking his head and telling an aide, "If I were not Alexander, I would like to be Diogenes."

Diogenes agreed with Epicurus that death was nothingness. He asked "Why should death be bad when we are not aware of its presence?"

The Athenian people loved the old eccentric. When a juvenile delinquent destroyed Diogenes' pottery jar, the Athenians punished the boy and gave Diogenes a new one. After Diogenes died, perhaps from eating a raw octopus, his followers placed the marble statue of a dog on his grave. The instructions he left—that his body should be thrown out to feed the wild beasts—were ignored.

Other skeptics proclaimed the meaninglessness of life and questioned the existence of the gods. Pyrrho of Elis (c. 360–272 B.C.) denied that any act was inherently honorable or dishonorable, just or unjust, since custom, which was infinitely variable, governed human action. Once he declared, "It matters not whether I live or die." A heckler (heckling philosophers was a favorite pastime of the Greeks) shouted, "Why don't you go kill yourself then?" After a pause, Pyrrho replied, "Because it matters not." Like David Hume, the first great modern skeptic, Pyrrho even questioned the reality of causation itself. Indeed, Pyrrho was that rare specimen of a skeptic who actually put his own philosophy into practice: legend has it that he was saved from harm by traffic, precipices, and dogs only by the vigilance of his less skeptical friends. Euhemerus (*Sacred History*) contended that each of the gods had been a human who had served his society so well in some way (e.g., Dionysus was the first to make wine) that it had worshipped him as a deity after his death.

THE CONTINUING INFLUENCE OF PLATONISM

The latter part of the Roman imperial period witnessed a revival of Platonism. The most influential of the Neoplatonists was Plotinus (A.D. 205–270), an Egyptian by birth who moved to Rome. Plotinus believed that the Absolute Being transmitted his powers through *nous* (pure intelligence), from which flowed the World Soul, from which, in turn, flowed human and animal souls. Plotinus counseled his followers to abandon material interests for intellectual meditation in order to lift themselves to an intuition of the nous and, ultimately, to a complete, ecstatic union with the Absolute Being. Plotinus claimed to have experienced the ecstasy of such a union a few times during his life. Plotinus's emphasis on contemplation over action, and metaphysical doctrines over moral concerns, separated him from most philosophers of his day. He had no interest in politics, sometimes even displaying hostility toward it. Elements of his Neoplatonic philosophy influenced the Christian theologian Augustine.

In the late eighteenth century, Immanuel Kant (*Critique of Pure Reason*) revived Platonism. A modern form of Platonism known as Idealism became the rage in Germany, influencing Friedrich Hegel and numerous others. Both independently and through the German idealists, Platonism also profoundly influenced the American Transcendentalists of the nineteenth century. In the 1960s, it combined with eastern mysticism to produce the New Age religious movement. The Platonic belief in the innate goodness of humans and in the power of intuition to grasp universal truths has played a leading role in the formation of modern utopianism, including the movements for global government and for the unification of the world's religions. While such utopianism can have catastrophic results, it can also temper the equally dangerous extreme of cynicism.

Even skeptics, who reject the reality of Plato's world of the forms, have often found certain elements of Platonism highly useful. For instance, many of the arguments advanced by the Pragmatist philosophers of the late nineteenth and early twentieth centuries concerning the mutability of the material world, regarding the limitations of human reason, and concerning the insufficiency of human language in expressing knowledge, can be traced to Plato's analysis of the world of the senses.

Furthermore, by promoting the theory of natural law and by initiating the theory of mixed government, Plato also provided the modern West with its chief safeguards against the excesses of the very utopianism that his theory of human nature has sometimes inspired. Modern republicans like John Locke deduced from natural law the existence of natural rights—specifically, the unalienable, individual rights of life, liberty, and property. (Thomas Jefferson's substitution of "the pursuit of happiness" for "property" was not intended to deny the right of property but to broaden the definition of natural right.) Meanwhile, the same modern republicans deduced from Plato's theory of mixed government the need not only to balance the power of economic classes within government, but also to balance the legislative, executive, and judicial branches of government, as well as the federal and state levels of government. Though based on a suspicion of government in general that was alien to the ancients, who lived in small, participatory republics, both federalism and the separation of powers were direct descendants of the theory of mixed government and its emphasis on the need for a governmental structure that balanced interests. The longevity of the U.S. Constitution is largely attributable to the shrewd manner in which the Founding Fathers adapted the two ancient theories of natural law and mixed government to the unique demands of a modern society.

6

+

Alexander the Great: Disseminator of Greek Culture

A lexander the Great created the largest empire in history up to his time. His conquests led to the transmission of Greek culture to other peoples of the Mediterranean and the Near East, even as submission to Macedon transformed that culture.

FOURTH-CENTURY GREECE

Spartan Domination

Having won the Peloponnesian War, the Spartans installed puppet oligarchies throughout the former Athenian empire and in Thebes and interfered in the internal affairs of other Greek states. These oligarchies were so ferocious that the Spartan king Pausanias allowed the restoration of democracy in their poleis after only a year or two, rather than face a massive rebellion.

Even so, the Spartan social system was ill-suited to the imperial policy the Spartans now pursued. The wealth that resulted from the control of Greece corrupted luxury-starved Spartan leaders, who began secretly violating the city's prohibition on private wealth. One war hero, Gylippus, hid gold under the tiles of his roof. After a servant informed on him, saying there were "owls" roosting under those tiles (Athena's sacred owl graced Athenian coins), Gylippus was forced to leave Sparta in disgrace.

Worse yet, constant warfare had dramatically reduced the number of Spartan citizens, and Greece remained restive. Indeed, even Corinth, Sparta's erstwhile ally, joined Athens, Thebes, and Argos in rebellion against Sparta, with some financial help from Persia. This so-called Corinthian War (395–386 B.C.), in which Lysander, Sparta's greatest general, was killed, was followed by continuous skirmishes that lasted another decade. The numerous wars of the fifth and early fourth centuries B.C. took such a toll on the Spartan army that only 1,200 citizens remained by 371 B.C.

The Battle of Leuctra

Their numbers diminished and their discipline weakened, the Spartans suffered an astonishing defeat at the hands of the Thebans at the Battle of Leuctra that year. Although the Spartan force at Leuctra outnumbered the Thebans and their allies 11,000 to 6,000, only 700 of the Spartan number were citizens; the rest were allies and perioikoi. When Epaminondas, one of Thebes's elected leaders, attempted to outflank the Spartan right wing, the Spartans were forced to shift their formation. Pelopidas, another Theban leader, struck the right wing quickly and with great force at that precise moment, crushed it and created confusion and panic throughout the Spartan army. As a result, the Thebans were able to rout the Spartans, killing 400 of their citizens, including King Cleombrotus. Even more humiliating for Sparta, the survivors ran ignominiously from the field. In fact, so many Spartans retreated that the Spartan people had to suspend the law depriving them of citizenship for cowardice.

The Thebans and their allies then invaded the Peloponnesus with 70,000 men, the first time in Spartan history a foreign army had entered Laconia. The army burned and plundered the territory, freed some helots, and restored Messenia to its former inhabitants, thereby undermining Spartan power and traditional Spartan culture.

But Thebes was not to lead Greece for long. Epaminondas, the leader on whom it depended, was speared to death, on the verge of victory, while fighting the odd new alliance of Athens and Sparta at Mantinea in 362 B.C. Pelopidas was killed in a different battle soon after.

Philip II of Macedon

Meanwhile, virtually unnoticed, the power of Macedon was growing. The Macedonians were a relatively primitive, tribal people who were closely related to the Greeks, but who possessed a distinct culture of their own. Macedon was not divided into democratic and oligarchic poleis like the rest of Greece but was governed by a single, centralized monarchy. By the fourth century B.C., Macedon had become wealthy enough to possess cities and a Hellenized aristocracy.

In 359 B.C., at the age of twenty-two, the brilliant Philip II seized the throne while serving as regent for his infant nephew after his brother had been killed in battle. Taken hostage by Thebes at the age of fifteen in 367 B.C. in order to guarantee the Theban-Macedonian alliance, Philip had learned the art of warfare from Epaminondas himself. Immediately after assuming power in Macedon, Philip decreed that his infantry be trained in complex tactical maneuvers and close-order drills and sent them on thirty-five mile marches. He also hired distinguished mercenary officers from various parts of Greece. Philip improved Epaminondas's phalanx by lengthening the standard eight-foot spear to eighteen feet and by fitting this *sarissa* with a heavier iron point and a stouter bronze butt spike. Held six feet from the butt, the fifteen-pound sarissa now extended twelve feet, thus allowing the soldiers' shields to be shortened by two-thirds and their bronze breastplates and helmets to be replaced with lighter leather. The greater length of the spear also meant that the first four or five rows of soldiers could thrust instead of the usual three. (The chief problem of Philip's phalanx was to keep the spears free of the enemy's ruined equipment and mutilated corpses.) To the phalanx Philip added cavalry (great numbers of horses, largely unavailable in southern Greece, grazed in the northern pasture land), armed with lances and broad, slashing swords. Having learned from the success of Thebes's "Sacred Band" the importance of esprit de corps within elite units, Philip created an elite cavalry unit known as "the Companions." (Indeed, the very name "Philip" means "horse-lover.") Philip learned to use his cavalry to drive the enemy onto the long spears of his phalanx, a hammer-and-anvil tactic that proved highly effective.

Having ended the threat posed by the primitive Illyrians of what is now Yugoslavia, Philip seized the Athenian colony of Amphipolis and other points in gold-rich Thrace in 357 B.C. Thracian gold and silver mines, which produced 1,000 talents per year, provided Philip with the means to expand his army. The following year the Thebans called on Philip for aid in their holy war against the Athenian ally Phocis for control of sacred Delphi. Philip was only too glad to help, thereby extending his influence into central Greece. In 355 B.C., Philip gained control of Thessaly by allying himself with some of its partisans in a civil war.

Unfortunately, even the extraordinarily eloquent and passionate orations of Demosthenes (the *Philippics*, 351–341 B.C.) could not persuade the Athenians to oppose Philip. The son of a sword manufacturer, Demosthenes had overcome a speech impediment to become one of the greatest orators in Western history, even helping to inspire Winston Churchill to oppose Adolf Hitler in the 1930s, at a time when few would. Demosthenes had begun studying rhetoric in order to prosecute the trustees whose mismanagement had cost him his father's estate. Able to recover only a portion of his inheritance, he had turned to speech writing for litigants to secure his livelihood. He had spent months at a time in an underground study, writing and practicing speeches before a full-length mirror, even shaving one cheek so that he would not be tempted to go out of the house and neglect his rhetorical training. Demosthenes now contrasted the apathy and corruption of contemporary Athens with the glorious Athens of the previous century, the Athens that had scorned the bribes and resisted the incursions of another set of barbarians, the Persians. Demosthenes warned of "the restless activity which is a part of Philip's very being and which will not allow him to content himself with his achievements and remain at peace." Demosthenes concluded:

> This peace that he speaks of is a peace which you are to observe towards Philip, while he does not observe it towards you. . . . If we will not fight him now in his own country we shall perhaps be obliged to do so in ours. . . . It is by deeds and actions, not by words, that a policy of encroachment must be arrested. . . . The Greeks see these things and endure them, gazing as they would at a hailstorm, each praying that it may not come their way, but no one trying to prevent it. . . . Heaven grant that the time may not come when the truth of my words will be tested with all severity.

But despite the warnings of Demosthenes, the Athenians adopted a policy of appeasement toward Philip, who bribed some Athenian leaders and convinced others that he was a friend who had no further territorial ambitions. Some Athenians even welcomed Philip's leadership in a joint invasion of Persia. They considered Greek unity more important than resistance to tyranny. Others were simply tired of war and the high taxes required to pay for it.

In 349–348 B.C., Philip conquered many cities of the Chalcidician League in northern Greece, several of which were Athenian allies. Having taken Olynthus, the league's capital, with the help of traitors, Philip then sold its entire population into slavery. In 348 B.C., with the help of traitors he had bribed, Philip used an army to set up puppet dictators in Euboea. The same year he seized the rest of Thrace. In 346 B.C., the Athenian Philocrates, who was also on Philip's payroll, negotiated a disastrous peace treaty with Macedon, in which Athens accepted the loss of Amphipolis, the historical equivalent of the Munich Agreement of 1938 between Neville Chamberlain and Hitler. With Athens's guard down, Philip conquered Phocis the same year. He now acquired the prestige of acting as the guardian of sacred Delphi. When Philip attacked Byzantium, thereby threatening Athens's grain supplies from the Black Sea region, Athens, Thebes, Corinth, and a few other poleis finally joined together to stop him.

The Battle of Chaeronea

It was too late, however. In 338 B.C., Philip destroyed the coalition's reserve force of 10,000 mercenaries in a surprise attack. He then engaged the coalition's main army at the decisive Battle of Chaeronea in Boeotia. Both sides possessed about 30,000 troops. Philip led the right wing of his army ahead of the rest of his force. He engaged the Athenians, who had not put an army in the field in twenty years, then withdrew up a hill in an orderly fashion. The inexperienced Athenians, thinking they had a rout, advanced incautiously, opening a gap between themselves and the Thebans. Philip's cavalry, stationed on the left and commanded by his eighteen-year-old son, Alexander, then struck the Thebans on their now exposed flank. Meanwhile, Philip turned and launched a counterattack against the Athenians, charging downhill. The Macedonians killed 1,000 soldiers and took another 2,000 captive. The rest of the coalition forces fled. The Macedonian infantry then rushed to help the cavalry slaughter the courageous Thebans, who refused to flee. Nearly all 300 of the Sacred Band, a unit that had never before been defeated, were killed at Chaeronea. Philip wept over their slain bodies, piled up where they had died defending one another in a futile effort. He buried them there in seven soldierly rows.

Philip was magnanimous toward Athens because he did not relish expending further resources on a siege of Athens and because he admired Athenian culture. He organized the Greek poleis into the "Corinthian League," which he dominated. Each polis was obligated to contribute men and supplies for a full-scale invasion of the Persian Empire.

But Philip would not live to see the invasion of Persia. In 336 B.C., he was stabbed to death by a Macedonian nobleman while walking in a procession at his daughter's wedding. The javelins of three pursuers killed the assassin before he could be questioned. While some contemporaries believed that the Persians, who feared Philip's planned invasion of their empire, had hired the assassin, others believed the assassin had been employed by one of Philip's wives, Queen Olympias of Epirus, who feared that the son produced by his latest marriage to young Cleopatra—not to be confused with the more famous Cleopatra who lived three centuries later—would threaten her son Alexander's ascension to the throne. Indeed, the three pursuers who killed the assassin all happened to be close friends of Alexander. More revealingly, Olympias placed a crown on the assassin's corpse, buried it, and dedicated the murder weapon (a short sword) to Apollo. Soon after, Alexander had Cleopatra's powerful uncle quietly liquidated and encouraged his mother to kill Cleopatra's infant son, his rival for the throne. Requiring little encouragement, Olympias exceeded her instructions, roasting both the infant and a daughter of Cleopatra over a charcoal brazier, then forcing Cleopatra to hang herself. A maenad in the cult of Dionysus, Olympias enjoyed sleeping in a bed filled with large snakes, an unintentional form of birth control that had driven Philip from her bed long before. She was also suspected of having administered drugs that caused brain damage to the child of another of Philip's wives.

THE VICTORIES OF ALEXANDER THE GREAT

Greek Rebellions Crushed

Alexander III was not yet twenty when he ascended the throne of Macedon. His features included blond hair that resembled a lion's mane, one gray-blue eye, one dark brown eye, and pointed teeth. He had a high-pitched voice, and he walked at a brisk pace, with his head bent slightly upward and to the left.

Within fifteen months, Alexander the Great, one of the greatest generals in history, had crushed Persian-financed rebellions in Thessaly, Thrace, Illyria, and Thebes. In Thebes, he slaughtered 6,000 inhabitants and sold the remaining 30,000 into slavery. He destroyed every building in the city except the temples and the house where the poet Pindar had lived.

At that point, Alexander's generals wanted him to marry and produce an heir, but he feared that those aristocratic families whose daughters were not chosen would lead a rebellion while he was away in Persia. His decision to delay the production of an heir would have unfortunate consequences for his empire.

The Invasion of the Persian Empire

In 334 B.C., Alexander crossed into Asia Minor with about 37,000 infantrymen and 6,000 cavalry. An additional 60,000 soldiers were held in reserve to await his call. The Persians rejected a Greek mercenary's wise suggestion that they engage in a scorched-earth policy, a tactic that might have forced Alexander back across the Hellespont due to a lack of supplies.

The Battle of Granicus

Alexander soon scored a victory at the Granicus River in northwest Asia Minor. Thirty thousand Persian infantry and 15,000 cavalry had positioned themselves across the deep and fast-running stream on a steep bank with thick alluvial deposits beneath. On the suggestion of Parmenio, his best general, Alexander marched downstream under cover of darkness, forded the river, and had most of his infantry across before the Persians detected his army. Recognizable by his magnificent armor and the tall white plumes on his helmet, Alexander was nearly killed in fierce cavalry combat. A javelin pierced his breastplate, and an ax severed his helmet, laying his scalp open to the bone. But the Persian infantry, far inferior to their cavalry, broke and fled. During the battle, the Persians suffered 2,500 casualties, and the Macedonians only 150. After the battle, Alexander slaughtered 15,000 to 18,000 Greek mercenaries who had dared to fight with the Persians and sent another 2,000 back to Macedon as slaves.

The victory at Granicus opened up all of Asia Minor to Macedonian conquest. But, lacking money to pay his rowers since Philip had died 500 talents in debt and Alexander had borrowed another 800 talents, Alexander was forced to send his fleet home.

The Battle of Issus

In 333 B.C., Alexander won a crucial victory at Issus, located at the crossroads between Asia Minor and Syria. Having covered his flanks with hills and the sea, so that the Persians could not use their superior cavalry and greater numbers to advantage, Alexander outflanked the Persian left, routing it and putting the whole army to flight. Darius III, who had just taken the Persian throne following the murder of Artaxerxes III, fled, leaving behind his mother, his wife, his children, and much wealth. The Persians lost 50,000 to 100,000 men.

The Siege of Tyre

Syria and most of the Phoenician ports fell soon after. The siege of Tyre lasted seven months due to the city's location on an island encircled by 150-foot walls. The capture of Tyre in 332 B.C. gave Alexander control of most of the Persian navy, thereby preventing an attack on Greece while he was in Persia. Alexander then killed about 9,000 Tyrians, crucifying 2,000 of them (it was Alexander who introduced crucifixion into the Western world), and sold another 30,000 into slavery.

The Sack of Gaza

Having then received a serious wound at the siege of Gaza in Palestine, Alexander proceeded to slaughter 10,000 of the town's males, selling the women and children into slavery. Alexander had the governor of Gaza dragged around the city until he died.

Egypt

Alexander spared Egypt since the province surrendered without resistance. The Egyptians proclaimed him Horus and the son of Osiris—in other words, a pharaoh. This proclamation, rather commonplace in Egypt, fascinated Alexander, since it seemed to corroborate the story his mother had told him just before his departure from Macedon. Olympias had implied that his real father was not Philip but a god. Eager to learn more about his divine origin, Alexander marched his army 300 miles through the Libyan desert to consult the oracle of Zeus-Amen at the Siwah Oasis. Although Alexander saw the oracle alone and claimed that he could reveal what the oracle said only to his mother, he thenceforth acted as though the oracle had declared him the son of Zeus-Amen, a scandalous claim to the Greeks, who did not worship living humans as gods. Indeed, the Macedonians refused to give their generals titles; even the lowliest soldier called the king "Alexander." To such a people, Alexander's behavior was shocking.

The Battle of Gaugamela

In 331 B.C., Alexander marched over 1,000 miles northeastward into the heart of the Persian Empire to face Darius III's main army at Gaugamela on the Tigris River. Darius then offered Alexander all of his empire west of the Euphrates River, 30,000 talents, his daughter's hand in marriage, and his son as a hostage. But when Parmenio advised, "If I were Alexander, I would accept this offer," Alexander replied, "So would I, if I were Parmenio." Though outnumbered by the Persian force of 100,000 infantry and nearly 50,000 armored cavalry (Alexander's army now consisted of about 47,000 men, only 7,250 of whom were cavalrymen), Alexander refused to launch a surprise attack at night, as Parmenio suggested, declaring his determination to demoralize the Persians by defeating them in broad daylight in an open plain. Nevertheless, he leaked Parmenio's plan to the Persians, so that they stayed awake all night and were exhausted by the time the battle was fought the following day.

In the brief but murderous Battle of Gaugamela, Darius showed his disgust with his infantry by holding them in reserve. Alexander's brilliant tactic—later imitated by John Churchill, the first duke of Marlborough, at Blenheim, and Napoléon Bonaparte at Austerlitz—was to draw as much of the Persian cavalry as he could into combat against his left wing, Parmenio's phalanx, which he made to look weaker than it actually was, and then to crush the weakened Persian center. His timing had to be perfect: If he attacked the center too soon, it would not be depleted enough, and the attack would be blunted; on the other hand, if he waited too long, his left wing might cave in from the Persian onslaught. Indeed, the Macedonian left might well have been surrounded if the Persian right had put as much energy into that objective as it put into plundering the Macedonian camp. Alexander waited patiently, and when a gap opened in the Persian line, he charged at the head of the Companions. In two or three minutes the battle was transformed. The Companions smashed through the Persian center. Fearing it would be surrounded, the Persian left then retreated. Darius fled again, as did the infantry. Alexander then turned back to slaughter the Persian right, the Scythian and Bactrian cavalry that was now penned between Alexander's cavalry and Parmenio's phalanx—yet another application of the hammer-and-anvil tactic. While Alexander lost only about 500 men, the Persians lost about 50,000 men, including much of their cavalry. Nevertheless, Alexander now had to give his soldiers huge bonuses to get them to continue eastward. They did not like the idea of marching farther and farther from home.

The Conquest of the Eastern Part of the Persian Empire

In 330 B.C., Alexander defeated 25,000 Persians at the Susian Gates, the mountain pass leading to Persepolis in what is now western Iran. The Persians initially forced the Macedonians into retreat by rolling boulders down on them. But by finding a pass that led behind the Persians, the Macedonians were able to attack them from two sides. Only 700 of the Persian cavalrymen escaped.

Alexander then seized and burned Persepolis, one of the chief cities of the Persian Empire. At that point, Darius's own satrap of Bactria (part of what are now Afghanistan, Uzbekistan, and Tajikistan) took the emperor hostage and ran him through with javelins when he refused to ride off with the satrap. Alexander ordered that the assassin's nose and ears be severed, followed by a public execution, the Persian penalty for regicide, and allowed Darius's body to be buried in the tombs of the Persian kings.

Alexander then admitted some Persians into the Companions and began dressing as a Persian king, wearing a blue and white diadem and a

white robe with a sash. Unfortunately, in the process of attempting to reconcile Persians to his rule, he was beginning to antagonize his own Macedonian soldiers. Nevertheless, from 330 to 327 B.C. Alexander conquered
Parthia in what is now eastern Iran, as well as Bactria, in fierce, mountain
guerilla fighting.

Paranoia

Increasingly paranoid, Alexander then ordered the murder of Parmenio
and of Parmenio's son Philotas, the head of the Companions, for treason.
Parmenio was stabbed to death and decapitated, while Philotas was tortured and then stoned to death before the troops. The hot-tempered and
often intoxicated Alexander even impaled Cleitus, who had tended
Alexander when he was a child and had saved Alexander's life at Granicus, with a spear, when Cleitus (who was also drunk) had rebuked
Alexander for putting on airs.

The Indian Campaign

In 327 B.C., despite thunderstorms and his first real encounter with ele-
phant cavalry (Darius had not used the fifteen elephants he had
brought to Gaugamela), Alexander defeated Porus, king of the Punjab
in western India, at the Jhelum River. The Macedonian horses refused
to go near the elephants, which hurled, impaled, and stamped on many
Macedonians, until the Macedonians surrounded the elephants, shot
their drivers full of arrows, and pierced the elephants' feet with
javelins and axes. In this battle, Alexander's army killed 20,000 of
Porus's soldiers.

The following year, Alexander wanted to proceed farther into India and
again offered huge bonuses, but his exhausted soldiers, who had marched
over 17,000 miles and had fought in many battles, refused to go farther. An
old soldier received thunderous applause at an officers' meeting when he
told Alexander, "Sir, if there is one thing above all others a successful man
should know, it is when to stop." Though Alexander was able to use "bad
omens" as a face-saving excuse for turning back, he was furious at his men.

Alexander's frustration and rage at having to turn back, compounded
by the opposition of fierce tribes, manifested itself on his voyage down
the Jhelum, Chenab, and Indus Rivers. At one point, he slaughtered Indian mercenaries with whom he had negotiated a truce. He also hanged
many Brahmans who encouraged the Indians to resist him. In fact,
Alexander may have killed as many as 80,000 people in the cities of the
southern Punjab.

The Return to Susa

Alexander and his army then sailed from the Arabian Sea into the Persian Gulf and marched northward. On the march back to Susa (325 B.C.), pounded by sandstorms, most of Alexander's army died from poisonous plants and snakes, from thirst, and from a sudden desert flood.

Dissension

Meanwhile, Alexander continued his attempt to meld together the Macedonian and Persian elites. By 330 B.C., Alexander had begun to suggest that Macedonian officers prostrate themselves before him in the Persian fashion. In fact, Alexander slammed the head of a newly arrived Macedonian against a wall for laughing at the Persians who prostrated themselves before the king. Now, in 324 B.C., acting like a Macedonian Reverend Moon, Alexander organized a mass wedding of ninety-two of his top officers to Persian women in a Persian-style ceremony. He himself took Stateira, daughter of Darius, as a wife. (Most of Alexander's forced weddings were repudiated following his death.)

Despite the fanciful claims of historians like Plutarch that Alexander sought to actualize "the brotherhood of man," his real purpose was practical—he wanted to assimilate Persian officers into his command structure and to create a Perso-Macedonian administrative class. For this reason, he gave 30,000 Persian youths Macedonian-style military training.

But Alexander's plan to allow the Persians to form part of his army prompted a mutiny among the Macedonians at Opis on the Tigris River in 324 B.C. When Alexander announced that he was letting some Macedonian soldiers return home and replacing them with Persians, the troops jeered: "No! Let us all go, and stay and fight your battles with your Persians and your father Amen!" Infuriated, Alexander had the leaders of the mutiny executed. In an emotional speech, he reminded his men of the hardships he had endured beside them: "Every part of my body—except my back—has been scarred, and there is no weapon, whether held in the hand or thrown, that has not left its mark on my flesh." He also reminded them of the fact that he had kept little wealth for himself, lavishing most of it on his men. Were they prepared to return to Macedon and tell its citizens that they had abandoned the king who had brought them honor and glory? Overcome with remorse, the soldiers wept and begged to remain. Alexander gladly forgave them and increased their pay.

The Death of Alexander

By then Alexander's empire was the largest in the world, stretching from the Adriatic Sea in the west to the Indus River in the east and from the Caspian Sea in the north to the Upper Nile in the south. The only battle Alexander ever lost was to a mysterious fever, aggravated by a wound suffered in India and by excessive drinking, a Macedonian habit. Some historians believe that the fever was induced by strychnine poisoning instigated by Antipater, the governor of Macedon in Alexander's absence. Antipater had just been ordered to Babylon by Alexander, obviously for execution. Not yet thirty-three, Alexander died at Babylon in 323 B.C. At the time, he was supervising the construction of a temple and the exploration of the Caspian Sea. He planned to extend his empire into the Arabian Peninsula. Olympias had many men killed on suspicion of poisoning her son.

THE DIFFUSION OF GREEK CULTURE

Alexander's conquests began the process through which Greek culture was transmitted throughout his vast empire. Alexander himself had imbibed Greek culture from the time he was thirteen, when Alexander's parents had employed Aristotle, the greatest living philosopher in Greece, to act as his tutor. Alexander brought Aristotle's annotated copy of the *Iliad* with him to Persia, keeping it under his pillow next to his dagger. Alexander wept because he had no Homer to recount his own exploits. During his march through Asia Minor, Alexander, who fancied himself another Achilles, stopped at what was believed to be Achilles' tomb in Troy and laid a wreath on it. Under Aristotle's influence, Alexander became interested in science as well. He included geographers, biologists, and zoologists in the Persian expedition.

Alexander established about thirty-five Greek colonies throughout the Near East. Simple garrisons, most of these settlements were composed of soldiers, located at strategic sites, and designed to offer protection against the empire's foreign and domestic foes. But some of the cities later developed into cultural centers. The greatest of the Greek centers, Alexandria (a name shared by many of these colonies), was located at the northwestern tip of the Nile delta on the site of a small fishing village. Possessing two fine harbors, Alexandria became the capital of Egypt, the largest city in the Greek world, and a center for learning, banking, and commerce. Alexandria became the port of transit from Africa and the Red Sea region and a manufacturing center for linen, jewels, cosmetics, papyrus, and glass. Planned by the Macedonian Deinocrates, the city was filled with gardens, parks, and fountains. Alexandria's streets were uncommonly wide (100 feet) and lined with shops. By 200 B.C., the city possessed a population of 500,000, including a Jewish population large enough to require three synagogues. Many of these Jews were landowners who also served as tax collectors or generals. Considered one of the Seven Wonders of the Ancient World, Alexandria's 440-foot lighthouse, located on the island of Pharos in the city's harbor, projected a beam that was visible at a distance of twenty miles. (An earthquake destroyed the lighthouse in the fourteenth century A.D.) Antioch and Pergamum, both located in what is now Turkey, were the other great commercial centers of the Hellenistic period that followed the death of Alexander. Commerce flourished throughout the empire, as Alexander unleashed hoards of Persian gold into the economy and standardized the coinage.

Koine (common Greek), a simplified version of the Attic dialect of classical Greek, became the standard written language of the Near Eastern aristocracy. In fact, the New Testament was later written in a vernacular form of koine with Semitic admixtures.

But Greek culture did not completely displace Near Eastern cultures. For instance, the Ptolemies, the Macedonian rulers of Egypt, depicted themselves wearing Egyptian garb, financed Egyptian-style temples, participated in Egyptian religious rites, and even married their own sisters as the pharaohs had. Meanwhile, officials of the Seleucid Empire used Near Eastern languages like Aramaic and cuneiform Akkadian in drafting some documents.

DIVISION AND DESTRUCTION

When Alexander died, his only heir was an embryo, a child later murdered at age thirteen. When asked on his deathbed to whom he bequeathed his empire, he whispered, "To the strongest." After forty years of bloody struggle between his former generals for control of the empire, it was divided into three parts, each controlled by a general. Ptolemy, who had been Alexander's personal staff officer and his governor of Egypt, ruled that province. Antigonus the One-Eyed, who had once saved Alexander's supply line in an important battle, ruled Macedon and much of Greece. The brilliant Seleucus, who had commanded Alexander's infantry, ruled the rest of Alexander's empire.

The easternmost portion of the Seleucid Empire was soon captured by an Indian ruler. The rest of the eastern Seleucid Empire fragmented into independent states, which were absorbed by the Parthians in the second century B.C. The western part of the empire also fragmented and fell to Rome. Egypt was conquered by Rome in the first century B.C. Greece revolted against the Antigonids, fragmented into a number of states, and was also conquered by the Romans.

One of these Greek states, the Achaean League, was an early model of a federal system. Reestablished from a looser version by four Peloponnesian poleis around 280 B.C., the league was governed by a representative body elected by the adult males of each member polis. This assembly met four times a year to formulate a common foreign policy and to enact economic legislation, such as laws regulating the coinage. At its height, the league successfully combined as many as sixty different poleis in rough equality and harmony under a single government and currency. Previous leagues had been empires, dominated by a single member, not federations of equal states. Another federation, the Aetolian League of central and northwestern Greece, varied representation according to population. The Founding Fathers of the United States cited both of these leagues as models in their debates at the Constitutional Convention.

ALEXANDER'S LEGACY

Alexander's conquests greatly extended the size and scope of Greek civilization. Yet, even as his conquests led to the dissemination of Greek culture over a much wider area, they also transformed it. The ideal of the versatile citizen, epitomized by Pericles, gave way to increasing military and economic specialization. New military tactics, involving the use of cavalry, mountain warfare, and precision rowing, required lengthy training. The average citizen could not undergo such training and perform his daily work as well. As a result, soldiers became specialists, and the crucial link between citizenship and the defense of one's polis, a connection that lay at the heart of Greek culture, was severed. While the explosion of trade produced greater prosperity, it also undermined the versatility the polis had traditionally encouraged. The greater the number of items that could be imported cheaply, the fewer local citizens had to make themselves and, hence, the fewer their skills. In addition, the increasing volume and complexity of trade caused many citizens to devote less time to public affairs and more time to their own businesses. The delicate balance the Greeks had attempted to maintain between individual freedom and social responsibility had been undermined. The individual and, theoretically at least, the world at large replaced the middle entity, the polis, as the greatest objects of concern.

Though Alexander's conquests partially Hellenized the Near East, they also partially easternized the Greek world. Democratic city-states now took a back seat to opulent kings, who, in Near Eastern tradition, often established cults dedicated to their own worship. These changes opened the Greek world to conquest by Rome.

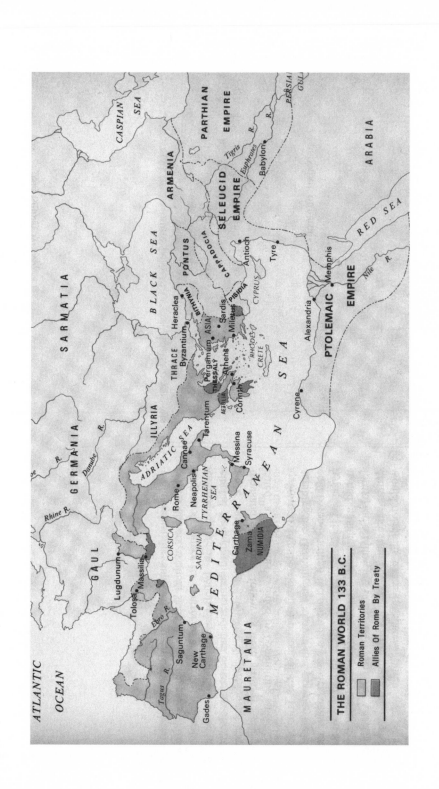

THE ROMAN WORLD 133 B.C.

☐ Roman Territories

☐ Allies Of Rome By Treaty

7

✛

Scipio Africanus: Defender of the Roman Republic

Just as Themistocles had saved Greek civilization at the Battle of Salamis in 480 B.C., so Scipio Africanus saved the Roman republic at the Battle of Zama in 202 B.C. Because of Scipio's victory, Rome, rather than Carthage, would dominate the Western world. It was the Romans who modified and spread Greek culture and, eventually, Christianity throughout the Mediterranean world and western Europe. But the Romans should not be viewed exclusively as the disseminators of the achievements of other peoples. They themselves contributed substantially to Western civilization. Their language, law, and architecture still exert a powerful influence over every Western nation.

THE REASONS FOR ROMAN SUCCESS

How is it that a small people possessing relatively poor soil and harbors came to rule over the largest empire in the world, spanning several million square miles and containing fifty million people? The Romans' geographical advantages and cultural traits account for much of their success.

Location, Location, Location

Around 1000 B.C., various Latin tribes migrated from the Balkans into central Italy and intermarried with the locals. Though familiar with iron, the Latins were mostly shepherds and herdsmen. During the ninth century B.C., some of these tribesmen settled on the Palatine and Esquiline Hills, two of

Rome's famed seven hills, overlooking a convenient crossing of the Tiber, the second largest river in Italy. Twenty miles from the sea, Rome was close enough for transportation and communication but distant enough to have warning of raiders. Located near valuable salt beds, Rome's hills were easily defensible and free from flooding. Most significantly, Rome was located at the crossroads between the Etruscans to the north and the Greeks to the south. The Romans learned much from both of these peoples.

By 700 B.C., the Etruscans had settled in Etruria, the land northwest of Rome. The Greeks called the Etruscans "Tyrrhenians," whence comes the name "Tyrrhenian Sea" for the gulf that separates Italy from Corsica and Sardinia. The precise origins of the Etruscans are not known for certain, but their language was not Indo-European, and in all probability they came from Asia Minor. The Etruscans were famous for their music and love of war. They also enjoyed dancing, hunting, wrestling, juggling, and feasting. Initially, the Etruscans cremated their dead, but in the late eighth century B.C. they began burying the deceased in stone coffins. In the following century, they hewed massive, lavish chamber tombs out of subterranean rock, often covering them with large mounds of earth. The walls of the tombs were painted. The dead were laid on benches or interred in sarcophagi, on the lids of which reclined stone images of the deceased. The Etruscans became fairly wealthy through agriculture, iron mining, and piracy. They traded fine pottery, candelabra, jewelry, mirrors, chariots, and leather for luxury goods from Greece, Phoenicia, and Egypt. Their cities were well planned and fortified. They were the first people to use a dental bridge (made of gold) to anchor a false tooth (made of wood or ivory) to the two adjacent teeth. Their women possessed a relatively high status, socializing with men to an extent impossible for a respectable Greek or Roman woman.

The Etruscans expanded southward to the Bay of Naples, intermarrying with the locals and organizing much of northern and central Italy and some of southern Italy into three different confederations of Etruscan-dominated city-states. By about 625 B.C., an Etruscan adventurer from Tarquinia, the wealthiest and most powerful of the Etruscan cities (forty miles north of Rome) had become king of Rome. Tarquinia's control of Mount Tolfa, which contained large deposits of iron, tin, and copper, contributed greatly to its wealth and power. This city of 25,000 people also produced metalwork, pottery, and linen, and traded widely. At that time, there was much freedom of movement between cities, and intermarriage between Etruscan and Latin aristocrats was common. In fact, more than a few Roman family names were Etruscan in etymology.

The Etruscans contributed much to Roman civilization. Etruscan kings transformed Rome from a collection of huts into a real city possessing streets, public buildings, markets, and temples. The Etruscans furnished such words as "Roma," "Italia" (meaning "calf-land"), "Tuscany" (from "Etruscan"), and

"Adriatic" (from the Etruscan settlement of "Hatria"). The Etruscans also contributed a few gods, the custom of making statues of deities, and the practice of prophesying by examining the entrails of sacrificial animals, by monitoring the flight of birds, and by following the positions of heavenly bodies. The Etruscans taught the Romans the art of construction, including the use of the arch. Their temples, shrines, private homes, aqueducts, and roads greatly influenced Roman architecture and engineering. When one of their kings drained the Forum, Rome's marshy central valley, which had previously been used as a burial site, it was the first step toward the Forum's eventual fame as the greatest marketplace in the world. The Etruscans also furnished the toga and introduced the *fasces*, an ax bound by a bundle of wooden rods tied together, as a symbol of executive authority. (The ax symbolized the power to put to death, the rods the power to whip. Seeking to use Rome's ancient glory to his advantage, Italian dictator Benito Mussolini later used the fasces as his symbol, whence comes "fascism." A century and a half before Mussolini, Thomas Jefferson had proposed using the fasces as Virginia's state symbol.) The Etruscans were also responsible for the Roman use of the color purple, which was the Etruscan state color, as a symbol of royalty. Finally, the Etruscans introduced chariot races and gladiatorial contests.

Between 750 and 500 B.C., the Greeks colonized southern Italy and Sicily, converting parts of these regions into what the Romans called Magna Graecia (Greater Greece). From these Greeks, via the Etruscans, the Romans learned the Greek alphabet, which they adapted into the Latin alphabet now used throughout the Western world. The Romans assimilated virtually the entire Greek religion (also via the Etruscans), merely changing the names of the gods. Zeus became Jupiter, Hera became Juno (whence comes the month of June), Hermes became Mercury, Aphrodite became Venus, Athena became Minerva, Ares became Mars, Hephaestus became Vulcan, Kronos became Saturn, Poseidon became Neptune, Artemis became Diana, Demeter became Ceres, and the demigod Heracles became Hercules. Only Apollo remained Apollo. Even more than the Greeks, the Romans tied religion to patriotism. Roman gods seemed to exist for no other reason than to strengthen and protect Rome. Appointed by the state, Roman priests were much more powerful than their Greek counterparts. The Romans also adopted Greek-style coins and pottery early in their history. Of course, the Romans would later assimilate Greek art, literature, science, and philosophy as a result of their conquest of the eastern Mediterranean.

Cultural Traits

The Romans possessed important cultural traits that also contributed to their success. The Romans were staunch pragmatists. Cicero once declared: "Whereas our ancestors respected tradition when Rome was at peace, they were invariably guided by expediency in time of war." The pragmatism of the Romans not only proved crucial to their military success, but also made them the greatest engineers of the ancient world.

The Romans were also tough and frugal. They prized strength over delicacy, power over agility, and utility over grace. They preferred *gravitas* (seriousness) to *levitas* (frivolity). They acquired this toughness the hard way, by scratching out a living on rocky, barren soil.

Romans subordinated themselves to the family and to Rome. In the recesses of the central hall of their houses, aristocrats kept wax busts and masks that realistically depicted the faces of illustrious ancestors. When a distinguished member of the family died, each mask was worn at the funeral by the family member most resembling the ancestor whose face was depicted in the mask. The family member even dressed himself according to the rank the ancestor had held. The eulogy was delivered by the most prominent living family member, who not only listed the achievements of the newly deceased family member, but also painstakingly recounted the achievements of the whole group of ancestors, who were understood to be present in the form of their masks and borrowed bodies. This ritual instilled in young men a desire to endure hardship and even death in order to win the glory of such a eulogy for themselves one day.

The doctrine of *pater familias* (the father of the family) dominated Roman family law. The patriarch of an extended family possessed absolute authority over the entire clan. Theoretically, he could even kill any member of the family and could sell his children as slaves, though such acts were exceedingly rare. (Regardless, it was not a good idea for a Roman son to tell his father he had wrecked the family wagon.) As in many other cultures, the worst crime was parricide. Anyone guilty of so heinous a crime was sewn up in a sack with a dog, a cock, a snake, and a monkey and hurled into the river or sea. Rome was regarded as an extended family, and it was but a small step from the doctrine of pater familias to the doctrine of *pater patria* (the father of the country) that later legitimated the reign of the emperors.

The Romans utilized a large collection of stirring myths to instill courage, selflessness, honesty, and patriotism in their children. According to one popular legend, around 506 B.C. Horatius Cocles saved Rome from an Etruscan army by single-handedly holding off the Etruscans while his comrades destroyed a bridge spanning the Tiber. Having no bridge left behind him, Horatius then recited a quick prayer to Father Tiber and hurled himself into the river. According to another legend, around 462 B.C. a delegation of Roman officials asked Cincinnatus, a Roman farmer who was busy plowing his three-acre farm, to assume dictatorial power over Rome for six months in order to expel the Aequians, a Latin tribe threatening the village. Wiping away the sweat and grime, Cincinnatus put on his toga and set about defeating the Aequians in only fifteen days. Cincinnatus immediately resigned his dictatorship and retired to the plow. (George Washington later modeled himself on Cincinnatus and encouraged the comparison. Lord Byron called Washington the "Cincinnatus of the West.") According to yet another account, in 340 B.C. Titus Manlius ordered the execution of his own son for leading a reckless attack on the enemy against orders. Manlius declared: "You have . . . subverted military discipline, on which the fortune of Rome has rested up to this day. . . . It is a harsh example we shall set, but a salutary one for the young men of the future." In another legend, around 250 B.C. Marcus Atilius Regulus, a Roman consul captured by the Carthaginians, was allowed to return to Rome to discuss peace terms and to negotiate the exchange of Carthaginian prisoners for himself; the Carthaginians made him pledge that he would return to Carthage if he failed. After arriving in Rome, Regulus urged the Senate to continue the war and dissuaded it from making the prisoner exchange, declaring that the Carthaginian prisoners were young and capable officers while he himself was old and worn out. True to his word, Regulus then returned to Carthage, though he knew that the enraged Carthaginians would torture him to death. In fact, they killed him through sleep deprivation.

But the greatest of all the Roman patriotic myths was the poet Virgil's myth of the founding of Rome. According to Virgil's *Aeneid*, Aeneas, son of the Trojan aristocrat Anchises and the goddess Venus, had led a few refugees out of Troy before it fell to the Greeks. The refugees experienced numerous adventures and encountered many hardships before reaching Italy, where they settled down with local Latin tribesmen. Thirteen generations later, two of Aeneas's distant descendants, Romulus and Remus, established Rome. Romulus and Remus were the sons of the war god Mars and Rhea Silvia, a priestess sworn to chastity. Rhea Silvia's uncle, the king of Alba Longa, angry with her for breaking her vows, rejected her claim that the father was Mars, imprisoned her, and had her infant sons exposed on the banks of the Tiber. But a wolf found and nursed Romulus and Remus until a herdsman discovered and raised the brothers. According to the myth, in 753 B.C. the brothers returned to the site where they had been exposed as infants and Romulus traced the outlines of Rome with his plow. Romulus killed Remus in a fit of rage over an insult and became the first king of Rome. This myth gave the Romans a noble origin and lineage; they were descended from Trojan heroes and from the god of war himself.

From such myths the Romans learned courage, discipline, persistence, patience, self-restraint, hard work, endurance, honesty, piety, dignity, and manliness. The last of these qualities was *virtus*, whence comes the English word "virtue." Indeed, most of these English terms are derived from Latin words. Many of the qualities they express were those of the farmer-soldier, who had to endure boredom, harsh weather, unforeseen calamities, and hard labor. Soldiers did not just fight; they had to dig ditches and build roads as well. Such traits were essential to success in the early struggle against nature and neighbors. In fact, Mars had begun as an agricultural god; it was Roman farmer-soldiers who converted him into the god of war.

Most importantly perhaps, the Romans possessed a sense of invincibility. The Roman historian Livy wrote: "It is as natural for Romans to win battles as for water to go downhill." This feeling of invincibility stemmed from the Roman belief that the gods would support them completely as long as they performed the proper rituals. Each Roman house possessed its own small shrine containing statuettes of the Lares, the household gods. Like the citizens of many other empires throughout history, the Romans possessed a sense of divine mission. When a Roman general celebrated a triumph, he proceeded through the city to the temple of Jupiter (later to the temple of Mars) and offered up to the god "the achievements of Jupiter wrought through the Roman people."

For this reason, perhaps no other people has ever been so obsessed with rituals. When the Romans declared war on another people (a frequent occurrence), one of the *fetiales,* a special group of priests, performed an ancient ceremony. After the enemy had rejected Roman demands, which were sometimes exorbitant in order to ensure their rejection, the fetial went to the enemy's border and, in the presence of at least three men of military age, announced to the gods: "Whereas the X have committed acts and offenses against the Roman people, and whereas the Roman people have commanded that there be war with the X, and the Senate of the Roman people has ordained, consented, and voted that there be war with the X: I therefore and the Roman people hereby make war on the X." The fetial then hurled a spear across the border into the enemy's territory, to symbolize the beginning of a state of war. When the Roman Empire became too large to accommodate such a practice, the Romans set aside a special, enclosed area outside the gates of Rome called the Campus Martius, which symbolized the enemy's territory in the war-making ritual. The Romans never went to war without performing this rite.

If a mistake was made during any ritual, however time consuming, the Romans began again from the beginning. They were willing to perform the same ritual as often as necessary until it was performed without error. It did not even matter that, in some cases, the meaning of the ritual had been completely forgotten.

Many of these rituals originated in elaborate family rites, handed down from father to son, for the purpose of appealing to Ceres (the goddess of agriculture), Vesta (the goddess of the hearth), and the Lares. Even the family meal was a religious ceremony during which the Romans offered prayers, incense, and libations to the gods. Other household rituals expelled evil spirits and pleased friendly ones. Legend even has it that a Roman once marched past the astonished Gauls besieging Rome and over to Quirinal Hill in order to perform a traditional family sacrifice that had to be performed on that day. After the Gauls left the city in rubble (c. 390 B.C.), there was a great cry to immigrate to the nearby town of Veii, but Camillus convinced the Romans that it would be impious to abandon the places in Rome where rituals must be performed. According to Livy, Camillus declared: "Surely it would be nobler to live like country shepherds amongst everything we hold sacred than to go into universal exile, deserting the gods of our hearths and homes."

Military victories reinforced the Roman sense of invincibility, which, in turn, produced more victories. On the few occasions when the Romans lost battles, they believed that the gods were merely teaching them a lesson in order to keep them from becoming too proud. Nearly all Roman authors cited piety as a crucial factor in the city's success.

THE ROMAN CONQUEST OF ITALY

Between the sixth and third centuries B.C., the Romans conquered all of Italy and established a republic. These two momentous developments were interrelated. The growing recognition of the rights of commoners created the internal harmony necessary for the defeat of external enemies, and the constant warfare highlighted the need to keep commoners happy by recognizing their rights.

The last of the seven kings who ruled Rome from about 625 to 509 B.C. was Tarquin the Proud, an Etruscan who had seized power and who ruled without Senate consultation. In 509 B.C., Tarquin was expelled from Rome. According to Roman legend, Lucius Junius Brutus (an ancestor of Caesar's assassin) and Publius (a name the authors of *The Federalist* later selected as their pseudonym) led the rebellion. Legend held that the Romans rebelled against Tarquin when Lucretia, the married daughter of a prominent Roman nobleman, stabbed herself through the heart after being raped by Tarquin's son. After the fall of Tarquin, Lars Parsenna, king of Clusium, took advantage of the turmoil to capture Rome, but a coalition of Latins and Greeks under Aristodemus decisively defeated Lars' son, Arruns, near Aricia, thus allowing Rome to resume its independence. In any case, the Romans so hated Tarquin that the very title of "king" became odious to them. Even centuries later, the Roman emperors, who had more power than Tarquin ever dreamed of possessing, adopted the designation "emperor" (*imperator*) to avoid the title of "king" (*rex*).

In 496 B.C., the Roman infantry suppressed a rebellion of the other Latin tribes that formed the Latin League, defeating a force composed mostly of cavalry at Lake Regillus. In 396 B.C., the Romans, under Marcus Furius Camillus, tunneled into the citadel of Veii, the Etruscan city with which they struggled for control of the salt beds at the mouth of the Tiber. The Romans captured and destroyed the rival city. Situated at a river crossing from which roads radiated in all directions, Veii was a trade and craft center located only nine miles from Rome. In capturing Veii, the Romans doubled the extent of their territory. By 390 B.C., the Latin League dominated central Italy.

That same year the invasion of Italy by 30,000 Gauls, fierce Celtic warriors from what is now France, threatened Rome's very existence. Having crossed the Alps and marched southward into Italy, the Gauls routed the Roman army, who escaped to Veii, leaving Rome open. Though a small Roman garrison held out on Capitoline Hill, the Gauls burned most of Rome. After seven months, the Roman patricians were able to bribe the Gauls into leaving the city. (The Gauls also left because other tribes threatened their northern territory. Naturally, Roman legend declared that they left because Camillus defeated them in battle.)

Though it took the Romans half a century to recover fully, they rebuilt their city and protected it with a new wall so sturdy that part of it still stands. The wall enclosed an area of 1,000 acres. By necessity, the city was rebuilt quickly and haphazardly, which was why, according to Livy four centuries later, "the general lay-out of Rome is more like a squatters' settlement than a properly planned city." But the Romans swore that never again would a foreign army enter Rome. Indeed, it was another eight centuries before one did.

The Romans' determination to resist conquest combined with population pressures to produce a policy that some historians have termed "defensive imperialism." In the quest for ever securer borders, the Romans eventually conquered all of Italy.

Four peoples, the Latins, Samnites, Etruscans, and Greeks, blocked the Roman conquest of Italy. Though plagued by disunity, the Latin tribes repeatedly rebelled and fought the Romans tooth and nail; the last tribe was not subdued until 338 B.C. The Romans dissolved the Latin League and forced each tribe to sign a separate peace treaty with them. The Romans then conquered Tarquinia by 311 B.C. Meanwhile, from 343 to 290 B.C., the Romans engaged in three fierce wars against the Samnite tribes of the hills of Campania (in southwestern Italy), who were distant relatives of the Latins. Though the Samnites possessed few towns, they were highly organized and disciplined, possessed twice the population and land of Rome, could retreat to mountainous country when in distress, and received some aid from the Etruscans and Gauls. Nevertheless, the Romans overcame numerous setbacks and defeated the Samnites and their allies decisively by 290 B.C.

It was during the Samnite Wars that the Romans moved from the phalanx, learned from the Greeks via the Etruscans, to the more maneuverable formations that later enabled them to conquer the entire Mediterranean basin and all of western Europe. Roman armies were now organized around small units called *centuries* led by *centurions*. A century equaled sixty to one hundred men. Two centuries equaled a *maniple*. Three maniples equaled a *cohort*. Ten cohorts (4,000 to 6,000 men) and 300 cavalry equaled a *legion*. When a Roman legion marched into battle, its sixty centuries did so in three lines, each able to coalesce into a mass or disperse into smaller contingents. Two lines (the *princeps* and the *triari*) watched the front line (the *hastati*) intently, preparing to exploit success or prevent collapse. Roman soldiers generally cast seven-foot javelins, then ran to meet the enemy with a razor-sharp, double-edged short sword (the *gladius*). They often used their rectangular shields offensively as battering rams. The second line cast their javelins over their friends' heads to impale the enemy before them.

The Roman conquest of the Samnites left only the Greeks of southern Italy to conquer. In 282 B.C., the Greek city of Tarentum, fearful of the growing Roman power, sank part of a Roman flotilla and called on the brilliant Greek general Pyrrhus of Epirus for aid. In 280 B.C., Pyrrhus brought 25,000 troops and 20 Indian war elephants to add to Tarentum's 15,000 soldiers, mercenaries, and large navy. After seeing the Romans in action, the sharp-witted Pyrrhus declared, "These may be barbarians, but there is nothing barbarous about their discipline."

Nor did it take long for Pyrrhus to see the superiority of the Romans' more flexible formations over the more rigid Greek phalanx. By then the phalanx employed mutually supporting rows of twenty-one foot spears. While it was highly effective in opening charges, it required level ground without obstructions and lost its effectiveness in subsequent fighting, because the soldier in the phalanx could not operate either singly or in small units, like the Roman maniples, which could wheel about to face danger from any direction.

Nevertheless, in 280 B.C. and again the following year Pyrrhus defeated the Romans, losing far fewer men than the Romans each time. But Pyrrhus could not afford his losses as well as the Romans. He could rely on far fewer reinforcements than the Romans, and each defeat seemed only to leave the Romans angrier and more determined to prevail. When a friend congratulated Pyrrhus on his second victory, he declared, "One more victory like that over the Romans will destroy us completely." This is the origin of the term "Pyrrhic victory," a victory that is so costly as to constitute defeat.

Pyrrhus withdrew to Sicily for three years, where he helped the Greeks rout the Carthaginians. Following his return to the mainland, his attempt to bribe the Roman general Fabricius failed, and he was forced to fight again. (Fabricius was so ethical he even informed Pyrrhus when Pyrrhus's physician offered to poison him for money.) This time the Romans defeated

Pyrrhus, and he returned home with only one-third of his original force. Three years later Pyrrhus was killed in a battle at Argos, when an old woman, alarmed at the sight of Pyrrhus engaging her son in combat, hurled a heavy roof tile at Pyrrhus and struck him below the helmet, knocking him unconscious. An Argive soldier then cut off his head.

By 275 B.C., the Roman army had subdued all of the Greek city-states of Italy. Only the conquest and colonization of the Po River valley, shortly after 200 B.C., remained to complete Roman control of the Italian Peninsula.

Roman Treatment of Conquered Italians

The Romans won the loyalty of the conquered Italians through lenient treatment. Although most subject states had to adhere to Rome's foreign policy, to supply troops for the Roman army, and to surrender 20 percent of their land (twenty-seven small Roman colonies were established in these lands by 250 B.C., thereby reducing Rome's population problems), the Romans demanded no tribute and allowed each state to retain its local self-government. Some cities were even allowed full Roman citizenship and given loot and land. Such leniency was extremely uncommon in the ancient world. As we have seen, the "enlightened" Greeks often slaughtered or enslaved conquered peoples. But Roman leniency in Italy proved extremely wise. During the Second Punic War (218–201 B.C.), when Hannibal and the Carthaginians invaded Italy, their failure to entice Italians into widespread rebellion saved Rome and proved fatal to Carthage. As Camillus had once put it, "By far the strongest government is one to which men are happy to be subject."

THE GROWTH OF REPUBLICAN GOVERNMENT

Until 509 B.C., the Romans were ruled by monarchs selected by the Senate and approved by the people. The Senate was a council of 300 former officeholders called *patricians* (fathers) who advised the king. Nearly all of the senators were landed aristocrats.

After the Romans expelled Tarquin, they established an oligarchy. In theory, two *consuls* (colleagues) replaced the king as the city's executive and legislature. (Tarquin's reign had produced the fear of a single executive.) The consuls were elected annually from the patrician class by the people, subject to ratification by the Senate. But, in reality, since the consuls were fatally weakened by their fractured power (they could veto each other's decisions) and exceedingly short terms, the real power in the Roman republic was held by the life-tenured Senate, which decided public policy and controlled the treasury. The Senate could veto any actions taken by the consuls. If the consuls disagreed with each other, the Senate could make executive decisions. The Senate also served as the supreme judicial body. During a time of emergency, the Senate had the power to substitute a dictator for the consuls for a period of six months. Common Romans, the *plebeians*, possessed very little power.

Republican Reforms

Within a few centuries, however, Rome moved from an oligarchy to a more republican government, a system in which common people possessed a greater voice. In 494 B.C., short of grain and tired of fighting wars for the benefit of the patricians, the plebeians withdrew to Aventine Hill. They threatened to secede and establish their own city. As a compromise, the patricians then allowed the plebeians to elect two *tribunes*. Eventually, these tribunes, whose persons were sacrosanct (to strike them was considered both a political and a religious crime), were granted the authority to halt any Senate measures they considered unfair by walking into the Senate chamber and shouting, "Veto!"—Latin for "I forbid!" They could block any magistrate from exercising his office. They were required to maintain an open house and were prohibited from leaving Rome overnight, so that plebeians could request their aid at any hour. The number of tribunes was gradually increased from two to ten.

In 451 B.C., the plebeians demanded a written code of laws, so that consuls could no longer interpret Rome's customary law to suit their own interests. Drafted by ten aristocrats called the *decemviri*, the legal code was inscribed on twelve tablets and set up in the Forum for all to see the following year. Roman children memorized the laws. The Law of the Twelve Tables was the first landmark in the illustrious history of Roman law. Like most of its contemporaries, the code, which was largely formalized from existing oral law, was harsh, allowing enslavement for debt. But its terse sentences represent the first indication of the Romans' uncanny talent for legal definition.

In 445 B.C., plebeians were granted the right to marry patricians. (In practice, only a plebeian who had acquired some wealth would be acceptable to a patrician woman.) In 421 B.C., the office of *quaestor* (the consuls' finance manager) was made elective and opened to plebeians, and the number of quaestors was increased to four. (Previously, the consuls had appointed them.) In 367 B.C., one of the two consulships was reserved for the plebeians; in 342 B.C., the other was opened to them. In 326 B.C., confinement and enslavement for debt were abolished. Livy later referred to this measure as "a new birth of freedom," a phrase later immortalized in Abraham Lincoln's Gettysburg Address.

In the mid-to-late fourth century B.C., new offices were created and opened to the plebeians. Most of the new offices possessed powers previously held by the consuls. One office was that of *aedile* (supervisor of the marketplace, public buildings, archives, traffic, water and grain supplies, and weights and measures and sponsor of games), while another was that of *praetor* (supervisor of courts). A third new office was that of *censor* (administrator of the census every five years, assessor of taxes, supervisor of public morals, awarder of state contracts, and confirmer of the lineage of senators). At about the same time, some wealthy plebeians (especially former officeholders) were admitted into the Senate.

In 300 B.C., every citizen was granted the right to appeal to the people against a death penalty. At about the same time, the college of *pontiffs* and *augurs* was opened to plebeians. The pontiffs presided over rituals and maintained the lore, while augurs recorded omens and predicted the future.

Most significantly, in 287 B.C. temporary dictator Quintus Hortensius transferred supreme legislative authority from the Senate to the *comitia tributa*, one of the Romans' three popular assemblies. The plebeians had gained each of these reforms by taking advantage of Rome's dependence on their military support. The patricians knew that if the plebeians refused to serve in the army, or left to form another city, they would be destroyed. The increased wealth of some plebeians also helped produce the reforms.

The Romans called the system of government that developed in their city a *res publica* (commonwealth). They believed it was a mixed government, a system in which the power of the one (in this case the two, the consuls), the few, and the many were balanced against one another. The Greek historian Polybius noted that the consuls needed to maintain good relations with the Senate because the Senate could block the flow of grain, clothing, and money to them in military campaigns, could replace them in the middle of a campaign if their year in office had expired, and could withhold triumphs and other prestigious awards. The consuls needed to maintain good relations with the people since they could find fault with the account that the consuls were required to submit at the end of their term and could reject the treaties they negotiated. Similarly, the Senate and the people were bound to one another by the Senate's control of lucrative contracts, by its dominance of the judicial system, and by the people's ability (through the tribunes) to veto the Senate's decisions. Likewise, the people needed to maintain good relations with the consuls since they served under them in the army.

But, although political power was certainly more balanced than it had been before the initiation of the republican reforms discussed earlier, the few still possessed more power than the many. The Senate still controlled the treasury. It could refuse to fund any measure passed by the comitia tributa. The patricians were also able to use their control of most Roman land to pressure many plebeians, including their own *clients* (various dependents, including tenant farmers, who worked patrician land for part of the crop), to vote the way they demanded. The patricians gave their clients jobs, protection, and legal aid (when called before the aristocratic

Senate) in exchange for their loyalty. Since most plebeians could not afford to hold office, because officials did not receive salaries, the patricians controlled most offices. Even the tribunes were hardly immune from their influence. The fact that tribunes and many other officeholders knew that they would automatically become members of the Senate after they left office often led them to support aristocratic interests. Similarly, the consuls, who were almost always patricians, who shared in the economic interests of that class, and who generally had relatives in the Senate, can hardly be considered to have served as an effective counterweight to that body. In addition, the balances between the consuls and the people were of unequal weight. A consul's fear that he might have a treaty rejected hardly balanced plebeian terror at the thought of opposing someone who, as a military leader, would have the power of life and death over them. Indeed, the imbalance between the patricians and plebeians was increasing at the very time that Polybius and Cicero were writing their odes to the Roman republic, as we shall see in the next chapter.

Nevertheless, the republic granted the plebeians greater rights than they had ever known. Hence, the plebeians felt that they had a stake in Roman military success. It is no accident that republics, such as Athens, Sparta, Rome, Carthage, France after the French Revolution, and the United States, have generally fought well.

THE FIRST PUNIC WAR (264–241 B.C.)

Carthage

The word "Punic" is derived from *Poeni*, the Latin term for the Carthaginians since Carthage had been founded as a Phoenician colony by settlers from Tyre. The Phoenicians had colonized the western Mediterranean (western Sicily, Sardinia, Corsica, Spain, and North Africa) by about 800 B.C. By 500 B.C., Carthage, located on the coast of what is now Tunisia, had become wealthy and powerful enough to dominate the other Phoenician colonies. The chief source of Carthaginian wealth was trade (especially in metals), and the chief source of Carthaginian power was a large navy. Thirty merchant princes played the leading role in governing Carthage. The Carthaginian senate, controlled by the aristocracy, possessed most of the power. The popularly elected magistrates (called *suffetes*) possessed only one-year terms, and the popular assembly was consulted only when the senators and suffetes could not agree. The Carthaginians possessed little art or literature. Their chief deities were Baal, a Canaanite-Phoenician god whose worship the Hebrew prophets of the Old Testament had denounced, and Tanit, a fertility goddess who became more prominent after the fifth century

B.C. The smaller size of the Carthaginian population, when compared with that of Rome, forced Carthage to rely too heavily on mercenaries.

The Cause of War

Rome and Carthage began to quarrel after the Romans conquered southern Italy, thereby extending their borders to within range of Carthaginian territory in Sicily. In 264 B.C., the First Punic War began as the result of a struggle over the strategic city of Messana (now Messina) on the northeastern tip of Sicily. When the Greek king Hiero II of Syracuse threatened to expel from Messana a group of Italian mercenaries called Mamertines, they begged both Rome and Carthage for protection. Carthage quickly provided troops. The Romans feared that if the Carthaginians controlled the Straits of Messina, the narrow strip of water that separates Sicily from the Italian mainland, they would be able to cross over into Italy without warning and to block Rome's most important sea-lane. Hence, the Romans dispatched an army, under Appius Claudius, to besiege Messana. Fearing that army, the Mamertines fooled the Carthaginian garrison into leaving the citadel and turned the city over to the Romans. After suffering a serious defeat at the hands of Appius Claudius, Hiero also defected to the Roman side, becoming the first of Rome's many client-kings.

The War

The First Punic War was a bloody struggle that lasted twenty-three years. Some contemporaries believed that the Carthaginians' economic and naval superiority ensured their victory. In fact, the Romans possessed so few ships at the beginning of the war they had to borrow vessels from the Greeks in southern Italy just to transport their army to Messana. Yet, the Romans managed to construct a fleet and train its crews in just a few months. The Roman ships were modeled on Carthaginian vessels but were heavier and slower, since the Romans liked to keep soldiers aboard for grappling and boarding enemy ships.

After defeating the Carthaginians in a naval battle at Mylae (260 B.C.) through these tactics, the Romans suffered a serious defeat in North Africa (255 B.C.), from which they were forced to withdraw. The Romans then lost two complete fleets and 200,000 men (mostly allied soldiers) in a series of other naval battles and storms.

But, unable to admit defeat, the stubborn Romans rebuilt their fleet each time. Rome was a pit bull that would not release its grip on the enemy's leg, no matter how many times it was beaten on the head or offered the milk bone of peace. In 242 B.C., the Romans' third fleet, under Gaius Lutatius Catulus, defeated the Carthaginian navy off the Aegates, a group of islands near the western coast of Sicily. Based on the false assumption that the Romans could not recover from the destruction of their previous fleets, the Carthaginians had allowed their own naval training to diminish. Meanwhile, the Romans had learned how to fight at sea. They had removed all nonessential equipment from their ships and had worked hard at rowing in unison. As a result, the Romans were able to sink 50 Carthaginian ships and capture 70 vessels containing 10,000 men at the Aegates. Although the Carthaginians had lost only 500 ships to the Romans' 700 during the war, they now faced the threat of another invasion. Carthage sued for peace on Roman terms.

The Peace

Under Lutatius's treaty, Carthage was forced to surrender Sicily and 3,200 talents over a ten-year period. A few years later, taking advantage of a rebellion against Carthage launched by mercenaries and Libyan slaves, Rome seized Sardinia and Corsica and demanded another 1,200 talents. The Carthaginians were furious but were in no position to resist the Romans.

The islands of Sicily, Sardinia, and Corsica were the first of Rome's overseas provinces, which it ruled less leniently than its Italian possessions. The provinces were taxed and disarmed. Sicily and Sardinia were placed under the rule of Roman praetors. Local leaders, operating under Roman direction, were allowed to continue governing the other provinces until 146 B.C., at which point they were replaced by Roman military governors, called *proconsuls* because they acted "for the consuls." The proconsuls ruled according to the Senate's stipulations, but the vagueness of the regulations created a tremendous opportunity for abuse.

THE SECOND PUNIC WAR (218–201 B.C.)

The Roman republic reached its peak during the Second Punic War. In this war, waged against Rome's most formidable adversary, wealthy and powerful Carthage, the Romans demonstrated their most impressive quality: the ability to maintain their courage and determination in the darkest hours. The defeat of Carthage was crucial to Roman survival and, hence, to the transmission of Greco-Roman civilization throughout western Europe. Victory in that war also made possible Roman conquest of the rest of the Mediterranean world.

The Causes

Although the First Punic War had weakened Carthage, the Carthaginians quickly regained their strength. Between 237 and 229 B.C., Hamilcar Barca, Carthage's greatest general, expanded Carthaginian territory in Spain.

(When the Romans asked Hamilcar what he was doing in Spain, he remarked snidely that he was fighting to obtain the money Carthage needed to pay its indemnity to Rome.) In 229 B.C., Hamilcar died covering a retreat that saved the lives of Hannibal, his brilliant son, and Hamilcar's staff. By 219 B.C., Hannibal (Grace of Baal) had further extended Carthaginian rule northward to the Iberus (now the Ebro) River. When news reached Rome that Hannibal had besieged Saguntum, an important Roman ally in Spain, the Romans were furious. When Carthage refused to repudiate Hannibal's act and turn him over to the Romans, Rome declared war (218 B.C.).

It is difficult to say which side was most responsible for the war. The Romans argued that, in besieging Saguntum, the Carthaginians had violated Lutatius's treaty, in which each side had agreed not to assault the other's allies. But Saguntum was not yet an ally of Rome when that treaty had been negotiated and, in a different treaty, the Romans had agreed that the area south of the Iberus River was a Carthaginian sphere of influence. Saguntum, which lay within that area, had been inciting other towns to resist Carthage—out of fear of the growing Carthaginian power and out of confidence that Rome would come to its aid. But while an examination of the treaties leads one to the conclusion that Rome was technically in the wrong, it is also true that the Carthaginians were exceptionally bitter toward Rome because of past humiliations and that both sides eagerly embraced the conflict.

Hannibal's Expedition

It was thought that the Second Punic War, like the first, would consist largely of naval battles, with some ground combat in Spain. No one expected that the Carthaginians would attack Italy from the north. But the Romans had not reckoned with the fierce determination of Hannibal. When Hannibal was only nine years old, his father had made him take a solemn oath, on an altar to Baal, to oppose Rome his whole life.

Hannibal now collected an army of 90,000 infantry, 12,000 cavalry, and 50 war elephants. He then subdued the tribes of northern Spain with remarkable speed. Leaving some troops behind in Spain under the command of his brother Hasdrubal, Hannibal then crossed the Pyrenees Mountains into what is now southern France with 50,000 infantry, 9,000 cavalry, and all 50 elephants.

One of Hannibal's greatest challenges lay in crossing the Rhone River, where the Volcae, a Gallic tribe, blocked his path. Hannibal secretly dispatched a party of his best men upstream to build a bridge and ford the river. They accomplished the task swiftly. The detachment then moved back downriver toward the Volcae, who remained unaware of their presence. When the detachment was in position, they informed Hannibal through smoke signals. Hannibal then began crossing the river. In their eagerness to slaughter the Carthaginians while engaged in a difficult river crossing, the Volcae rushed to the waterfront. The Carthaginian detachment that had forded the river then emerged from hiding and attacked the Volcae in the rear, throwing the whole army into utter panic.

Hannibal then faced the difficult task of leading his thirty-seven remaining elephants across the river. The elephants followed all of their Indian drivers' orders but one: they refused to go into the water. So Hannibal had rafts constructed and fastened to the docks in such a way as to appear to be mere extensions of the docks. The elephants confidently followed their drivers onto the rafts up to the edge of the water. Imagine their surprise when the rafts were cut loose from the bank, and they began to float across the river. Some panicked and overturned the rafts. Nevertheless, none of the elephants drowned, since they could hold their trunks above water to breathe and to discharge water. Many of the drivers were not so fortunate, however.

Hannibal and the Alps

Hannibal then proceeded to the Italian Alps. Contrary to popular myth, the reason the Romans were surprised that Hannibal crossed the Alps to attack them was not because the Alps were impassable, though they were certainly difficult to cross. (The Gauls crossed the Alps constantly.) Rather, the Romans were surprised that Hannibal would risk so large an army by leading them through a mountainous area inhabited by Gauls, whom the Romans considered fierce and treacherous. But many Gallic tribes whom the Romans had treated harshly favored the Carthaginians. They supplied Hannibal and showed him safe passes through the mountains. (It is true that one tribe, the Allobroges, ambushed Hannibal, inflicting heavy casualties. On that occasion, wounded horses, laden with baggage, fell off the precipices or collided with those before and behind and with horrified soldiers, who plunged to their deaths. But the canny Hannibal defeated the tribe and took their city, thereby intimidating neighboring tribes into cooperating with him.)

Having ascended the Alps, the Carthaginians then encountered the problem of descending its steep, icy slopes. The elephants proved a mixed blessing; they terrified the Gauls, who had never seen such monstrous animals, but they were difficult to lead across mountain passes.

Hannibal managed to reach the Po River in northern Italy with 20,000 infantry, 6,000 cavalry, and a bunch of skinny elephants. (There had not been enough grass in the snow-capped mountains.) It had taken him only five months to march from New Carthage (now Cartagena) in Spain to the Alps and only fifteen days to cross the mountains.

The Battle of Trebbia

After Hannibal defeated a Roman cavalry force, Gauls serving in the Roman army rebelled and massacred Roman soldiers. Reinforcing his army with Gallic allies, Hannibal then routed 40,000 Romans, under Tiberius Sempronius Longus, at the Trebbia River (218 B.C.). In this battle, Hannibal employed what was to become his favorite tactic: he enticed Sempronius into an ambush. Hannibal ordered a small force to attack Sempronius and withdraw, thereby drawing him into a ravine. Hannibal's main force then attacked the Romans on all sides from its positions on the overhanging riverbanks. Hannibal then armed his force with the larger shields and sturdier swords captured from the Romans in the battle.

The Battle of Lake Trasimene

Fearful of assassination attempts by treacherous Gallic chieftains (he even wore a collection of different wigs and other disguises to elude them), Hannibal then marched his men into Etruria via an obscure road that led through the marshes. The men traveled four days and three nights with little sleep, periodically collapsing on top of dead pack animals in order to keep above the water. Hannibal himself lost the vision in one eye from an infection exacerbated by sleeplessness.

By laying waste to the countryside, Hannibal managed to entice another Roman army, under the rash Gaius Flaminius, into pursuing and attacking him at a preselected position. Hills lay to Hannibal's left and Lake Trasimene to his right. Flaminius believed the hills provided sufficient cover for his flank. He was wrong. Aided by a thick mist, Hannibal had hidden detachments in the hills, who now fell on the Romans from the side and rear. Fifteen thousand Romans were killed, including Flaminius himself, and another 15,000 were captured. Hannibal lost only 1,500 men, mostly Gallic allies.

Hannibal's victories stunned and terrorized the Roman people. They had been so confident of victory that large numbers of them had followed Flaminius's army carrying chains and fetters in the hope of capturing Carthaginian slaves. Fortunately for Rome, Hannibal lacked the engines and supplies required for a siege, so he turned away from the city, crossed the Apennines, and ravaged Italy's Adriatic coast.

The Strategy of Fabius

The Romans used the respite to declare a state of emergency and appoint the fifty-eight-year-old Quintus Fabius Maximus dictator. A religious man, Fabius improved public morale by attributing the Roman defeats to a lack of piety, rather than to cowardice or ineptitude. Fabius wisely decided that Hannibal was too brilliant, and his Carthaginian veterans were too experienced (having fought with Hannibal in Spain for many years), for the Romans to oppose him in open battle. Fabius's strategy was to follow Hannibal but to avoid major engagements with him. Fabius knew that the Romans possessed two important advantages. First, while the Romans, as the native power in Italy, would always be well supplied, the Carthaginians would have to scavenge for supplies ceaselessly. Second, unlike the Romans, the Carthaginians could not easily receive reinforcements in Italy. Hence, Fabius kept his army intact and pounced on every small detachment Hannibal dispatched to forage for supplies. Through this war of attrition, Fabius gradually depleted Hannibal's force. Fabius kept to the mountains overlooking Hannibal's army—out of the reach of Hannibal's superior cavalry, but close enough to pounce on Carthaginian stragglers and foragers. Everywhere the victorious Hannibal marched, Fabius followed.

Fabius's strategy frustrated Hannibal. Hannibal could not defeat a force he could not fight. The losses Fabius inflicted on Hannibal's army were imperceptible to most observers, but not to Hannibal, who shared Fabius's farsightedness.

Fabius under Attack

But Fabius's strategy was as unpopular in Rome as George Washington's Fabian strategy was in the United States during the Revolutionary War. (During the early years of that war Washington consciously followed Fabius's model in avoiding major battles with the better-trained and more experienced British soldiers.) Many Romans considered Fabius a coward. They called him "Hannibal's *pedagogus*" (a pedagogus was a male slave who walked his master's children back and forth from school). When Fabius's friends begged him to risk a battle in order to save his reputation, he replied, "In that case I should be an even greater coward than they say I am."

Hannibal was one of the very few who realized that Fabius's strategy was the wisest and the most dangerous to his army. Hence, in order to discredit Fabius's strategy among the Romans, he adopted the cunning tactic of sparing Fabius's country villa while laying waste to the surrounding countryside. As Hannibal expected, some Romans then charged Fabius with colluding with the enemy. Fabius shrewdly dispelled the charge by selling the estate and contributing the proceeds to the repayment of Rome's public debt.

But the Roman people remained frustrated. When Fabius moved to punish his rash subordinate, the cavalry commander Municius Rufus, for attacking the enemy against orders, the Romans appointed Municius codictator with Fabius. The appointment of codictators was an unprecedented act.

Fabius Vindicated

Now freed from Fabius's wise restraint, Municius allowed Hannibal to lure him into an ambush at Gerunium. Hannibal hid some of his men in the small ditches and hollows of a plain. When Municius attacked his decoy force, situated on a hill, the other detachment came out of hiding and attacked the Roman force in the rear and on the flanks. If Fabius had not moved quickly to reinforce Municius, he would have lost his entire force. After seeing the vigor of Fabius's successful counterattack, Hannibal told his aides, "Haven't I kept telling you that the cloud we have seen hovering over the mountain tops would burst one day like a tornado?"

To the credit of both men, Fabius did not gloat or criticize, and Municius placed himself and the remnants of his army under Fabius's command. The strategy of Fabius, whom the Romans nicknamed "the Delayer," had been vindicated.

The Battle of Cannae (216 B.C.)

Hannibal's greatest victory occurred at Cannae, on the southwestern Adriatic coast, when he had only a ten days' supply of food left and his Spanish allies were considering desertion. The Romans had ended the dictatorships of Fabius and Municius and had transferred control of the armies to the duly elected consuls, Lucius Aemilius Paulus and Gaius Terentius Varro. Although Fabius was able to persuade Paulus of the wisdom of his defensive strategy, Varro was too ambitious to heed such warnings.

On one of Varro's days to command (the consuls alternated the command), he attacked Hannibal at Cannae with 80,000 infantry and 6,000 cavalry. Hannibal possessed only 40,000 infantry and 10,000 cavalry. Hannibal placed his army with its back to a strong, choking wind. The fighting was close and desperate, but Hannibal routed the Romans in the same fashion that Miltiades had routed the Persians at Marathon. He kept his center weak, filling it with Spaniards and Gauls, and kept his wings strong, filling them with his Carthaginian infantry and cavalry. Hannibal himself led the weak center, so that it held long enough to ensure that its feigned retreat did not occur too soon. When the Carthaginian center executed its cautious retreat, the Romans foolishly pursued too far too fast, thereby allowing the victorious Carthaginian wings, led by well-trained Numidian cavalry, to close in and slaughter them. Though well armored in front and behind, Roman soldiers were vulnerable on their flanks, which the Carthaginians struck with javelins.

Rather than taking advantage of his great numerical superiority to outflank the Carthaginians or to hold a force in reserve that might be sent wherever it was needed, Varro had massed the bulk of his army in the center along a one-mile front, thereby fatally reducing his soldiers' ability both to get at the enemy and to escape Hannibal's trap. Varro compounded this error by filling his wings with his least experienced troops. (Because of the previous disasters at Trebbia and Lake Trasimene, the Romans were short of experienced soldiers.)

At Cannae, the Carthaginians slaughtered 50,000 Roman soldiers (including a bleeding and dejected Paulus, who refused a Roman soldier's offer of a horse for his escape) and captured another 10,000. Astonishingly, the Carthaginians lost only 4,000 Gauls, 1,500 Spaniards and Carthaginians, and 200 cavalry.

The Romans perceived the defeat at Cannae as the greatest calamity in their history. Looking for the cause of divine disfavor, they discovered that two of their priestesses called Vestal Virgins were no longer such; against one they carried out the prescribed punishment, burying her alive, while the other was allowed to commit suicide. Indeed, the Romans became so desperate for the favor of the gods they even briefly adopted the ancient Carthaginian practice of human sacrifice, burying alive a pair of Gauls and a pair of Greeks in the Forum. (Ironically, by that time the Carthaginians themselves had abandoned the practice of their Phoenician forebears of sacrificing small boys to Baal.)

Only the commanding presence of Fabius (and the guards he placed at the city gates) kept many citizens from fleeing Rome. In order to prevent the people's confidence from declining even further, Fabius even prohibited public lamentation for the dead. He also cut the property qualification for infantry service in half, and even offered 8,000 slaves their freedom in exchange for such service, in an effort to replace the army lost at Cannae. Better yet, because Hannibal now possessed fewer than 20,000 troops and was not equipped for siege warfare, he still did not march on the city.

The Battle of Cannae secured Hannibal's place as one of the greatest generals in history. Legends of his brilliance abound. Hannibal had once even outfoxed Fabius. Fabius had trapped Hannibal in a valley at Casilinum because Hannibal's guide, misunderstanding his Carthaginian accent, had led him to the wrong place. Hannibal ordered the guide beaten and crucified. There was only one pass out of the valley, and Fabius had posted a detachment to block it. But Hannibal had used nightfall and a clever ruse to mask his movements. The ruse had consisted of several thousand cattle with torches tied to their horns, which Hannibal stampeded in the direction of Fabius's camp. Fooled by the sound of so many thundering hooves and by the sight of so many flickering lights into believing that Hannibal was hurling his whole army at Fabius, the detachment at the pass had rushed to Fabius's aid, leaving the opening unguarded. Hannibal's army had then slipped through the deserted pass.

The Loyalty of the Italian Allies

But Hannibal's impressive victories proved as futile as his pillaging of Italy. The Romans displayed their usual determination to persevere, and most of their well-treated Italian allies refused to join the Carthaginians. The Italians realized that they had little to gain and much to lose from a Carthaginian alliance. Except for the Gallic villages of northern Italy (which was not then considered part of Italy), only a few Italian cities joined the Carthaginians. (Rome put down these revolts between 211 and 209 B.C. Fabius captured Tarentum and massacred its inhabitants; Marcellus seized Syracuse on a festival night, but spared most of its inhabitants. It was in the latter siege that Archimedes unleashed his diabolical inventions on the Romans.) Naples even voluntarily contributed forty platters of gold to the Roman treasury.

The most remarkable and crucial fact about the Second Punic War was that the vast majority of Italians suffered death and destruction alongside the Romans for sixteen years rather than defect to the enemy. Their loyalty, combined with the gradual depletion of Hannibal's forces, undermined the Carthaginian war effort.

Scipio's Spanish Victories

In 210 B.C., twenty-four-year-old Publius Cornelius Scipio was elected proconsul for Spain. The young man had fought his first battle at the age of seventeen. At the head of a troop of cavalry, Scipio had saved his wounded father from being surrounded. Scipio refused an award for his heroism, saying, "The action was one that rewarded itself." Having survived the rout at Cannae, Scipio had broken up a meeting of dejected officers who, considering Rome lost, were considering escaping overseas to serve as mercenaries for some king. As he was to do so many times, Scipio had reminded the officers of their duty and had inspired them with a new sense of confidence. After the Carthaginians defeated and killed Scipio's father in Spain, Scipio alone among the Romans volunteered to take the Spanish command.

Scipio then set about instilling confidence in the Roman people, the Roman soldiers in Spain, and the Spanish allies. His generosity soon secured the support of most of the Spanish tribes.

In 210 B.C., Scipio captured New Carthage, Carthage's greatest city and largest supply center in Spain. Overconfident after conquering nearly all of Spain, the Carthaginians had left the port city garrisoned by only 1,000 men. Discovering from local fishermen that the sea ebbed dramatically in the late afternoon each day, Scipio told his men that Neptune, the sea god, had come to him in a dream and promised aid. Scipio then assaulted the city from the usual approaches, attempting to scale its high walls. When this conventional approach failed, and the hour came for the tide to ebb, Scipio dispatched a special force to scale the eastern wall. The soldiers were astonished by the rate at which the ocean was receding, thereby allowing them to set up their ladders and scale the wall. Remembering Scipio's promise of help from the sea god, the soldiers were greatly encouraged. The Carthaginians had left the eastern wall virtually unmanned, since they had not expected an attack from that quarter.

Scipio then defeated Hasdrubal at Baecula, an inland city in southeastern Spain, in 208 B.C. Doubting that Scipio would attack his strong position on a ridge, Hasdrubal had allowed his men to grow careless. Scipio used his heavy infantry to attack Hasdrubal's flanks, while his light infantry held the center. Hasdrubal lost one-third of his 25,000 men.

Scipio then won another important victory at Ilipa in 206 B.C. Near the end of each day, Scipio marched his soldiers out of their quarters in the same formation: his Roman legions were positioned in the center, his less reliable Spaniards on the wings. After staring across at each other for a while, each army would then return to its quarters. Then one day Scipio attacked the Carthaginian camp before dawn, with his Spaniards in the center and his Romans on the wings. The Carthaginians mustered in their customary formation, with the Carthaginians in the center and their Spanish allies on the wings. Thus, the Roman infantry and cavalry were able to fall on and rout the Carthaginians' Spanish allies. With their wings crushed, the Carthaginians were forced to retreat. The pursuing Romans slaughtered most of the fleeing Carthaginians. Out of the initial force of 70,000, only 6,000 Carthaginians escaped. Unlike many generals, both ancient and modern, Scipio understood the importance of pursuit.

Scipio's victory at Ilipa drove the Carthaginians from Spain and caused the defection of King Masinissa of Numidia (eastern Algeria) to the Roman side. Scipio had been cultivating Masinissa, the brilliant commander of Carthage's Numidian cavalry, ever since the Battle of Baecula. After the battle, Scipio had released Masinissa's young nephew, who had been captured when thrown from his horse, and dispatched him to his uncle on a charger, bearing a golden ring and draped in fine clothing as gifts of Scipio. When combined with Scipio's Spanish victories and Masinissa's disgruntlement with Carthage, Scipio's cultivation of Masinissa succeeded in securing an alliance that would pay huge dividends in North Africa. Because the Carthaginians did not treat their allies as well as the Romans did, they proved far less loyal.

The Death of Hasdrubal

Forced from Spain, Hasdrubal moved to aid Hannibal in Italy. But in 207 B.C. the Romans, having intercepted a dispatch from Hasdrubal to Hannibal that revealed his destination, surprised and routed Hasdrubal at Metauros in northern Italy. Out of 30,000 Carthaginians, 10,000 were killed, including Hasdrubal himself, to only 2,000 Romans. Another 10,000 Carthaginians were taken prisoner. Hannibal would get few reinforcements. His first inkling of the disaster came when the Romans flung his brother's head on the ground in front of his outpost.

The North African Campaign

The Romans were now prepared to strike their first direct blow at Carthage. The Senate granted Scipio, fresh from his conquest of Spain, its reluctant permission to land a force in North Africa. The cautious (and perhaps envious) Fabius opposed the daring expedition so vehemently he would not allow funds to be voted for it. Scipio had to pay for the expedition out of his own income. Furthermore, the Senate assigned Scipio minimal forces. Aside from Scipio's own recruits, the Senate granted him only the discredited remnants of the Fifth and Sixth Legions, legions that had been decimated by Hannibal in the shameful defeat at Cannae.

But Scipio, who was fully aware that the rout at Cannae had been the fault of the imbecilic Varro and not the result of any cowardice on the part of the soldiers, was delighted to command these battle-hardened veterans. A master at instilling confidence in troops, Scipio now took full advantage of the intense desire of his soldiers to avenge their fallen comrades, to wipe away the personal humiliation and stigma of Cannae, and to reward Scipio's own faith in them. With his own recruits, Scipio filled these neglected legions to full strength for the first time in over a decade, a move that further restored the morale and the esprit de corps of the resurrected legions.

After a year of training and preparation, Scipio sailed for North Africa in 204 B.C. Using a peace conference to spy out the Carthaginian camp at Utica, he discovered that the soldiers' huts were wooden structures built close together. Therefore, Scipio attacked the camp at night, setting its buildings ablaze and slaughtering the bewildered soldiers who often emerged from their huts unarmed, thinking that the fire was an accident. When another Carthaginian army rushed in to help put out the fires, it, too, was ambushed and slaughtered.

Scipio then defeated another Carthaginian army on the plains before Carthage. The Carthaginians became so confused and panic stricken that they surrendered Tunis, only fifteen miles from Carthage, without a fight. After sixteen years of brilliant victories but no knockout blow, Hannibal was forced to return home to face the dire threat posed by Scipio's army.

The Battle of Zama

In 202 B.C., Hannibal faced off against Scipio's legions at Zama, eighty miles southwest of Carthage. Both had about 40,000 troops, though Scipio's force was greatly superior in cavalry. The fact that Hannibal had never been defeated as a commander did not intimidate Scipio, perhaps because neither had he. In fact, when Carthaginian spies were caught lurking about his camp, Scipio ordered an officer to give them a personal tour of the place and send them back, an act of bravado that impressed Hannibal.

Hannibal planned to use his eighty elephants to launch the opening assault, hoping that their charge would disrupt the Roman lines. While his Carthaginian and Numidian cavalry held off that of the Romans and Masinissa, the Roman infantry would wear themselves out on the mercenaries and Carthaginian civilians Hannibal placed in the front lines. (Since the Carthaginians, unlike the Romans, did not require military service of their civilians, the Carthaginian civilians now pressed into service were poor fighters.) When the Roman infantry was exhausted from the sheer energy required to kill all of these worthless masses of troops, he would then unleash his trained veterans on them.

But Hannibal's cunning and ruthless plan was thwarted by a clever stratagem of Scipio. Recalling that the Carthaginians' elephants at Ilipa had become so confused at one point in the battle that they had charged into the Carthaginian center, Scipio ordered a tremendous blare of trumpets along the front lines as Hannibal's elephants charged to begin the Battle of Zama. Frightened by the trumpets, some of the elephants wheeled around and collided with Hannibal's Numidian cavalry. The other elephants followed the path of least resistance, the semicircular line that Scipio had purposely left open for them, where they were urged along by Roman darts and javelins, only to emerge and crash into the Carthaginian cavalry on the opposite side. Instead of wreaking havoc on the enemy, the elephants had scattered both wings of Hannibal's cavalry. Taking advantage of the chaos, Scipio's cavalry charged Hannibal's disoriented cavalry, driving the horsemen from the field and pursuing to ensure that they would not return.

Meanwhile, the rest of the battle proceeded as Hannibal planned. The Roman soldiers tired themselves killing mercenaries and Carthaginian civilians. Indeed, the civilians proved so cowardly, leaving the mercenaries to bear the brunt of the Roman attack, that the mercenaries finally turned on the civilians and struck many of them down. There were so many bodies and severed limbs, and there was so much gore on the ground, that the Romans had great difficulty maintaining their footing, much less advancing. When they were finally able to advance, Hannibal struck them with his well-rested veterans.

The Carthaginians then had the better of the battle, and victory seemed at hand, when Scipio's cavalry returned. Surrounded by Roman veterans and Masinissa's horsemen, the Carthaginian infantry was beaten to a pulp. Twenty thousand Carthaginians were killed, and almost as many captured, to the Romans' 1,500.

The Peace

Under the terms of the treaty of 201 B.C., 500 out of the 510 ships of the Carthaginian fleet were towed out to sea and set ablaze, in what might be called the funeral pyre of Carthaginian supremacy. The Romans also forced the Carthaginians to pay a huge indemnity of 10,000 talents, to relinquish their war elephants, and to cede Spain and southern France to the Romans. Henceforth, Carthage could not wage war outside of Africa and could not wage war within Africa without Roman consent. Yet, such was the weakness of the Carthaginian position that Hannibal physically pulled an astonished Carthaginian senator from the podium when the senator proposed rejecting the treaty terms. Hannibal was amazed that the Romans did not kill or enslave every Carthaginian in retribution for his destruction of Italy. Rome now controlled all of the western Mediterranean.

Hannibal set about reducing corruption in the Carthaginian government and placing the city's finances on a sounder basis. Angered by his attacks on them, corrupt politicians and judges in Carthage joined with Roman senators led by Cato the Elder to accuse Hannibal of continuing to plot war against Rome. Against the protest of Scipio, Hannibal was called to Rome to stand trial on these charges. Hannibal fled to the Seleucid Empire, where he did indeed stir up opposition to the Romans. In 183 B.C., Hannibal poisoned himself when the king of Bithynia (in Asia Minor) surrounded his house with the purpose of killing him in order to win favor with Rome.

Scipio was given the title "Africanus" in honor of his North African victories. Some people wanted to make him a perpetual consul and dictator but he rebuked them. He even refused to allow statues of himself to be erected.

After helping to defeat the Seleucid king Antiochus III at Magnesia, Scipio was later tried on the preposterous charge of giving Antiochus favorable peace terms in exchange for a bribe, an accusation made by his implacable foe Cato the Elder. On the first day of his trial, which ironically fell on the anniversary of the Battle of Zama, Scipio stood and, with all eyes fixed on him, credited the gods for his famous victory. He then declared that he was going to the Capitol to sacrifice to the gods in order to "give them thanks for having, on this day, and at many other times, endowed me with both the will and ability to perform extraordinary services to the commonwealth." He added: "Such of you also, Romans, who choose, come with me and beseech the gods that you may have commanders like myself." The entire audience followed Scipio, leaving his accusers alone in a deserted Forum. Scipio refused to attend the rest of the trial, and the charges were dropped. He remained at his estate at Liternum, never visiting Rome again. Scipio left instructions that his body should be buried on his estate, where he died in 183 B.C.—ironically, the same year as Hannibal, his erstwhile foe and fellow enemy of Cato.

Shamelessly vindictive, Cato then succeeded in having Scipio's brother Lucius convicted of the same charge of accepting a bribe from Antiochus. When the praetor attempted to collect the imposed fine, which was equal to the alleged bribe, he discovered that the value of Lucius's entire estate did not equal the fine—strong proof of the brothers' innocence.

Just as Themistocles had been exiled by rivals after saving Greek civilization at Salamis, Scipio spent his final years, after saving the Roman republic at Zama, in a self-imposed exile caused by the less justifiable attacks of his own rivals. Like the democratic society of Athens, the Roman republic seems to have been far better at producing saviors than at dealing with the repercussions of their success. Invariably, winners in the quest for military glory had to deal with envious and suspicious competitors, men determined to level those who had grown so great as to pose a potential threat to other glory-seekers and to the republic itself. But, though no one can deny that the ancient republics displayed a disgraceful ingratitude to their military heroes, ingratitude proved less fatal than the alternative extreme of granting them excessive power, a mistake that would eventually play a leading role in the destruction of the Roman republic.

THE LEGACY OF SCIPIO AFRICANUS

Scipio Africanus had succeeded in defending the Roman republic against the serious threat posed by Carthage and in setting Rome on the path to conquering and ruling the whole Western world. Ironically, Scipio's very success—the Roman victory in the Second Punic War—would ultimately contribute to the downfall of the republic and lead to the rise of the emperors.

8

Julius Caesar: Destroyer of the Roman Republic

It was Julius Caesar who gave the tottering Roman republic the final push that plunged it over the cliff of despotism. Having conquered Gaul for the Roman empire, Caesar found himself in a quarrel with Pompey that led to his dictatorship over Rome. Though Caesar proved a capable dictator, his vanity and ambition led to his assassination, which led the republic into further chaos that ended only with the accession of Augustus as the first Roman emperor.

ROMAN EXPANSION IN THE
EASTERN MEDITERRANEAN, 200–133 B.C.

The destruction of the Carthaginian military power during and after the Second Punic War opened the Mediterranean world to Roman expansion. When King Philip V of Macedon allied himself with the Carthaginians during that war, even sending 4,000 Macedonians to fight with Hannibal at Zama, the Romans defeated him and, in the process, conquered Illyria. After the war, the Romans responded enthusiastically to the call of Pergamum and Rhodes for aid against Philip. In 197 B.C., a Roman legion under Titus Flamininus defeated Philip at Cynoscephalae in Thessaly, killing 20,000 Macedonians and capturing another 11,000.

As in most of the Romans' other battles against the Macedonians and Greeks, the chief cause of Roman victory was the army's ability to take advantage of the phalanx's woeful lack of maneuverability. Relying on the careful overlapping of heavy, twenty-one-foot-long spears, the phalanx was highly effective in opening charges but required level ground without obstructions and a perfect coordination between soldiers that the Romans, with their more maneuverable maniples, quickly learned to disrupt. The Romans surged into the inevitable gaps in the phalanx that formed during battle and assaulted the enemy from the side and rear. When the enemy had to turn their bulky, unwieldy spears to face such threats, they inevitably lost the close coordination on which the phalanx depended.

As a result of the victory at Cynoscephalae, the Romans were able to impose a treaty on Philip that limited him to 5,000 troops, deprived him of his elephants, and fined him 1,000 talents. Furthermore, the treaty prohibited Philip from waging war outside Macedon without Roman permission.

In 190 B.C., the Romans halted a Seleucid invasion of Greece that King Antiochus III had undertaken on the advice of Hannibal and of the Aetolian League, which desired territory in the Roman protectorate of Macedon. Though outnumbered 74,000 to 30,000, Scipio Africanus and his brother Lucius defeated Antiochus at Magnesia in Asia Minor. The Romans stripped the Seleucid emperor of his navy, his elephants, and a large sum of money.

In 168 B.C., the Romans, under Lucius Aemilius Paulus (a descendant of the Paulus who had died at Cannae), defeated a coalition of Greeks, led by Perseus, Philip V's successor, at Pydna in Macedon. Under orders from the Senate to treat the rebels harshly, Paulus sold 150,000 inhabitants of Epirus into slavery. The Romans also deported 1,000 leaders of the Achaean League to Rome. One of these hostages was the historian Polybius.

In 148 B.C., when anti-Roman sentiment flared in Greece as a result of the Senate's policy of supporting oligarchies there, the Romans burned Corinth. They then converted all of Greece into a collection of provinces governed by a Roman proconsul.

Under the Roman Empire, Greece was transformed from a place of political and military significance into a center for study and tourism. Long after the Spartans had abandoned their own unique political and social systems, they refrained from formally repealing their most famous laws so as to attract wealthy Roman tourists. Romans traveled hundreds of miles to see the reenactment of the notorious Spartan custom of flogging their boys until they fell unconscious—an ancient practice now performed in a specially built theater, not for discipline's sake, but as a tourist attraction. The Romans looted Greece for slaves, books, and art. The employment of well-educated Greek slaves was one of the principal means through which Roman aristocrats were "Hellenized."

In 133 B.C., when Attalus III, the king of Pergamum, died without an heir, he left his kingdom to Rome. Fearing a popular revolt when he died, he knew that the Romans would maintain law and order and would continue to follow his policy of favoring the aristocrats over the masses. The Romans had now conquered almost the whole Mediterranean basin.

THE THIRD PUNIC WAR (149–146 B.C.)

Meanwhile, the Romans had dealt a final, crushing blow to Carthage. Although the Romans had stripped Carthage of most of its armed forces and empire after the Second Punic War, some Romans remained obsessed by the fear that Carthage would threaten Rome again one day. Hence, in the mid-second century B.C., when Carthage revived economically, Roman extremists demanded the complete destruction of the city.

Cato the Elder

The leader of the anti-Carthaginian faction was the austere Cato the Elder. "Cato" was not the Roman's original name, but an epithet meaning "wise" or "experienced." The red-haired, grey-eyed Cato was an old-fashioned Roman, a man who displayed great harshness toward slaves. Despising weakness and luxury, Cato ate and worked beside his own slaves. His hero was Manius Curius, who had led the Romans to victory against the Samnites and against Pyrrhus, but who had tilled his little farm with his own hands and whose diet had consisted mainly of boiled turnips. Cato admired simple Fabius and despised flamboyant Scipio. Equating simplicity with virtue and extravagance with vice, Cato was alarmed at the growing influence of Greek culture in Rome. When addressing an Athenian audience in Latin, he was appalled at the number of words his Greek translator required to express the same sentiments. He concluded that the Greeks were mere bladders of wind—cunning talkers, rather than pragmatic doers. (While it is true that a florid rhetorical style was then in vogue among the Hellenistic Greeks, Cato probably also had a poor translator.)

Having become censor in 184 B.C., Cato set about purifying Roman society of "the extreme luxury and degeneracy of the age," even expelling Scipio's brother from the Senate for holding drinking parties. He expelled another senator for embracing his wife in the presence of his daughter, placed stiff taxes on luxury items, severed the pipes by which people diverted the public water supply free of charge, and demolished houses that encroached on public land.

A relentless enemy of Carthage, Cato completed every Senate speech, no matter the topic, with the refrain, "Carthage must be destroyed!" He once brought a basket of large North African figs into the Senate chamber to show the senators what the literal fruits of a Roman conquest of Carthage would look like.

The War

In 149 B.C., the extremists received their wish. Rome presented a series of outrageous demands to Carthage, including one that all Carthaginians leave the city and settle at least ten miles inland, a move that would destroy the Carthaginian economy. When the Carthaginians refused, the Romans, under Scipio Aemilianus, besieged the city. Though often on the verge of starvation, the Carthaginians fought heroically for three years.

When the Romans took the city in 146 B.C., they killed every male Carthaginian and sold every woman and child into slavery. The Romans then reduced all of the buildings to rubble. Although the popular legend that the Romans plowed up the city and poured salt into the ground, so that nothing would grow there for many years, is probably false, the Romans did forbid the resettlement of Carthage for a quarter of a century. (Julius Caesar later rebuilt it.) Rome then annexed the remaining Carthaginian territory. Ironically, Cato the Elder had died in the first year of the Third Punic War. He did not live to see the enemy crushed.

THE EFFECTS OF THE NEW ROMAN EXPANSION

By making apparent the tremendous importance of the plebeians to the army, the first phase of Roman expansion, the gradual conquest of Italy, had helped produce a republican form of government. By contrast, the Romans' rapid conquest of the Mediterranean basin helped destroy the same republic. By further increasing the already vast inequalities of wealth between the rich and the poor, the new Roman expansion generated class warfare, which, in turn, produced the chaos and violence that paved the way for the emperors.

The Decline of the Popular Assemblies

The new Roman expansion strengthened the position of the wealthy and undermined that of the poor. The sudden and extensive expansion of Roman territory transformed Rome from a village into an imperial center, housing a host of foreign and domestic supplicants. It is estimated that the city possessed nearly 750,000 people by the mid-second century B.C. Under such conditions, the average Roman found it difficult to participate in government, even to the small extent that he had before. The popular assemblies became far too large to make the swift decisions required of an empire. Hence, both the Senate and the aristocratic proconsuls whom they appointed to govern the provinces wielded great power. The aristocrats had always held the upper hand, of course, but the commoners were now losing what little power they had once possessed.

Inequalities

Ever increasing numbers of commoners lost their land and became the clients of the aristocrats. Moving to Rome, they were forced to support their masters' political interests in order to earn a living. Between 233 and 133 B.C., a mere twenty-six noble families furnished three-quarters of the consuls; no more than ten families furnished half. Some aristocrats possessed armies of client-bodyguards.

How were the commoners driven off their farms and into clientage in Rome? First, long-term military service overseas had forced many soldiers to neglect their farms. Second, Hannibal's soldiers had destroyed many farms. Third, the commoners could not compete with the massive amounts of produce grown on the aristocrats' plantations (the *latifundia*). The Senate sold aristocrats these plantations in the conquered territories, as well as a slave labor force, consisting mostly of prisoners of war, at a relatively low price. The Senate sold the land in large blocks, so that only the wealthy could afford it. The Senate also "rented" some of the land to aristocrats, and when the wealthy renters began to consider the land their own—building homes and family tombs on it and using it for dowries— the Senate did nothing to resist such claims. Some owners of the latifundia took advantage of new farming techniques to grow grapes and olives, while others continued to cultivate grain and to raise sheep and cattle. Small farmers could not compete with this large-scale production, which depressed prices. The potent combination of neglect, property damage, and depressed prices forced many veterans to sell their farms to aristocrats, move to Rome, and become their clients. Those whom the overseas wars had enriched exploited those whom they had impoverished.

The "Punic Curse"

Rome suffered a general moral decline that many observers attributed to the "Punic Curse," since the incredible wealth that helped produced the decline was the indirect result of the Roman conquest of Carthage. Newfound luxury undermined the traditional Roman values of frugality, discipline, honesty, and respect for law, the values on which the republic depended. Aristocrats sought profit with a ruthless abandon. Vote-buying and ballot box stuffing proliferated. The crushing poverty and slum environment of the commoners rendered them equally cruel and lazy. The new class of merchants, moneylenders, tax collectors, and government contractors spawned by the rapid growth of the empire proved equally corrupt. The low-born wealthy were called *equites*, members of the equestrian order, because they could afford to maintain a horse and serve in the cavalry.

Roman proconsuls and tax collectors plundered their provinces shamelessly, both for Rome and for themselves. Far from the prying eyes of the Senate, and largely ignorant of local cultures, the underpaid and overworked proconsuls extorted as much wealth as possible from the helpless inhabitants of their provinces. One proconsul explained that he needed to extract three fortunes from his province—one to pay the debts incurred in bribing senators to obtain the position, another to bribe the jury at his trial for corruption, and a third fortune to last the rest of his life.

The Romans also treated their slaves harshly. As a result, there were slave revolts in 139, 134–131, and 104–101 B.C. The largest slave rebellion occurred in 73–71 B.C., when the Thracian gladiator Spartacus, who had served as an auxiliary in the Roman army, led 70,000 slaves in revolt. The slave army defeated five separate Roman forces and plundered much of Italy before the rebels were finally overwhelmed at Lucania, their leader killed in battle. The Romans crucified 6,000 of the rebels and lined the Appian Way, Rome's main highway, with their rotting corpses.

THE AGRARIAN REFORM MOVEMENT OF THE GRACCHI

Tiberius Gracchus

In 133 B.C., at the age of twenty-nine, Tiberius Sempronius Gracchus, a grandson of Scipio Africanus, was elected tribune. Tiberius recognized that growing inequalities between the rich and the poor threatened traditional Roman values and the republic itself. He decided that the way to return Rome to its old values was to restore the backbone of the Roman republic, the small farmer. Accordingly, Tiberius proposed that the comitia tributa reenact a law of 367 B.C. (which had never been enforced) limiting the size of estates in the public lands (land rented out by the state) to roughly 300 acres per person. (In ancient times, due to primitive technology, 300 acres was considered a vast estate. Most small farmers possessed only a few acres.) Although this 300-acre plot would then become the renter's permanent property, the surplus land would be confiscated and allotted to the landless, who would pay a small rent to the state. Tiberius's moderate proposal even included compensation for the excess land the aristocrats would have to surrender, land that was not really theirs. Tiberius declared: "The wild beasts that roam over Italy have their dens and holes to lurk in, but the men who fight and die for our country enjoy the common air and light and nothing else. It is their lot to wander with their wives and children, houseless and homeless, over the face of the earth. . . . The truth is that they fight and die to protect the wealth and luxury of others, and though they are called masters of the world, they have not a single clod of earth that is their own." Slogans scrawled on nearly every portico, monument, and wall in the city urged Tiberius to proceed with land redistribution.

The comitia tributa passed the law, but the Senate bribed the tribune Marcus Octavian (an ancestor of Augustus) into vetoing it. Corrupted from its original purpose of blocking the aristocratic acts of the Senate, the tribunal veto power was now being used to block the popular will.

Infuriated, Tiberius responded by pushing through a second law that lacked a compensation provision. He pleaded with Octavian either to change his position or resign for the sake of justice and the republic. Octavian seemed moved but refused. Tiberius then persuaded the comitia tributa to remove Octavian from office and pass the bill again. The impeachment of a tribune was unprecedented, but Tiberius argued that the people could move from office any official they elected. However, the Senate, which controlled the treasury, refused to allocate sufficient funds for the enforcement of the land redistribution law. Intent on ensuring the enforcement of the new act, Tiberius attempted to bypass the Senate by using funds Attalus III of Pergamum had bequeathed to Rome.

Violating an almost sacred custom against consecutive terms, Tiberius ran for reelection as tribune. He spoke of the need to reduce the term of military service (it was nearly thirty years) and to give the people the authority to hear appeals from the patrician-dominated juries.

On election day near the end of 132 B.C., fearing that Tiberius intended to make himself a king, a crowd of senators and their clients marched on Tiberius and clubbed him and 300 of his followers to death. The senators threw all of the bodies into the Tiber River, thereby denying them a proper burial. Other followers were banished or executed without trial. The traditional Roman reverence for law was giving way to corrupt, unconstitutional acts.

Gaius Gracchus

Gaius Sempronius Gracchus, Tiberius's younger brother by nine years, was elected tribune for the year 123 B.C. So many people poured into Rome from the rest of Italy to support Gaius that there was not enough shelter for them. Gaius was a passionate orator, in sharp contrast to Tiberius, who had possessed an almost Olympian calm. In fact, Gaius ordered one of his slaves to strike a soft tone on an instrument whenever Gaius's passion overcame him during a speech. After hearing the tone, Gaius would become aware of himself and regain his composure.

As tribune, Gaius pledged to secure the enforcement of Tiberius's agrarian law so that Roman colonies could be established at Tarentum, Capua, and Carthage, areas the Romans had depopulated. Gaius cultivated equestrian support by appointing equites to special juries that tried proconsuls for corruption and by issuing contracts to their tax collection companies. These private companies, which collected taxes for Rome in the provinces, were allowed to collect surplus taxes as profit. (It is no wonder that tax collectors were the most hated figures of the New Testament.) Gaius also prevented food riots and profiteering in times of famine by persuading the comitia tributa to purchase grain and store it in warehouses. The food would then be sold to the poor of Rome at cost, slightly below its market value. (Politicians later turned this price stabilization measure into a dole, which they manipulated for personal advantage.) Aristocrats hated the measure, fearing that it would undermine the dependence of the poor on them for food and, with it, the master-client relationship. Gaius also pleased the poor and angered the aristocrats by offering free seats at the gladiatorial contests. (The aristocrats rented seats to the poor.) Gaius persuaded the comitia tributa to insist that no one under the age of seventeen be conscripted into the army and that soldiers be issued free clothing. He supported the construction of roads, to the benefit of country farmers.

But Gaius lost the support of poor Romans by advocating the extension of full citizenship to Rome's Latin allies and the "Latin right" for its other Italian allies. The first step toward citizenship, the Latin right included the granting of citizenship to the leaders of a foreign people. Fearing that they would lose control of the comitia tributa to non-Romans, the poor citizens of Rome zealously guarded their privilege of citizenship. Due to a loss of support among the poor, combined with electoral fraud, Gaius suffered a defeat in his bid for a third term near the end of 122 B.C.

Gaius's defeat led to some minor skirmishing between factions, which provided the Senate with a pretext to declare martial law at the beginning of 121 B.C. The Senate ordered the Italian allies who supported Gaius to leave the city and called for the murder of Gaius himself. His supporters proved cowardly: rather than aiding him in evading the assassins that pursued him, Gaius's followers merely shouted at him to run faster. Knowing that the consul Opimius had agreed to reward Gaius's murderer with the weight of his head in gold, the assassin cleverly emptied the brain and filled the skull with molten lead, thereby increasing its weight to nearly eighteen pounds. Three thousand of Gaius's followers were also arrested and executed. The bodies of the victims were hurled into the Tiber, their property was confiscated, and their wives were even forbidden to mourn publicly.

The Romans' failure to enact Gaius's citizenship law, combined with Rome's growing harshness toward its Italian allies, eventually led the Italians to revolt (90–88 B.C.). Having loyally endured the horrors and hardships of two centuries of constant warfare on behalf of Rome, many Italians were furious at the Romans' unwillingness to grant them full citizenship. The Italians feared that, without voting rights, they might be dispossessed of their land to make room for Roman veterans. After this "Social War" (so called because the Latin term for the Italian allies was *socii*), Rome was forced to grant citizenship to all Italians south of the Po River. Those to the north of the Po, mostly Gauls, were granted the Latin right.

THE FIRST ROMAN CIVIL WAR: MARIUS VERSUS SULLA

Rome was increasingly divided between two factions, the Optimates, who favored the aristocrats, and the Populares, who favored the poor. (Even the leaders of the Populares were generally wealthy.) This schism led to three bloody civil wars in Rome.

Marius

In 107 B.C., Rome faced a grave crisis. A violent and corrupt Numidian king named Jugurtha (the grandson of Masinissa) was waging war with his brother for complete control of Numidia, in contradiction to the settlement the Romans had imposed. Soldiers under Jugurtha (though perhaps not acting on his order) even murdered Roman merchants who had sided with his brother. Partly because Jugurtha had bribed some of the senators, the Senate was reluctant to act against him at first. (According to the Roman historian Sallust, Jugurtha made the famous statement about Rome: "Here is a city put up for sale, and its days are numbered if it finds a buyer.")

Furious at the Senate, the comitia tributa ordered the consul Gaius Marius, an *eques*, to proceed to North Africa and crush Jugurtha. It was the first time the assembly had ever insisted on assigning a general to a command, a power traditionally reserved for the Senate. A hard-bitten soldier from the country town of Arpinum, Marius declared regarding the aristocrats: "They call me vulgar and unpolished, because I do not know how to put on an elegant dinner and do not have actors at my table or keep a cook who has cost me more than my farm overseer. All this, my fellow citizens, I am proud to admit." He also expressed pride at not having studied Greek literature.

In 106 B.C., Marius defeated Jugurtha's army. Having captured and imprisoned Jugurtha through the treachery of an ally soon after, the Romans starved him to death. In 102 and 101 B.C., Marius followed this triumph with a successful defense of Italy against two large Germanic tribes, one of which had routed a Roman army and inflicted 80,000 casualties a few years earlier.

Marius's army was composed of landless citizens (he disregarded the small property qualification for service in the army) whom he personally equipped with javelins that broke on impact so that the enemy could not throw them back. Marius also made the army more mobile by having soldiers carry their own entrenching tools and other equipment rather than relying on vulnerable baggage trains. Marius transformed the Roman army from a militia equipped by, and loyal to, Rome, into a professional army equipped by, and loyal to, its commander. He used the threat of armed force to overcome Senate opposition to the distribution of land in North Africa to his troops—a tactic unheard of during the early days of the republic. But at least Marius did not yet take the opportunity to seize Rome. He contented himself with being elected consul six years in a row between 105 and 100 B.C., though Roman law prohibited consuls from holding office two consecutive terms.

Sulla

In 88 B.C., King Mithridates VI of Pontus (northeastern Asia Minor) led Greece and Asia Minor, both severely oppressed by corrupt proconsuls, tax collectors, and moneylenders, into revolt against Rome. Mithridates slaughtered 80,000 Italian men, women, and children living in his territory. Both the Senate and the comitia tributa claimed supreme authority to put down the revolt, and each selected its own general. While the comitia tributa chose Marius, the Senate selected Lucius Cornelius Sulla, who had once served as Marius's quaestor but was now his rival.

After failing to find and kill Marius, who fled to North Africa, Sulla set sail for the East. Marius then returned to Rome in Sulla's absence, allowing his troops to loot and murder and even execute a few Optimates, including a consul. Having put down Mithridates' revolt in 86–85 B.C., Sulla then returned to Rome to rout Marius's army, which had been weakened by the leader's death from pleurisy. Thousands of Romans died in the civil war, including many senators; the Senate had been reduced from its usual 300 members to about 150.

In 82 B.C., the Senate appointed the victorious Sulla dictator for an unlimited term, another unconstitutional act, and assigned him the task of revising the Roman political system. Sulla transferred almost all government functions to the Senate, leaving the popular assemblies and the tribunes virtually powerless. He removed equites from juries, returning nearly all judicial power to the Senate. To hobble popular leaders, he prohibited men from holding the same office twice within a ten-year period. To weaken the position of tribune, by depriving it of ambitious leaders, he prohibited former tribunes from running for higher offices and restricted the tribune's veto power.

Worst of all, Sulla "proscribed" (listed for execution) his own enemies and the enemies of his friends. His soldiers killed 30,000 to 50,000 people, so many that even the Senate begged him to stop. The victims included forty senators (Populares) and 1,600 equites, whose property Sulla confiscated and distributed among his 120,000 troops. Indeed, some Romans may have been killed purely for their property. Sulla expanded the Senate from 150 to 600 members, packing it with his own supporters.

But Sulla was not personally ambitious. He wanted only to "cleanse" Rome by restoring the Senate to a dominant position. In 81 B.C., he voluntarily surrendered power. After serving as consul in 80–79 B.C., he returned to his rural estate and died peacefully in 78 B.C. If Rome had escaped a permanent dictatorship, it was due solely to the fact that Marius and Sulla still possessed a few scruples about openly assuming such power. Rome would not be so fortunate in the future.

THE SECOND ROMAN CIVIL WAR: POMPEY VERSUS CAESAR

Pompey's Conquest

The First Civil War accelerated the trend toward factionalism and personal ambition. In 70 B.C., and again in 67 B.C., Pompey (Gnaeus Pompeius) and Marcus Licinius Crassus were elected consul (partly through vote-buying), though Pompey was below the legal age for that position. Though they had supported Sulla during his dictatorship, Pompey and Crassus won the favor of the masses by repealing nearly all of Sulla's laws. They reduced the senatorial representation in juries to one-third and restored the tribunician power.

In 67 B.C., over Senate objections, the comitia tributa gave Pompey temporary dictatorial power to clear the Mediterranean of the pirates who had proliferated as a result of the Senate's neglect of the navy. With a fleet of nearly 1,000 ships, the pirates had captured or looted nearly 400 towns. Proceeding methodically, Pompey cleared the sea of pirates in three months, thereby ending the threat to Rome's grain supplies.

As part of an effort to put down yet another revolt led by Mithridates, Pompey then spent four years conquering the remaining part of the Seleucid Empire, which included Syria, Armenia, Phoenicia, Pontus, and Cilicia (southeastern Asia Minor). He also conquered Judea (Israel), an independent kingdom that had successfully revolted against the Seleucids a century earlier. Thousands of Jews threw themselves to the ground before Pompey and begged him not to desecrate the Great Temple of Jerusalem by entering it since no Gentile could enter the temple without desecrating it. This display only convinced Pompey that the temple must contain great riches, so he barged in, even marching into the Holy of Holies, its innermost sanctum. The Roman historian Tacitus later declared: "It is a fact well known that he found no image, no statue, no symbolical representation of the Deity; the whole presented a naked dome; the sanctuary was unadorned and simple." When the dumbfounded Pompey emerged from the temple, he exclaimed in wonder, "It is empty; there is nothing there but darkness!" Pompey's reaction typified Roman confusion concerning the Jews and their worship of an invisible, omnipotent God. Nevertheless,

Pompey's conquests greatly added to the wealth and power of both Rome and himself.

The First Triumvirate

When Pompey returned to Rome in 62 B.C., the Senate refused to grant his soldiers the land he requested for them. Pompey had made the mistake of disbanding his army too quickly, leaving him with no leverage over the Senate. In frustration, Pompey then formed what historians call the First Triumvirate, an alliance with Crassus and Julius Caesar, in 60 B.C.

Famous for putting down Spartacus's slave rebellion, with a little help from Pompey, Crassus was the second wealthiest man in Rome. (Pompey was the wealthiest after he returned from his eastern conquests.) Crassus had amassed his vast fortune partly by purchasing the estates of Sulla's victims at a discount and partly by purchasing other houses at an even greater discount during the periodic fires that plagued the wooden city. Whenever a fire erupted, Crassus's slaves negotiated with the neighbors of the fire victims. As the fire spread closer to their homes, the desperate neighbors sold their homes for next to nothing. Once Crassus's agents had purchased the houses for him, his specially trained fire brigades, standing nearby, could then begin to extinguish the fires. Public fire departments did not yet exist.

Though a member of one of the oldest aristocratic families in Rome, Julius Caesar established himself as a champion of the masses. (Nearly proscribed by Sulla as a young man, Caesar was the nephew of Marius and had subsequently married the daughter of one of Marius's allies.) Tall, fair, thin, and epileptic, Caesar possessed a broad face and lively, dark brown eyes. Though he was bald, he tried to cover it up by combing his thin strands of hair forward (a gambit that has never worked in any era). He valued luxury and developed a reputation as a womanizer, even having affairs with the wives of his fellow triumvirs. His enemies also accused him of having had an affair with King Nicodemes of Bithynia in order to secure his patronage. One political opponent called Caesar "the Queen of Bithynia . . . who once wanted to sleep with a monarch, but now wants to be one." Once, when Caesar was listing his obligations to Nicodemes before the Senate, Cicero interrupted, saying: "Enough of that, if you please! We all know what he gave you, and what you gave him in return." Caesar first became associated with Crassus in 65 B.C., when Caesar borrowed large sums of money from him, cash that Caesar then used to curry favor with the masses by funding lavish gladiatorial games.

The triumvirate secured Caesar's election as consul in 59 B.C. When Caesar's colleague proved uncooperative, Caesar threatened him so fiercely he stayed home the rest of the year, leaving Caesar, in effect, as sole consul. Caesar also once had Cato the Younger forcibly removed from the Senate

House to stop a filibuster. Caesar repaid his fellow triumvirs for their support in obtaining the consulship by securing legislation that remitted taxes to Crassus's equestrian supporters and granted land to Pompey's veterans. Caesar then requested and received the proconsulship of Cisalpine Gaul (northern Italy), Transalpine Gaul (southern France), and Illyria, while Crassus secured command of the army in the East, and Pompey received an absentee command in Spain that allowed him to remain in Rome.

In 53 B.C., Crassus was killed while attempting to conquer Parthia, a new Persian empire east of the Euphrates River. Crassus had foolishly advanced into open country east of the Euphrates, where the Parthians, under Suren, surrounded the Romans and pummeled them with arrows supplied steadily by a train of 1,000 camels. Unwilling to risk a night attack on the enemy, Crassus then abandoned 4,000 wounded soldiers, fleeing to Carrhae under cover of night. Lacking adequate supplies, Crassus was forced to negotiate. The Parthians killed him treacherously, under a flag of truce. Ten thousand of his soldiers were taken prisoner. Fortunately for the Roman position in Syria, Orodes, the king of Parthia, then had Suren killed as a potential rival.

Caesar's Conquests

Caesar, who had wept as a young man because he had accomplished nothing at the same age at which Alexander the Great had conquered a vast empire, now spent nine years subduing the rest of Gaul (what is now France, Belgium, southern Holland, Germany west of the Rhine, and most of Switzerland). One of the greatest generals in history, Caesar always made a careful reconnaissance, and in a hard-fought battle always sent all the horses away, including his own, so that his soldiers would know that without victory there was no chance of escape. He inlaid his soldiers' weapons with silver and gold, which gave them such pride in their arms that they were especially careful not to be disarmed in battle. Ordinarily lax, he insisted on strict discipline whenever the enemy was in the vicinity. He made a point of becoming acquainted with all his centurions, of heeding their advice, and of rewarding loyal service. Caesar himself was so loyal to his troops he once disguised himself as a Gaul in order to reach them when the enemy had surrounded them. Caesar's intense loyalty to his soldiers, whom he called "comrades," was matched only by their fidelity to him. Caesar's legions never mutinied throughout the Gallic War, a record of loyalty unmatched by any other army of the period.

In 57 B.C., Caesar annihilated the Helvetii near Bibracte, routed the Germanic Ariovistus in Alsace, and destroyed the Nervii on the Sabis River. In 55 B.C., and again the following year, Caesar's attempts to invade what is now Great Britain, also inhabited by Celtic tribes, were thwarted by storms, which prevented him from receiving vital supplies and cavalry units. Caesar then put down several revolts among the Gallic tribes in France.

Caesar's greatest victory in the Gallic War came at Alesia (near modern Dijon) in 52 B.C., a victory that broke the back of Gallic resistance. While besieging an impregnable Gallic town situated atop a hill and manned by 80,000 Gauls, Caesar was himself surrounded by an even larger force. He instructed his soldiers to construct a double ring of siege works, the inner ring alone extending ten miles. Caesar himself occupied a good observation post, from which he could follow the action in each part of the battlefield and dispatch reinforcements wherever they were needed. The brilliantly conceived siege works allowed Caesar to maintain the siege of Alesia while warding off the large Gallic army that surrounded his own. The shortage of food in Alesia became so severe that one Gallic leader even seriously suggested eating those too young and too old to fight. When the Gauls on each side of the Romans launched a simultaneous night attack, many of them fell into camouflaged pits and impaled themselves on sharpened stakes. Nevertheless, by attacking the Romans at their weakest point, the Gauls nearly succeeded. Only Caesar's timely dispatch of reinforcements prevented them from breaching the Roman line. Caesar then made a sortie and routed the larger force, sending the survivors scrambling to their individual homes and forcing the surrender of the smaller force in Alesia. Plutarch estimated that Caesar's legions killed as many as 1 million people and enslaved another million during the course of the Gallic War.

In conquering Gaul, Caesar acquired a fortune in plunder, which he used to bribe Roman officials and to curry favor with the Roman people. In preparation for another campaign for the consulship, Caesar kept his name before the Roman public by publishing his *Commentaries on the Gallic War*, a memoir in which Caesar wrote of himself in the third person to present the illusion of objectivity. Caesar's *Commentaries*, one of our most important sources concerning the early Gallic and Germanic tribes, was written so well it is still used as a Latin primer. Its simple but nonrepetitive prose is as free of colloquialisms as it is of pedantry. Even Cicero, whose style was far more florid, admired Caesar's lucid, graceful writing, remarking of his sentences: "They are like nude figures, upright and beautiful, stripped of all ornament and style as if they had removed a garment." Cicero also considered Caesar a great orator, calling his rhetorical style "elegant as well as clear, even grand and in a sense noble."

Civil War

But Pompey and the Senate had grown jealous of Caesar's victories. The death of Julia, Caesar's daughter and Pompey's beloved wife, in 54 B.C., combined with the death of their common ally Crassus the following year, had removed powerful motives for cooperation between the former triumvirs.

In 49 B.C., two enemies of Caesar were elected consul with Pompey's tacit consent. The Senate then ordered Caesar to disband his army and return to Rome. A tribune vetoed the order but was physically removed from the Senate chamber, a violation of the sanctity of tribunes. When Caesar balked at the Senate's order, the Senate retreated, voting overwhelmingly (370–22) in favor of a compromise proposal that both Caesar and Pompey disband their armies, but the proposal was vetoed by a different tribune. In fact, Caesar even proposed surrendering all but two legions and relinquishing command of Cisalpine Gaul and Illyria. Pompey was willing to accept this compromise, but the consuls refused.

Fearing for his life should he disband his army, his sole protection against his enemies, Caesar crossed the Rubicon River with his army. He understood that this act was tantamount to a declaration of war against the Senate (hence the phrase "crossing the Rubicon" to signify the performance of an act that cannot be reversed). Indeed, Caesar hesitated at the river, but then declared, "Let the die be cast!" and plunged the republic into another civil war.

Pompey and most of the Senate fled eastward. After defeating the large armies of Pompey's legates in Spain, Caesar crossed the Adriatic Sea to face Pompey himself. Caesar besieged Pompey's army at Dyrrachium (in Epirus), but Pompey's force broke through and slaughtered 1,000 of Caesar's men. Caesar thought Pompey could have won the civil war had he pursued and annihilated Caesar's army after the battle. But, fearing an ambush, Pompey allowed Caesar to retreat eastward.

The Battle of Pharsalus

Caesar was able to reorganize his troops, restore their morale, and make a decisive stand at Pharsalus in Thessaly in 48 B.C. According to Caesar's admittedly subjective account, Pompey's overconfident officers "were already starting to squabble openly among themselves about rewards and priesthoods and were assigning the consulships for years to come, while some were claiming the houses and property of people in Caesar's camp. . . . They were thinking not of how to win but of how to exploit the victory."

If so, Pompey's officers greatly underestimated Caesar's legions. Though outnumbered more than two to one (47,000 to 22,000), Caesar's troops were more experienced and more loyal than Pompey's. Many offered to serve without pay; none deserted, though Caesar allowed any centurion who wished to join Pompey to do so. When deprived of food and supplies at one point, Caesar's stalwarts had eaten grass, prompting Pompey to exclaim: "I am fighting wild beasts!"

When Pompey attacked with his left wing, composed of cavalry and archers, Caesar dispatched fresh, carefully selected reinforcements to face them. They managed to encircle and massacre Pompey's left wing, thereby turning his flank and initiating a rout of his whole army. Caesar had instructed his infantrymen to thrust their lances at the faces of Pompey's cavalrymen rather than hurling them. As Caesar expected, the handsome, inexperienced, young cavalrymen shrank from facial disfigurement. Six thousand of Pompey's troops were killed in the battle; the rest surrendered. Generally magnanimous, Caesar would not allow the slaughter of any soldier who surrendered, shouting to his army: "Spare your fellow Romans!" Surveying the Optimate dead, Caesar cried, "They would have it thus!"

Pompey fled to Egypt. Wishing to please Caesar, Egyptian officials used treachery to assassinate Pompey and sent his head to Caesar. But Caesar wept at the sight and ordered the murderers put to death. He then dallied with Cleopatra VII, the Macedonian queen of Egypt, who, on their first meeting, had herself smuggled to him in a carpet, from which she emerged nude.

Caesar did not defeat the last of Pompey's scattered forces until 45 B.C. When defeat was certain for his republican army in North Africa, Cato the Younger, the great grandson of Cato the Elder, fell on his sword at Utica. After putting down a revolt in Pontus, Caesar celebrated a triumph. One of the decorated wagons in the triumphal procession bore a banner that declared: "Veni, Vidi, Vici" ("I came, I saw, I conquered").

CAESAR'S RULE

From 48 to 44 B.C., Caesar was first the unofficial, and then official, dictator of Rome. He was magnanimous—in retrospect, more than was wise—even appointing some of his former opponents to high offices and restoring the statues of Pompey that had been pulled down by some of Caesar's more zealous followers. In addition, Caesar put down the street gangs that had paralyzed the city. He reduced Rome's debt through more efficient administration. He rebuilt much of the city. He reduced the number of the unemployed from 320,000 to 150,000 through a public works program and through the decree that at least one-third of the laborers in the latifundia must be free men. He established both Italian and provincial colonies for his veterans and for 80,000 poor Romans, the fulfillment of the Gracchi's dream. Caesar also canceled all interest on debts incurred during the recent civil war, an inflationary period. He planned a public library. As *pontifex maximus* (chief priest), he introduced the "Julian calendar" of 365 and one-fourth days, the calendar employed in Europe until Pope Gregory XIII modified it (removing one leap day every two centuries) in 1582. Caesar also restored order in the provinces. He removed many incompetent and corrupt procon-suls from office and ejected them from the Senate. In a momentous move, Caesar extended Roman citizenship to numerous non-Italians for the first time, namely, to the people of Cisalpine Gaul and to the chieftains of Transalpine Gaul. He even admitted some Gauls into the Senate, thereby ac-celerating the assimilation of Gaul. Rome was beginning to conceive of the empire more as a community and less as a field of exploitation.

CAESAR'S ASSASSINATION

But Caesar's arrogance offended some aristocrats. With the consent of a fearful Senate, he placed statues of himself among those of the ancient kings. He wore semiregal dress, sat on a golden throne in the Senate House, and allowed the Senate to rename the month of Quintilis after himself (July). One statue depicted him with a globe beneath his feet. When the senators came to him bringing honors, he remained seated, like a patron receiving clients. Finally, one of Caesar's underlings, Mark Antony (Marcus Antonius), attempted to crown Caesar at a festival. Although Caesar re-fused the crown three times, the incident further alarmed some senators, who perceived Caesar as testing the waters for a return to monarchy.

Although the Senate agreed to extend his dictatorship from the initial ten years to life in February 44 B.C., some senators began plotting his as-sassination. One month later, a group of conspirators, led by Marcus Ju-nius Brutus and his brother-in-law Gaius Cassius Longinus, stabbed Cae-sar to death with daggers—ironically, in Pompey's Theater, where Caesar had called a meeting of the Senate. The senators attacked Caesar with such frenzy that they wounded each other and drenched themselves with Caesar's blood. Brutus supposedly stabbed him in the groin. Caesar fell dead at the foot of Pompey's statue, his body riddled with wounds.

Caesar had often refused a bodyguard, saying it was better to die once than to live in constant fear of death. Clutched in Caesar's dying hand was a detailed warning of the assassination plot given him by an acquaintance of Brutus and his friends. Caesar had attempted to read the note several times but had been interrupted by supplicants each time. He was fifty-five years old and planning a campaign against the Parthians when he died.

Cassius was a praetor who had distinguished himself by repelling a Parthian invasion of Syria in 51 B.C. Brutus was a descendant of the leg-endary Lucius Brutus, who had expelled King Tarquin from Rome (and who had supposedly killed his own sons for conspiring to restore Tar-quin). Brutus idolized his uncle, the republican martyr Cato the Younger, even marrying his daughter Porcia. Though Brutus had taken Pompey's side in the civil war, despite the fact that Pompey had executed his father, because he considered Pompey more likely to restore the republic, the victorious Caesar had befriended Brutus. One rumor even claimed that Brutus was really Caesar's son, though this was probably untrue. (When Brutus was born, Caesar was barely fifteen. However, Caesar did have an affair with Brutus's mother, Servilia, when Brutus was twenty-two. This misunderstanding probably accounts for the Roman historian Seutonius's claim that Caesar's last words were "And you, son?" Shakespeare later substituted the more plausible "Et tu, Brute?")

It was said that Brutus, the Stoic republican, had acted because he hated dictatorship, and the fiery Cassius because he hated the dictator. While Caesar's supporters had placed crowns on his statues, to encourage the people to make him king, Brutus's fellow republicans had scrawled messages on his desk every day reminding him of his ancestral duty to oppose monarchy. Nothing so moved a Roman as an appeal to family tradition.

Caesar's death plunged Rome into chaos that led to a third Roman civil war. In turn, that bloody war would eventuate in the rise of the first Roman emperor, Caesar's grandnephew Augustus.

CAESAR'S LEGACY

Caesar's conquest of Gaul extended Roman civilization into northern Europe. The Romans were so successful in assimilating Gaul that France would play a leading role in the preservation of classical civilization during the Middle Ages. Though conquered by the Germanic Franks in the fifth century A.D., France would remain a Latin nation, as reflected in its language even today.

While Caesar's conquests made him an object of emulation for future generals, his crucial role in the downfall of the Roman republic made him the greatest villain of modern republicans. The Founding Fathers of the United States uniformly despised Caesar. In a famous part of Patrick Henry's Stamp Act Speech of 1765, Henry compared King George III with Caesar, declaring: "Caesar had his Brutus, Charles the First his Cromwell, and George III [cries of "Treason!"] may profit by their example." In 1771, John Adams compared the Tory Thomas Hutchinson, the new royal governor of Massachusetts, with Caesar: "Caesar, by destroying the Roman Republic, made himself a perpetual Dictator; Hutchinson, by countenancing and supporting a System of Corruption and Tyranny, has made himself Governor." Both Adams and Thomas Jefferson compared Alexander Hamilton with Caesar. Adams wrote: "When Burr shot Hamilton, it was not Brutus killing Caesar in the Senate-House, but it was killing him before he passed the Rubicon." Though Hamilton's references to Caesar in his correspondence were uniformly negative, Jefferson claimed that

Hamilton had once told him, "The greatest man that ever lived was Julius Caesar." Ironically, Hamilton wrote to George Washington implying that Jefferson was a Caesar: "It has aptly been observed that Cato was the Tory—Caesar the Whig of his day. The former frequently resisted—the latter always flattered the follies of the people. Yet the former perished with the Republic, [while] the latter destroyed it." A month later, Hamilton wrote an article in the *Gazette of the United States* in which he stated concerning Jefferson: "But there is always a first time, when characters studious of artful disguises are unveiled; when the vizor of stoicism is plucked from the brow of the Epicurean; when the plain garb of Quaker simplicity is stripped from the concealed voluptuary; when Caesar coyly refusing the proffered diadem is seen to be Caesar rejecting the trappings, but tenaciously grasping the substance of imperial domination."

Nor did these recurrent attempts to brand one's political opponent as a Caesar—a cunning, ambitious individual seeking to overthrow the republic—end with the founding generation. When Andrew Jackson withdrew funds from the national bank in order to destroy it, an act many considered unconstitutional, Henry Clay compared Jackson's action with Caesar's entrance into the Roman treasury, sword in hand, to collect the funds necessary to prosecute his military campaign against Pompey. The Whigs' attempts to brand Jackson as another Caesar were so numerous and so passionate that one newspaper blamed the first presidential assassination attempt in American history on the overheated rhetoric. While the deranged house painter Richard Lawrence almost certainly acted from a more personal motive (insanity, perhaps caused by sniffing too much lead paint) than from adherence to Whig rhetoric when he unsuccessfully attempted to shoot Jackson, the Whigs had clearly demonstrated Caesar's continued utility as the leading bogeyman for republicans of every political persuasion.

9

✛

Cicero: Statesman, Philosopher, and Republican Martyr

Perhaps the most influential figure of classical civilization was a Roman statesman, orator, essayist, and philosopher named Cicero. Considered a martyr for republicanism as well as one of the greatest orators in history, Cicero became the role model for many Western statesmen over the centuries. His eloquent speeches and writings on behalf of popular sovereignty, natural law, and mixed government enshrined those crucial theories at the center of Western civilization.

CICERO'S DEFENSE OF THE REPUBLIC

Catiline's Conspiracy

The son of an eques from the country town of Arpinum, the home of Marius, Marcus Tullius Cicero (106–43 B.C.) was never fully accepted, either by the snobbish Senate elite or by the demagogic leaders of the masses, whom he despised. Nevertheless, in 63 B.C. Cicero became one of the few equites ever elected consul. Almost immediately, while Pompey and his army were away fighting in the eastern Mediterranean, Cicero faced a rebellion led by a corrupt, debt-ridden aristocrat named Lucius Sergius Catilina, who had just lost a second consecutive election for the consulship. Catiline conspired to kill the consuls, seize power, and win popular support through the cancellation of debts and the redistribution of land.

An ardent defender of the republic, Cicero acted quickly to thwart Catiline's plan. Catiline fled north to Etruria, while Cicero denounced Catiline in a series of famous speeches. In 62 B.C., a Roman army defeated and killed Catiline at Pistoria. Catiline's coconspirators in Rome were executed.

Cicero and Caesar

Two years later, Caesar, Pompey, and Crassus asked Cicero to join their alliance because they prized his renowned oratorical ability. Though membership in so powerful a collective would have held great financial and political advantages for Cicero, he refused the alliance out of loyalty to the republic. Although Cicero sided with Pompey in the civil war a decade later, on the assumption that Pompey was more likely to restore the republic, and though Cicero's cowardly brother and nephew blamed him for their own decision to side with Pompey, the victorious Caesar spared Cicero's life.

The Assassins' Mistakes

The assassins of Julius Caesar made two mistakes. First, on the insistence of Brutus, they decided not to kill Caesar's chief lieutenant, Mark Antony. Although some Romans despised Antony for his excessive drinking (he once vomited at a Senate meeting after partying the whole night) and womanizing, his soldiers loved him because he ate and slept alongside them. He had commanded Caesar's left wing at Pharsalus with distinction. Cicero complained regarding the assassination of Caesar: "That affair was handled with the courage of men and the policy of children. Anyone could see that an heir to the throne was left behind."

Second, the assassins allowed Caesar a public funeral, at which Antony read his will. The people were moved to tears on learning that Caesar had bequeathed to each Roman citizen seventy-five drachmas and the use of one of his gardens. Driven to a frenzy by grief when Caesar's blood-stained body was carried through the Forum, the mob even tore to pieces a man named Cinna, mistaking him for an assassin of Caesar who bore the same name. The mob then attempted to burn the houses of Brutus and Cassius. The assassins were forced to flee Rome. Many believed that a comet, which shone for seven days, was Caesar's soul.

The Second Triumvirate

Caesar's chief supporters, Antony, Marcus Aemilius Lepidus, and Octavian, eventually settled their differences and formed the Second Triumvirate. Lepidus was the proconsul of Spain. Octavian, newly arrived from military training in Illyria, was Caesar's grandnephew and (as the will revealed) adopted son. Caesar had no legitimate son of his own, and his only daughter had died childless. With his usual shrewdness, Caesar had seen more promise in the eighteen-year-old Octavian than Antony did; Antony sneered that he was a "mere boy, owing everything to a name."

The triumvirs slaughtered all opponents, including 300 senators and 2,000 equites, confiscated their property, and redistributed it among their supporters. In fact, it has been estimated that one-fourth of all Italian land changed hands as a result of the Second Triumvirate's proscriptions and evictions.

CICERO'S DEATH

Among the most prominent victims of the triumvirate was Cicero. The triumvirs ordered Cicero's execution in 43 B.C. He tried to escape by sea but bad weather and sea sickness forced him back to land near his villa at Formiaea. There he was slain, after commanding his slaves to leave him and save themselves.

Antony ordered Cicero's head and hands nailed above the rostrum in the Forum, where Cicero had spoken out against him in fourteen speeches, popularly called the *Philippics* after Demosthenes' famous speeches against Philip II of Macedon. According to Plutarch, horrified Romans saw in the putrefying remains "not so much the face of Cicero as the soul of Antony." Octavian acquiesced in the murder but later, as the emperor Augustus, called Cicero "an eloquent and learned man and a true lover of his country." Livy added regarding Cicero: "If one weighs his faults against his merits, he was a great man, of high spirit, worthy of remembrance; to sound his praises would require a Cicero for his eulogist."

CICERO'S ACHIEVEMENTS

Cicero contributed more than any other Roman to making the Latin language a supple and sophisticated tool of expression. For nearly two millennia every educated European and American read Cicero. Cicero astounded both ancients and moderns with the eloquence of his 106 orations, his 900 surviving letters, and his numerous political and philosophical essays. His majestic style, balanced clauses, and rhythmic cadences so dominated Latin prose that the highly respected rhetorician Quintilian said Cicero was "the name, not of a man, but of eloquence itself."

Cicero was the acknowledged master of each of the three types of rhetoric: deliberative, apodeictic, and forensic—speeches for the Senate building, for the funeral hall, and for the courtroom. His rhetorical texts advocated careful attention to every aspect of public speaking: care of the throat, breath control, tone variation, carriage, expression, eyebrow movement, gestures, toga arrangement, stride, and the production of tears. But he also emphasized the hollowness of eloquence devoid of knowledge and reason. Adopting a middle position between the terse Attic style made famous by Thucydides in Greek and Sallust in Latin, and the verbose Asianic style, Cicero drafted speeches that were copious without being redundant. While varying his vocabulary, he avoided meaningless synonyms, selecting each word for its peculiar force. The rhythm of his sentences was natural, not the artificial product of superfluous words or unconventional word order. The Roman Longinus later wrote: "Cicero, like a spreading conflagration, ranges and rolls over the whole field; the fire which burns within him, plentiful and constant, is distributed at his will, now in one part, now in another, and fed with fuel in relays." His speeches were so persuasive that, as consul, he convinced the masses to oppose debt relief and land distribution.

Like Mark Twain or Winston Churchill in later times, Cicero became so famous for his wit that the witticisms of others were often attributed to him. (Yet, according to Cicero, Caesar was shrewd enough, when collecting clever sayings, to distinguish Cicero's witticisms from those falsely accounted to him.) Though Cicero's humor was essential in court, often distracting jurors from the legal weaknesses of a case, his biting wit earned him many enemies. When a snobbish aristocrat sneered, "Who is your father?" Cicero replied, "I can scarcely ask you the same question since your mother has made it rather difficult to answer." When Crassus said that no member of his family had ever lived past sixty, then reversed himself, asking, "What could I have been thinking when I said that?" Cicero replied that he must have been trying to elicit applause. When a young man accused of having given his father a poisoned cake said angrily that he would give Cicero "a piece of his mind," Cicero replied, "I would prefer it to a piece of your cake." When the demagogue Clodius was acquitted of adultery by a jury he had bribed, he told Cicero, who was the prosecutor, that the jury had not believed his evidence. Cicero replied: "You will find that twenty-five of them trusted in my word since they voted against you, and that the other thirty did not trust yours, since they did not vote for your acquittal until they had actually gotten your money in their hands." While tribune, Clodius later had Cicero banished and his villas destroyed.

Cicero's speeches, epistles, and essays, many of which were gathered for posthumous publication by his faithful secretary, freedman, and friend Marcus Tullius Tiro, have shed more light on the stresses and strains of the late Roman republic than any other historical source. They reveal the strengths and weaknesses of the Roman aristocracy, a group who were cultured, proud, patriotic, intensely political, vain, and self-interested. Perhaps the greatest compliment Cicero ever received came from his nemesis, Julius Caesar, who declared that Cicero's achievement was greater than his own: "It is better to have extended the boundaries of the Roman spirit than of the Roman empire."

Cicero's *On Duties* (44 B.C.), written after the fall of the republic had driven him from politics, were his last musings on life, proper behavior, and the duties of public office. Cicero's ominous warning foreshadowed the downfall of many future republics: "The armed forces stationed to attack the state are more in number than those which defend it; for it takes only a nod of the head to set in motion the reckless and the desperate—indeed of their own initiative they incite themselves against the state. The sound elements [of society] rouse themselves more slowly. . . . At the last moment [they] are stirred into belated action by the sheer urgencies of the situation." Cicero saw the horror of tyranny not merely in its destruction of liberty but in its corruption of morals as well. He considered *On Duties* his manifesto and his masterpiece.

Cicero's elegant prose placed the Greek doctrines of popular sovereignty, mixed government, and natural law at the center of Western thought. Although Cicero did not explicitly discuss the theory of popular sovereignty, his political writings assumed that no form of government—whether monarchy, aristocracy, democracy, or mixed government—was legitimate unless the people consented to it. (Even the later edicts of the emperors were thought to have the force of law not merely because the emperor willed it, but because the people supposedly consented to that mode of legislation.) Furthermore, Cicero's *Republic* (51 B.C.) attributed Roman success to the republic's allegedly mixed government.

A philosopher as well as a statesman and political theorist, Cicero helped popularize the crucial theory of natural law. Though entertaining an eclectic mix of opinions on various philosophical issues, Cicero was largely Stoic on the question of natural law. He conceived of the universe as "one commonwealth of which both gods and men are members." Natural law was not handed down by the gods, but was the glue that connected them to humans in the one great organism of the universe. Humans discerned natural law through a combination of reason and intuition. He wrote regarding Nature and Man:

It is true that she gave him a mind capable of receiving virtue, and implanted at birth and without instruction some small intimations of the greatest truths, and thus, as it were, laid the foundation for education and instilled into those faculties which the mind already had what may be called the germs of virtue. But of virtue itself she merely furnished the rudiments; nothing more. Therefore, it is our task (and when I say "our" I mean that it is the task of art) to

supplement those mere beginnings by searching out the further developments which are implicit in them, until what we seek is fully realized.

Concerning natural law, Cicero wrote:

> This law, my lords, is not a written but an innate law. We have not been
> taught it by the learned; we have not received it from our ancestors; we have
> not taken it from books; it is derived from nature and stamped in invisible
> characters upon our very frame. It was not conveyed by instruction but
> wrought into our constitution. It is the dictate of instinct. . . . There cannot be
> one law now, and another hereafter; but the same eternal immutable law
> comprehends all nations, at all times, under one common master and gover-
> nor of all.

Cicero used the two analogies of sparks and seeds to clarify his position. At one point, he stated that humans are all sparks temporarily separated from the Great Flame (the World Soul), but a spark might be extinguished by a bad upbringing. On another occasion he argued that
the seeds of virtue were manifested in the social nature of humans, in
their "gregarious impulses." (The two analogies differed somewhat:
nurturing a seed into a full-grown plant generally requires more conscious effort than keeping a flame lit.) Like most of the classical
philosophers, Cicero possessed an optimistic conception of nature and,
hence, of human nature, writing: "Great-heartedness and heroism,
and courtesy, and justice, and generosity are far more in conformity
with nature than self-indulgence. . . . Our nature impels us to seek what
is morally right." Those who violated natural law were punished, not
by the "penalties established by law, for these they often escape," but
by "their own degradation." The reward of virtue was self-respect and
the respect of others: "The reputation and the glory of being a good
man are too precious to be sacrificed in favor of anything at all."
     Cicero's philosophical treatises, written late in life as he grieved over
the deaths of both his daughter Tullia and the Roman republic itself,
noted the need to endure old age patiently and expressed confidence in
the existence of an afterlife. He noted: "Great deeds are not done by
strength or speed or physique; they are the products of thought, and character, and judgment. And far from diminishing, such qualities actually increase with age. . . . If some god granted me the power to cancel my advanced years and return to boyhood, and wail once more in the cradle, I
should firmly refuse. Now that my race is run, I have no desire to be
called back from the finish to the starting point!" The marvelous nature of
the human mind convinced him that it "cannot be mortal." He added: "It
is only after liberation from all bodily admixture has made them pure and
undefiled that souls enter upon true wisdom. . . . I look forward to meet-

ing the personages of whom I have heard, read, and written. . . . I am leaving a hostel rather than a home. . . . As I approach death I feel like a man nearing harbor after a long voyage: I seem to be catching sight of land."

Although Cicero's philosophical ideas were hardly original—he once conceded, "I supply only the words, and I don't lack those!"—"supplying the words" is at least as crucial to the popularity of a philosophy as supplying the ideas. Indeed, in Cicero's case supplying the words involved inventing a whole new Latin vocabulary that could correspond to technical terms in Greek philosophy.

Cicero's only literary failures were his poems, which were so bad they have given joy to countless generations of critics. Tacitus claimed that the verses written by Caesar and Brutus, though no better than Cicero's, were more fortunate since fewer people knew of their existence. The Roman satirist Juvenal wrote that if Cicero's prose had been of the same quality as his poetry, he would never have had to fear the vengeance of Antony.

CICERO'S LEGACY

So influential was Cicero that the late republican period of Roman history is sometimes referred to as "the Ciceronian Age." His writings influenced the early Church Fathers of Christianity. Ambrose used Cicero's *On Duties* as the model for an important manual on Christian ethics. Jerome read Cicero so much that he thought he heard God ask him once, "What art thou?" When Jerome replied, "A Christian," God answered, "No, thou art not a Christian, but a Ciceronian." In remorse, Jerome swore never to read worldly books again. But Jerome's writings continued to show the imprint of Cicero in both style and substance. When taunted with this, Jerome replied that his promise had been for the future; it was impossible for him to forget what he had already learned. In the *Confessions,* Augustine claimed that it was Cicero's *Hortensius* that had led him to love virtue.

Early medieval Christians loved Cicero so much that Pope Gregory the Great threatened to burn his writings because their charm diverted young men from the Scriptures. Boethius wrote a commentary on Cicero. Venerable Bede compiled collections of Cicero's famous statements. Alcuin, the leading figure of the "Carolingian Renaissance," found time to read the Roman's works, and Einhard, the famous biographer of Charlemagne, quoted from Cicero's *Tusculan Disputations.* Dante used *On Duties* 1.13 as the basis for his classification of sins in the *Inferno.* The poet found consolation for the death of Beatrice in Cicero's essay on *Friendship,* which presented arguments for an afterlife.

Petrarch, the "Father of the Renaissance," loved the musical quality of Cicero's writings. He began reading Cicero as a small child. His devotion to the Roman so hindered his legal studies that his father burned all of his volumes of Cicero. But, on seeing his son's tears, Petrarch's father rescued one of Cicero's rhetorical works from the flames. As soon as Petrarch was of legal age, he dropped his legal studies and began collecting and reading Cicero's works again. Indeed, Petrarch's dogged pursuit of all the Ciceronian manuscripts he could find probably saved some of the more obscure works from oblivion. Petrarch was instrumental in the final victory of classical Latin, as exemplified by Cicero, over the less elegant, scholastic Latin that had developed during the Middle Ages.

Indeed, some of the lesser figures of the Italian Renaissance became so zealous on behalf of Ciceronian Latin that they refused to use any word Cicero himself had not used. Naturally, this ridiculous prohibition created confusion as new manuscripts were discovered. These zealots evidently forgot Cicero's statement in *On the Nature of the Gods:* "In discussions it is not so much the authorities that are to be sought as the course of reason. In fact, the authority of those who profess to instruct is often a hindrance to their pupils; for they cease to use their own judgment, but accept what they know to be approved by one whom they respect."

Although Desiderius Erasmus, the great Catholic reformer, despised the slavish worship of Cicero, he too admired the Roman. In fact, Erasmus issued his own edition of the *Tusculan Disputations,* writing in the introduction: "Certainly I have never loved Cicero more than I do now."

Erasmus's Protestant counterpart, Martin Luther, agreed, calling Cicero "a wise and industrious man, [who] suffered much and accomplished much." Luther added: "I hope our Lord God will be merciful to him and to those like him."

Modern republicans deduced from Cicero's theory of natural law the concept of natural rights, which forms the basis of those bills of rights that distinguish democratic nations from the rest of the world. John Locke also recommended the study of Cicero for eloquence, epistolary style, and morals.

Eighteenth-century deists used Cicero's two chief arguments for the existence of God—humans' intuitive connection to him and the order of the universe—as the basis for their rejection of the need for divine revelation. Voltaire especially liked Cicero's essay *On Divination,* which was directed against superstitious belief in magic and augury. Frederick the Great, who carried Cicero's works with him on his military campaigns, ordered their translation into German. Cicero's writing style influenced Montesquieu and Edward Gibbon.

Eighteenth- and nineteenth-century orators ranging in ideology from Edmund Burke to Robespierre studied and admired his speeches. The "Great Triumvirate" of American antebellum orators, Daniel Webster, Henry Clay, and John C. Calhoun, were all admirers of Cicero.

Cicero's very character or, rather, an idealized version of it, became the model for future Western statesmen. Along with Socrates and Demosthenes, Cicero became the symbol of the statesman who sacrifices short-term popularity, which can only be purchased by vice, for long-term fame, which can only be purchased by virtue.

For instance, John Adams idolized Cicero throughout his whole life. In the autumn of 1758, Adams gloried in the fact that law, his chosen profession, was a "Field in which Demosthenes, Cicero, and others of immortal Fame have exulted before me!" That winter he confessed to his diary the pleasure he derived from reading Cicero's orations aloud: "The Sweetness and Grandeur of his sounds, and the Harmony of his Numbers give Pleasure enough to reward the Reading if one understood none of his meaning. Besides, I find it a noble Exercise. It exercises my Lungs, raises my Spirits, opens my Porrs, quickens the Circulation, and so contributes to [my] Health." Indeed, after a family quarrel a few days later, Adams "quitted the Room, and took up Tully to compose myself." In 1774, Adams urged an aspiring politician to adopt Cicero as his model. He wrote regarding Cicero's term as quaestor at Lilybaeum in Sicily: "He did not receive this office as Persons do now a days, as a Gift, or a Farm, but as a public Trust, and considered it as a Theatre, in which the Eyes of the World were upon him." Adams added that when Rome was short of grain, Cicero managed to feed the city without treating his own province unfairly.

When Adams, one of the greatest orators of his day, rose before the Continental Congress on July 1, 1776, to rebut John Dickinson's contention that American independence would be premature, the New Englander thought of Cicero. He recorded in his diary: "I began by saying that this was the first time of my Life that I had ever wished for the Talents and Eloquence of the ancient Orators of Greece and Rome, for I was very sure that none of them had ever had before him a question of more importance to his Country and to the World."

Adams's admiration for Cicero outlived the American Revolution. Adams spent the summer of 1796, several months before assuming the presidency, rereading the Roman statesman's essays. In 1803, Adams quoted Cicero regarding the true public servant: "Such a man will devote himself entirely to the republic, nor will he covet power or riches. . . . He will adhere closely to justice and equity, that, provided he can preserve these virtues, although he may give offence and create enemies by them, he will set death itself at defiance, rather than abandon his principles." No one followed this ethic better than Adams. In the 1760s, he had refused the lucrative and prestigious position of admiralty court judge because he considered the juryless British courts unconstitutional. In 1770, he had sacrificed his popularity to defend the British soldiers accused of murder in the Boston Massacre. As president, in 1799–1800 he had made peace with Napoleonic France, leaving Thomas Jefferson the glory of the Louisiana Purchase three years later, at the expense of his own reelection. While no other founder yearned so much for popularity, none so continually sacrificed it to a strict code of ethics. It is not fanciful to suppose that, when making such painful decisions, Adams found consolation in contemplating the Roman statesman's sacrifices and the eternal glory they had earned him.

Adams continued to express admiration for Cicero in the correspondence of his twilight years. In 1805, Adams wrote:

> The period in the history of the world the best understood is that of Rome from the time of Marius to the death of Cicero, and this distinction is entirely owing to Cicero's letters and orations. There we see the true character of the times and the passions of all the actors on the stage. Cicero, Cato, and Brutus were the only three in whom I can discern any real patriotism. . . . Cicero had the most capacity and the most constant, as well as the wisest and most persevering attachment to the republic.

In 1809, Adams poured out his heart in another letter:

> Panegyrical romances will never be written, nor flattering orations spoken, to transmit me to posterity in brilliant colors. No, nor in true colors. All but the last I loathe. Yet, I will not die wholly unlamented. Cicero was libeled, slandered, insulted by all parties—by Caesar's party, Catiline's crew, Clodius's myrmidions, aye, and by Pompey and the Senate too. He was persecuted and tormented by turns by all parties and all factions, and that for his most virtuous and glorious actions. In his anguish at times and in the consciousness of his own merit and integrity, he was driven to those assertions of his own actions which have been denominated vanity. Instead of reproaching him with vanity, I think them the most infallible demonstration of his innocence and purity. He declares that all honors are indifferent to him because he knows that it is not in the power of his country to reward him in any proportion to his services.
>
> Pushed and injured and provoked as I am, I blush not to imitate the Roman.

Adams was all too successful in his lifelong attempt to emulate Cicero. Adams's integrity, which found its greatest expression in his unwillingness to endorse party favoritism, led to unpopularity in both parties; and his responses to critics were often marked by the same petulance and vanity as the Roman's. The only difference between Cicero and Adams was that Cicero, uninfluenced by Christian notions of humility, had found nothing shameful in vanity. Indeed, as a man who had ascended from the equestrian order, a "new man" intruding on the traditional prerogatives of the nobility—not unlike Adams, who was of middle-class origin—Cicero may have considered it necessary to remind the Romans of his accomplishments. Perhaps it is for this reason that Cicero boasted only of his service to Rome, never of his unparalleled eloquence, the attribute for which he was universally admired.

Other Founding Fathers also idolized Cicero. James Wilson cited the Roman statesman more often than any other author in his 1790 lectures to law students at the College of Philadelphia (now the University of Pennsylvania). Wilson exulted: "The jurisprudence of Rome was adorned and enriched by the exquisite genius of Cicero, which, like the touch of Midas, converts every object to gold." He called Cicero's *On Duties* "a work which does honour to human understanding and the human heart." Similarly, John Marshall, who patterned his portrayal of George Washington, in his famous five-volume biography of the first president, on Cicero, told his grandsons that *On Duties* was "among the most valuable treatises in the Latin language, a salutary discourse on the duties and qualities proper to a republican gentleman." Benjamin Rush and Thomas Paine quoted Cicero repeatedly concerning natural law. Benjamin Franklin cited Cicero often on the importance of hard work and virtue.

It was not originality of thought that made Cicero the most influential of all the ancients. Rather, it was originality of expression, combined with a martyr's death, that endeared Cicero to statesmen throughout Western history.

10

Augustus: Founder of the Roman Empire

Although the Romans conquered most of their territory during the days of the republic, the term "Roman Empire" is often used to refer to the period when emperors governed Rome (27 B.C.–A.D. 476). The first of these emperors was Augustus. Augustus administered the empire so mildly and so capably that he succeeded in reconciling the Roman people to imperial rule. It is no exaggeration to state that the order, peace, and prosperity Augustus restored to the empire, coming in the wake of three bloody civil wars, saved Greco-Roman civilization from extinction. On the other hand, Augustus's very success also paved the way for the despotism of Caligula, Nero, and other maniacal rulers.

THE THIRD ROMAN CIVIL WAR: ANTONY VERSUS OCTAVIAN (AUGUSTUS)

The Battle of Philippi

In 42 B.C., the two largest armies in Roman history faced each other. The army of the Second Triumvirate defeated the republican army of Brutus and Cassius in two battles at Philippi in Macedon. In the first battle, Brutus routed Antony's force, while Octavian's army (Octavian himself was too ill to be present) routed Cassius's force. Unaware of Brutus's success and thinking that all was lost, Cassius committed suicide. He fell on the same sword with which he had stabbed Caesar. Brutus called Cassius "the last of the Romans." In this first battle, the triumvirate lost twice as many troops as their opponents (16,000 to 8,000).

But in the second battle, Cassius's soldiers, demoralized by the death of their fiery leader, were easily routed, thereby bringing defeat on Brutus's forces as well. When one of Brutus's aides implored him not to take his own life, pleading tearfully, "We must escape," the Stoic replied: "Yes, we must escape, but this time with our hands, not our feet." He ordered one of his servants to hold his sword while he plunged himself into it. His wife, Porcia, suffocated herself.

Like most of the Roman republican martyrs, Brutus was hardly the saint of legend. A greedy man, he had once ordered a representative to collect, by force if necessary, repayment of a loan from the people of Salamis in Cyprus. Brutus was charging the townsmen 48 percent interest, though the maximum interest rate allowed in the province was 12 percent.

But, whatever Brutus's faults, he was shrewd enough to predict that Octavian and Antony would soon be fighting each other. The Senate declared Julius Caesar a god, thereby granting added prestige to his adopted son Octavian, who had already curried favor with the Roman people by supervising the distribution of the funds Caesar had willed them.

Antony versus Octavian

The triumvirate ruled the Roman Empire as virtual dictators. In 40 B.C., they formally divided the empire between them. Octavian received the western empire, except for North Africa, which went to Lepidus, and Mark Antony received the eastern empire. At the same time, Antony married Octavian's sister Octavia to cement the alliance between them. Octavian evicted Lepidus from the triumvirate in 36 B.C., after Lepidus's attempt to seize Sicily from Octavian failed when most of his troops deserted to Octavian.

At first glance, it appeared that Antony held the upper hand against Octavian, since he controlled Egypt, Rome's most important province. But Octavian's control of Italy allowed him to impress the most important men of Rome with his administrative talents.

Antony then sealed his own fate by falling in love with Cleopatra. Though not particularly beautiful, Cleopatra was extremely intelligent, knowledgeable (having mastered numerous languages), and charming. The couple entertained themselves by going about Alexandria dressed as slaves and ridiculing people. (Since most citizens never imagined that this pair could be the rulers of Egypt, Antony was beaten several times.) The couple held lavish parties at which Cleopatra dressed as Isis and Antony as Bacchus.

When Antony dispatched formal letters of divorce to Octavia, who was a kind and virtuous woman much beloved by the Roman people, Octavian used the act as a pretext for waging war against Antony. He seized Antony's will from the Vestal Virgins and publicly revealed its contents. In the will, Antony made his sons by Cleopatra his heirs, even declaring that they would inherit Parthia, which had not been conquered. Romans were outraged at the eventual prospect of being ruled by men who were only half Roman. The people also discovered that Antony's will ceded control of three Roman territories to Cleopatra. Finally, the will declared that if Antony died in Rome, his body must be sent back to Cleopatra in Alexandria. Octavian cleverly used Roman xenophobia to attract broad support, claiming that Antony would transfer the capital of the empire to Alexandria. For propaganda purposes, Octavian declared war on Cleopatra, not Antony, claiming that Antony was acting under some sort of spell cast by this evil, eastern woman. Nevertheless, Octavian's brazen act of seizing a will from the Vestal Virgins antagonized some Romans; one-third of the senators and both consuls bet their lives on Antony.

The Battle of Actium

In 31 B.C., Octavian's navy, under the leadership of Marcus Vipsanius Agrippa—a brilliant admiral of low birth who had built and trained a fleet from scratch—destroyed or captured three-quarters of Antony's fleet at Actium in Greece. Although Octavian possessed only 400 ships to Antony's 500, Octavian's ships were more maneuverable and manned by better rowers. At a crucial point in the battle, Antony's center and left, perhaps alarmed by an enemy maneuver, began to retreat, forcing Antony to signal Cleopatra to escape with the war chest. Antony joined her squadron with forty ships of his own, leaving the remainder of his fleet to be destroyed or captured.

When Agrippa captured Antony's bases in the Peloponnesus, thereby severing the supply line to Antony's army in northern Greece, his 130,000 malaria-ridden soldiers, abandoned by their commander, surrendered. Octavian then cornered Antony in Egypt. When Antony heard a false rumor that Cleopatra had committed suicide, the fifty-three-year-old soldier stabbed himself through the stomach. Yet, he lived long enough to die in Cleopatra's arms.

The thirty-nine-year-old Cleopatra, the last of the Ptolemaic rulers of Egypt, committed suicide after Octavian captured her and the city of Alexandria in 30 B.C. According to Plutarch, Cleopatra chose to die from the bite of an asp, because the numerous experiments she had conducted on condemned prisoners convinced her that it was the least painful form of death. There may be some truth to this story, but it is also true that the asp was the representative of the Egyptian sun god, and its effigy encircled the crown of Egypt to protect the royal line. Cleopatra may have chosen the asp to represent the sun god rescuing his daughter Isis from humiliation. In any case, the asp was smuggled to her under a basket of figs.

Octavian approved the completion of the mausoleum Antony and Cleopatra had begun and allowed their burial together in the same tomb. Octavia, ever virtuous, took it upon herself to raise the three children produced by her philandering husband and Cleopatra, as well as the children from Antony's previous marriage. But Octavian killed Caesarion, Cleopatra's young son by Julius Caesar, whose potential claim as Caesar's heir made him a dangerous rival.

Octavian then annexed Egypt and placed it under his personal control, the first such arrangement in Roman history. Mopping up operations against Antony's allies continued until 27 B.C. Octavian returned to Rome with so much gold that the interest rate immediately plunged from 12 to 4 percent.

After a full century of chaos and violence, in which the Roman republic had proved incapable of maintaining any semblance of peace or order, Rome was now thoroughly prepared for the rule of an emperor.

THE NEW ARRANGEMENTS

When Octavian returned to Rome in triumph after defeating Antony and Cleopatra, he declared before the Senate that the republic was restored. Of course, this was a charade. Everyone knew that Octavian wielded the supreme power and that it rested on his status as *imperator* (victorious general), commander of the army, whose soldiers took an oath of allegiance to him. Fearful of Octavian's power and, even more, of the continual civil wars that had nearly destroyed Rome, the Senate heaped awards, honors, and titles on him. The most famous of his titles was Augustus (Consecrated One), a title previously reserved for the gods. The month of Sextilis was changed to August to commemorate the month when Octavian had entered Alexandria, thereby ending the civil war. Another of his titles (after 2 B.C.) was *pater patriae* (Father of the Country). He called himself the *princeps civitatis* (First Citizen), a title that had been granted to elder statesmen during the republican period. For this reason, historians often refer to Augustus's reign as the Principate.

In return for the honors the Senate bestowed on him, Augustus transferred most of the legislative and judicial functions from the popular assemblies and the courts to the Senate. This, too, was a charade, since Augustus's control of appointments to the Senate and the senators' fear of the army turned the body into the emperor's rubber stamp, its authority resting entirely on his good will. In 23 B.C., the people granted Augustus tribunician powers, thereby awarding him prestige as a "protector of the people," as well as the authority to veto Senate legislation. In 19 B.C., his consular power, which included the authority to convene the Senate and set its agenda, was extended for life. Augustus controlled the outer provinces directly, through the army and through the *legati* he appointed to govern them, and controlled the inner provinces indirectly, through his power to reject the proconsuls appointed by the Senate. He also possessed the power to make treaties and the authority to intervene in senatorial provinces. He could draw from the treasury any time he wanted, as well as from the vast personal wealth he had acquired during the civil war. (Indeed, from his own estate he contributed to the fund for discharged veterans and paid some other imperial expenses, so that he was comparatively poor when he died.) After 12 B.C., he served as *pontifex maximus* (Chief Priest). Although Augustus was careful not to portray himself as a god in Rome, he allowed himself to be worshipped by the foreign peoples of the provinces, on the grounds that it rendered them more obedient to the Roman will.

But perhaps the greatest source of Augustus's power was his own humility. Unlike his granduncle and adoptive father Julius Caesar, Augustus generally eschewed the appearance of arrogance. Even while consolidating power beyond the dreams of most kings, Augustus was careful to avoid the trappings of monarchy. He understood that although Romans of all classes thirsted for the stability offered by one-man rule, centuries of republican tradition had instilled in them a fierce hatred of the very word "king." Augustus's humility and magnanimity, when joined with his fiction of a restored republic, set the exhausted Romans at ease.

AUGUSTUS'S ACCOMPLISHMENTS (27 B.C.–A.D. 14)

Peace and Prosperity

The reign of Augustus was one of unprecedented peace and prosperity. During his rule, the doors to the temple of the god Janus, closed only in times of complete peace, were closed three times. The doors had been closed only twice in the centuries before Augustus.

When combined with the construction of durable roads throughout the empire, peace made extensive trade and travel possible. The increase in trade produced prosperity. Merchants even dispatched 120 ships per year to India via the Red Sea to trade their pots and other goods for Indian spices, jewels, and ivory and for Chinese silk. Augustus also increased prosperity by establishing an efficient monetary system, made possible by elaborate mining facilities and augmented by local small change. Gold and silver coins were minted at Lugdunum (Lyons), while the senatorial mint in Rome produced copper and bronze coins. The images on Roman coins were frequently changed, allowing emperors to highlight their own recent accomplishments, or to introduce their chosen successor to the provinces.

During the few periods of war in Augustus's forty-one year reign, his generals extended the empire's northeastern frontier to the Danube River. Augustus established a professional army of twenty-eight legions, stationed it on the frontier, and largely succeeded in keeping it out of politics. The army proved a tremendous Romanizing influence. Towns sprouted around its camps (e.g., Cologne, Mainz, and Baden), as Roman soldiers intermarried with native women, settled down on their pensions, and became local dignitaries. After twenty-five years of service, foreigners who served in the auxiliaries were issued a pair of bronze tablets called a *diploma* (double tablets) that granted them full citizenship. Augustus also maintained fleets throughout the Mediterranean to transport troops and to suppress piracy.

Efficient Administration

Augustus also reduced the number of senators from 900 to 600, making the Senate more efficient. He appointed honest and efficient legati to govern the outer provinces. Respecting local cultures to a large extent, the legati emphasized provincial autonomy and local self-government. This pluralism was one of the wisest of Rome's policies. It enabled the Romans to hold together a vast empire of innumerable ethnic groups with a minimum of rebellion and to avoid an inefficient, centralized bureaucracy, thereby allowing them to maintain taxes at a tolerable level.

Augustus established a periodic census to monitor changes in the population, wealth, and resources of each province, thereby allowing him to shift the tax burden from those provinces least able to pay. Most money raised in the provinces remained there, to cover the expense of local administration; few provinces provided a surplus for Rome. Augustus reduced the number of taxes collected by private tax collectors. He assigned equites, as well as aristocrats, to financial posts, to the governorship of small provinces, to the command of armies, and to the Praetorian Guard, the palace guard of 9,000 men.

Augustus constructed another forum in Rome to relieve congestion in the original. It was narrower than he originally planned because he could not bring himself to evict the owners of the houses that would have to be demolished. He also cleared the Tiber of rubbish to improve navigation and to help prevent floods.

Augustus must rank as one of the most skillful and energetic administrators in history. In fact, he once expressed astonishment that Alexander the Great had devoted so much energy and attention to conquering an empire and so little to administering it properly.

Piety and Morality

Augustus rebuilt eighty-two temples destroyed during the civil wars, revived old priesthoods, and restored religious festivals. Holding to traditional Roman frugality, he lived in a modest house on Palatine Hill (the word "palace" derives from the more lavish royal houses later constructed there), ate frugally, and dressed in simple clothes made by his female relatives. At the same time that he banished Ovid for his more lascivious poems and for a mysterious scandal perhaps involving Augustus's promiscuous daughter Julia, Augustus also exiled his daughter for adultery. Concerned about the decline of traditional Roman values and fearing depopulation, he passed laws rewarding the production of legitimate children and penalizing adultery, bachelorhood, and childlessness.

The Patronage of Virgil

Augustus also added crucial imperial support to his adviser Gaius Cilnius Maecenas's long-standing patronage of poets. One poet Maecenas supported was Virgil (Publius Vergilius Maro; 70–19 B.C.), the master of Latin poetry. Virgil's *Eclogues* (c. 42–37 B.C.) and *Georgics* (36–29 B.C.) reinvigorated the pastoral theme, a theme first pursued by Hesiod and later by the Alexandrian poets. Alarmed by small farmers' abandonment of their farms and migration to the cities (in some cases, they were forcibly expelled from their farms to make way for the veterans of the civil wars), Virgil portrayed the rural lifestyle as the happiest and most virtuous. Virgil wrote: "Pallas [Athena] can keep her cities, but let the woods beyond all else please you and me."

The *Eclogues* consisted of ten brief, melodious, enigmatic, unpretentious poems. The locale was a composite of Arcadia, Sicily, and northern Italy, but was, above all, Virgil's own imaginative creation, existing nowhere in the real world. Virgil cast a sensuous, enchanted light on rural life, tempered by the good-natured banter of shepherds. His fourth eclogue, written while Augustus and Antony were still allies (40 B.C.), expressed the widespread belief that a savior would appear who would rescue the world from its many troubles. The theory that Virgil thought the savior would be the child of Antony and Octavia, Augustus's sister, has been discredited, leaving the matter a mystery. Early

Christians, noting Virgil's references to "the virgin," to a divine child who would rule the world in peace, to the "nullification" of sin, and to the destruction of "the snake," later believed that the poet had received a vision of Jesus from the Holy Spirit.

The *Georgics* celebrated the beauties, labor, and rewards of the farm, a place situated comfortably between the extremes of the savage wilderness and the corrupt city. In this poem, one of the most influential in Western literature, Virgil demonstrated true genius. His problem was a most difficult one: how to write a great poem that was also a manual of practical advice for farmers. Virgil succeeded by virtue of his incredible descriptive power and through his charming ascription of human sentiment to every element of nature. Rather than write, "Don't plant your crops too early," Virgil warns the farmer never to "entrust too early to reluctant soil a whole year's hopes." He ends the second Georgic with the pleasing line: "By now we have traversed a course of many leagues; high time to unyoke the steaming necks of our horses." In Virgil's capable hands even a storm seems beautiful. In his vivid imagination, rivers feel boats on their backs, ants put aside food for old age, bees engage in "mob violence," "the endive revels in the brook it drinks," green river banks "delight in parsley," and a bull who loses a joust for a heifer anguishes over "lost love" and goes into "exile," quitting "his stable and ancestral kingdom." The poet even manages to inject suspense into an otherwise mundane instruction to keep the pens clean: "Often beneath neglected pens there lurks a dangerous viper, shrinking from the daylight, or an adder, curse of cattle, such as love to creep into the shelter of dark buildings and stab the herd with poison." His description of a fallen ox, the victim of a deadly plague, is strangely moving: "Sadly the plowman goes to unyoke the mate that mourns his brother, and leaves the plow stuck there, its work unfinished. No shade of lofty trees, no luscious meadow, can cheer that beast again."

The *Georgics* dispensed advice concerning the cultivation of crops, the growing of trees, the raising of livestock, and the keeping of bees. Some of the advice was quite good. For instance, Virgil advised crop rotation over 1,700 years before it sparked the modern Agricultural Revolution. (Nonetheless, Virgil had a poor understanding of bees. Future dead white male and defender of patriarchy that he was, he thought bees were led by "kings" rather than queens and praised them for their sexual abstinence. He evidently accepted the myth that young bees were not produced by copulation, but were gathered from the flowers that mysteriously generated them. In other words, Virgil was not the right person to teach children about "the birds and the bees.")

In the *Georgics,* Virgil exhorted his fellow Romans to help regenerate the community after a century of civil war by returning to the plow. He wrote:

> How lucky the farmers are—I wish they knew!
> The Earth herself, most just, pours forth for them
> An easy living from the soil, far off
> From clashing weapons. Though the farmer has
> No mansion with proud portals which spits out
> A monster wave of morning visitors
> From every room, nor do his callers gasp
> At inlaid columns, bright with tortoiseshell,
> Or gold-embroidered clothes or bronzes from
> Ephyre, nor in his house is plain white wool
> Dyed with Assyrian poison, nor does he
> Corrupt his olive oil with foreign spice,
> He has untroubled sleep and honest life.
> Rich in all sorts of riches, with a vast
> Estate, he has all the leisure to enjoy
> A cave, a natural pond, a valley where
> The air is cool—the mooing of the cows
> Is ever present, and to sleep beneath
> A tree is sweet. Wild animals abound
> For hunting, and young people grow up strong,
> Hardworking, satisfied with poverty.
> Their gods are holy; their parents are revered.
> Surely, when Justice left the earth she stayed
> Last with these folk, and left some tokens here.

The pastoral theme was as much a staple of classical history as of classical poetry, of course. Classical historians considered Sparta and republican Rome models not merely because they had possessed mixed governments, but also because they had been agricultural societies. Greek and Roman historians credited the triumph of Sparta and Rome over their vice-ridden, commercial adversaries, Athens and Carthage, as much to their pastoral virtues as to their government form.

Virgil celebrated the mythic past of the Italian countryside, its olive-laden vines, its perpetual spring, and its freedom from harmful plants and animals. He exulted: "Hail, great mother of harvests, land of Saturn, mighty mother of men; in your honor I tell of the things of that art of husbandry which from ancient times has been your glory; I dare to unseal those sacred springs, and through Roman towns I sing the song which Hesiod sang to the Greeks. . . . I will be the first, if life is granted me, to lead the Muses in triumph from Greek Helicon to my native land."

Virgil also painted a vivid portrait of the high cost and unstoppable momentum of civil war. He wrote: "No due honor attends the plow. The fields, bereft of tillers, are all unkempt and in the forge the curved pruning-hook is made a straight hard sword. . . . Impious War is raging. As on a race-course, the barriers down, out pour the chariots, gathering speed from lap to lap, and a driver, tugging in vain at the reins, is swept along by the horses and the heedless, uncontrollable car."

Virgil's greatest masterpiece was the *Aeneid* (29–19 B.C.), an epic poem modeled on Homer's *Iliad* and *Odyssey*. The poem told the story of the Trojan Aeneas, who escaped the Greek destruction of Troy and moved to Italy, where his descendants founded Rome. The *Aeneid* effectively conveyed the Roman mission to conquer and "civilize" the world. The Sibyl of Cumae (the Roman version of the oracle of Delphi) guides Aeneas, newly arrived in Italy, to the underworld, where his father Anchises reveals to him the future glory of Rome. After his return to the earthly world, Aeneas even visits the site where his descendants, Romulus and Remus, are destined to establish the city. The god Vulcan gives him a shield engraved with designs that convey a further forecast of Rome's grand destiny. A depiction of the Battle of Actium, in which Augustus will defeat Antony and Cleopatra, forms the center of the shield. To Virgil, Augustus's victory represented the triumph of Roman civilization over eastern barbarism. The last four books of the *Aeneid* concern wars between Aeneas's Trojan émigrés and the Latin tribes, wars ended by Aeneas's marriage to Lavinia, a Latin princess. The *Aeneid* is an *Odyssey* (a voyage-adventure epic) followed by an *Iliad* (a war epic).

Although Aeneas is a soldier like Achilles and the leader of a traveling band like Odysseus, his dedication to public service contrasts with the individualism of the Greek heroes. His epithet is "the pious." Aeneas brings both his household gods and his aged father to Italy with him. His travels afford him numerous opportunities to lay aside his arduous destiny for a comfortable life in an existing city. His greatest temptation of this kind occurs in ancient Carthage. The goddess Venus (Aeneas's mother) makes Queen Dido of Carthage fall in love with him and offer him a permanent home. Aeneas stays in Carthage a year, until Jupiter sends Mercury to recall him to his duty. Dutiful Aeneas, though heartbroken, stoically follows the will of fate in opposition to his own desires. Aeneas abandons the desperate Dido, who commits suicide, after calling down a curse of deadly enmity between her descendants and Aeneas's. She cries out to Carthage: "Pursue his seed with your hatred for all ages to come. Let no kindness or truce be between the nations."

Although the myth of Aeneas and Dido could be used to justify the Roman destruction of Carthage, by surrounding it with an aura of inevitability, Virgil's poem displays a rare sympathy for most of Aeneas's defeated enemies—tragic figures swimming desperately against the majestic stream of Roman history. At the end of the poem, Aeneas hesitates before finally killing Turnus, his Latin rival and king of the Rutulians; the destiny of a city yet to be born has forced the noble Aeneas to abandon or destroy those whom he would much prefer to spare. (Historic distance from a defeated foe, be it Troy for the Greeks, Carthage for the Romans, or the England of George III for Americans, often produces a certain magnanimity no less enlightened for its belatedness.) Concerning the Romans, Virgil has Jupiter declare: "For these I set no limits, world or time, but make the gift of empire without end." He adds that Rome's fate is to "bring the whole world under law's dominion."

Though Virgil had been under intense pressure from Maecenas to write an epic about Augustus, the poet had quickly realized that contemporary history is almost never a suitable subject for an epic. If familiarity does not necessarily breed contempt, it at least impedes the aura of grandeur essential to the epic form. Furthermore, the Battle of Actium, the moment of Augustus's triumph, had witnessed very little that might be considered heroic fighting; Augustus certainly had not killed hundreds with his own hands like Achilles or Hector. To have made Augustus the central character of an epic poem would have been to turn the poem into a farce. In addition, if Augustus were made the subject of the epic, there could be no sympathy for his defeated foes, which would remove a large portion of the pathos, the tragic element, that makes the *Aeneid* such a masterpiece. It is precisely because we feel the pain of the abandoned Dido and of the vanquished Latins that we can appreciate the human cost of Rome's fated success. Virgil's brilliant solution to the problem of how to make Augustus a focus of the *Aeneid* without actually making him its central character was perhaps the only solution that could have preserved the poem's grandeur. His solution was to use the stirring story of Aeneas to present Roman history as a progression culminating in Augustus. Virgil shrewdly presents the Battle of Actium as a tableau on a shield rather than as a narrative. The real focus of the *Aeneid* is neither Augustus nor Aeneas. It is Rome.

Finally, the poem serves one other purpose: to reconcile the recently enfranchised Italians with Rome. Jupiter and Juno agree to assuage the Latins' grief over their defeat by making the Italians themselves a source of Rome's future strength: "Italian hardiness will make Rome great." In this way, the vanquished Italians join the winning side and reconcile themselves to Roman destiny through participation in it. So wrote the poet from Cisalpine Gaul, the last part of Italy to be enfranchised.

Shortly before his death, Virgil instructed his friends to burn the *Aeneid*, perhaps because he had left some incomplete lines scattered throughout the poem. Fortunately for Western literature, Augustus ordered that the nearly finished work be published rather than burned.

One of the most revered poems in Western history, the *Aeneid* influenced Dante Alighieri, Geoffrey Chaucer, John Milton, Alfred Lord Tennyson, and numerous other poets. Dante's *Divine Comedy* and Milton's *Paradise Lost* were both modeled on the *Aeneid*. Indeed, Dante selected Virgil to represent all that was wise and good in the pagan world, assigning him the task of guiding the narrator through the *Inferno* and the *Purgatorio*, the first two portions of the *Divine Comedy*.

The Patronage of Horace

The second greatest poet of the Augustan Age was Horace (Quintus Horatius Flaccus; 65–8 B.C.), a native of southern Italy. Horace's father, a former slave and collector of auction payments, sacrificed much to secure his son a rigorous education in Rome and Athens. Although Augustus and Antony confiscated Horace's estate in retribution for his fighting with Brutus at Philippi, Maecenas, on the recommendation of Virgil, later made certain that Horace received the patronage of the magnanimous Augustus, including a famous Sabine farm.

Horace's *Epodes* (c. 41–31 B.C.) assaulted social abuses and praised the rural lifestyle, though sometimes with a palpable sense of irony. Horace wrote:

> Happy the man who, free from business worries and free from interest owing, like the men of the old days, tills with his oxen his ancestral fields. . . . He keeps away from the Forum and the proud threshold of the powers that be. . . . He likes to recline now under an ancient oak, now on the thick grass. Meanwhile the brooks flow between the high banks, birds warble in the woods, and springs bubble with running water, a sweet invitation to repose. But when the wintry season of thundering Jove brings back rains and snows, either with his pack of hounds he drives the fierce boars into the traps, or arranges large meshed nets on polished sticks to snare the greedy thrushes. . . . If a modest wife does her part in tending the house and her dear children . . . piles high the sacred hearth with dry firewood, waiting for the return of her tired husband, gathers in a pen made of wattles the fat ewes in order to milk their distended udders, and, drawing from the keg new sweet wine, prepares a meal which she had not to pay for . . . amid such feasts, what joy to see the sheep returning home from pasture, the wearied oxen dragging along the upturned plowshare and the young slaves, industrious swarm of an opulent house, seated around the resplendent Lares.

But the sly poet could not resist adding, "So says Alfius, a moneylender, on the point of turning farmer," leaving the reader in doubt as to the seriousness of the portrait. (Thomas Jefferson once planned to inscribe an abbreviated version of this passage near a small, Greek-style temple he hoped to build on his burial ground. Of course, as a fervent supporter of agriculture and the rural lifestyle, Jefferson omitted the poem's ironic ending.)

In these early verses, written before the triumph of Augustus, Horace also lamented Rome's disastrous civil wars. He wrote:

> Into what, what, do you wickedly plunge? Why do your hands draw swords from scabbards? Perhaps too little Latin blood has been spilled on battlefields

or Neptune's realm? And not that Romans might burn the haughty towers of emulous Carthage; not that the scatheless Briton might trudge in chains down the Sacred Way; but that in fulfillment of Parthian prayers the city might die by her own right hand. . . . So it goes: a bitter fate pursues the Romans, and the crime of fratricide, since the blood of Remus ran on the earth, the bane of his successors. . . . What Hannibal, whom parents wished away, could not destroy or tame, this impious generation of fated stock will waste and the land belong once more to beasts of prey.

Horace also wrote of the agonies of love. To the mysterious man who had stolen his lover's affection, he wrote bitterly: "And you, whoever you are, who amble happy and proud in my misfortune, though perhaps you are rich in flocks and land . . . and your beauty surpasses that of Nireus, alas, you shall bewail her favors transferred to another, and I shall laugh last."

Horace's *Satires* (35–30 B.C.), a collection of poems written in hexameters yet conversational in flow, rejected wealth and power and emphasized the need for serenity. They mocked familiar social types in a general and genial manner and displayed the remarkable variety of theme and tone that was to become one of Horace's trademarks.

Influenced by Alcaeus, Sappho, and the Hellenistic poets, Horace's *Odes* (c. 23–13 B.C.) were remarkably succinct. Alfred Lord Tennyson once called his lines "jewels five words long that on the stretched forefinger of all time sparkle forever." The theme of more than a third of the poems is friendship. Indeed, many of the verses are addressed to friends, offering advice and encouragement. Another third deal with the tribulations of love, with human nature, and with the countryside in a detached, charming, and ironic way. Horace declared: "Thrice happy the couple who are not torn apart by quarrels but are held in a bond of unbroken love which only death dissolves." He resolved to let others write epic poems about heroes while he wrote of the epic struggles between the sexes: "Flippant as ever, whether afire or fancy free, I sing of banquets and 'battles' of eager girls with neatly trimmed nails against the young men." A small group of odes glorify Augustus in gratitude for priceless peace. (Yet Horace also demonstrated genuine respect for Cleopatra, Augustus's fallen foe: "Resolved for death, she was brave indeed. She was no docile woman but truly scorned to be taken away in her enemy's ships, deposed, to an overweening Triumph.") Painfully aware of the approach of death, Horace resolved to live life to the fullest: "Pallid Death knocks impartially at the doors of hovels and mansions. . . . Be wise, decant the wine, prune back your long-term hopes. Life ebbs as I speak—so seize each day, and grant the next no credit. . . . Happy the man, and happy he alone, who can call today his own; he who secure within, can say, 'Tomorrow, do your worst, for I have lived today.'"

Horace's *Epistles* (c. 20 B.C.), which included influential literary criticism (especially in the *Ars Poetica*, an epistle on the art of poetry), revealed a kindly, tolerant, humane, realistic, and self-deprecating man. Against the literary critics who favored only archaic verse he argued: "Suppose the Greeks had resented newness as much as we do, what would now be old? And what would the people have to read and thumb with enjoyment, each man to his taste?" He defined a literary critic as "a grindstone which sharpens steel but has no part in the cutting."

Horace was buried next to Maecenas, his friend and patron, on Esquiline Hill in Rome. His poems, like Virgil's, held an honored place in Roman education within less than a century and influenced countless generations of poets.

The Patronage of Livy

Augustus also encouraged Livy (Titus Livius; 59 B.C.–A.D. 17), one of the greatest of the Roman historians. Livy wrote the *History of Rome* over a period of about thirty years, beginning in 26 B.C. A prose epic of 142 "books" (a classical "book" was roughly equivalent to one of our chapters), only 35 of which survive, the *History* charted the Roman past from the foundation of Rome to 9 B.C.

Livy's *History* was extremely patriotic. As R. H. Barrow put it: "[In Livy] Rome is the heroine inspiring Romans to heroic deeds to fulfill her destiny. Virgil and Livy perfected the language for showing the Roman at his noblest in action and character." Livy boasted: "If any nation deserves the privilege of claiming a divine ancestry that nation is our own." Indeed, Livy attributed Rome's success to its traditional values. He wrote: "I hope my passion for Rome's past has not impaired my judgment; for I do honestly believe that no country has ever been greater or purer than ours or richer in good citizens and noble deeds; none has been free for so many centuries from the vices of avarice and luxury; nowhere have thrift and plain living been for so long held in such esteem."

Although those parts of the *History* that concern Livy's own time have been lost, he made it clear in other passages that, although he admired the republican age above all, he was grateful to Augustus for restoring peace and order. (In Augustan Rome praise for the republic was not only permissible but encouraged, since Augustus claimed to have restored it.) Livy also echoed Augustus's fear of a moral decline. Livy wrote: "The might of an imperial people is beginning to work its own ruin. . . . Of late years wealth has made us greedy, and self-indulgence has brought us, through every form of sensual excess, to be, if I may so put it, in love with death both individual and collective." (In modern times, Pope John Paul II has referred to the prosperous, modern West as a society "in love with death." Did he borrow the phrase from Livy?) Livy referred to "the sinking of the foundations of morality as the old teaching was allowed to lapse, then the final collapse of the whole edifice, and the dark dawning of our modern day when we can neither endure our vices nor face the remedies needed to cure them." He added: "The study of history is the best medicine for a sick mind; for in history you have a record of the infinite variety of human experience plainly set out for all to see; and in that record you can find for yourself and your country both examples and warnings, fine things to take as models, base things, rotten through and through, to avoid."

Livy wrote with astonishing skill and charm, in a style famously fluent and colorful. Yet most modern historians have judged Livy's work solid and dependable—aside from Livy's first ten books, which began with Aeneas and which were more mythological than historical.

THE FAILURES OF AUGUSTUS

The Loss of Varus's Legions

Aside from the exile of his own daughter, Augustus's greatest source of sorrow was the loss of three Roman legions under Publius Quinctilius Varus in the Teutoburger Wald in A.D. 9. The Romans were on the verge of conquering Germany when a group of Germanic tribes, led by Hermann, chief of the Cherusci, ambushed and slaughtered Varus's army. Hermann had served in the Roman army as an auxiliary, under the name of Arminius, and had even been awarded Roman citizenship and equestrian rank for his services. Varus was marching to suppress a fictitious revolt reported by German conspirators when his legions were ambushed. He committed suicide when the battle was lost. Augustus made the anniversary a national day of mourning. He once beat his head on a door and shouted, "Quinctilius Varus, give me back my legions!" The Roman failure to conquer the Germanic tribes allowed these tribes to conquer Rome four centuries later.

Tiberius (A.D. 14–37)

But perhaps Augustus's very success as a ruler constitutes his greatest failure. At best, his reign was a mixed blessing for Rome: by making the Roman people content to live under an emperor, Augustus paved the way for the likes of Tiberius, Caligula, and Nero.

When Augustus died in 14, there was no question as to his successor. All but one of his male relatives had passed away, some rather mysteriously, and a reluctant Augustus had been forced to adopt his stepson Tiberius, the son of his third wife Livia Drusilla by a previous marriage, as his own son and successor. Indeed, Tacitus speculated that Livia had engaged in a long sequence of poisonings designed to secure the succession of her son. Among the heirs of Augustus who died unexpectedly were his nephew Marcellus (23 B.C.), his favorite general and son-in-law Marcus Agrippa (12 B.C.), and his grandsons Lucius (A.D. 2) and Gaius (A.D. 4). Tacitus even hinted that Livia poisoned Augustus himself, in order to prevent a reconciliation between the emperor and Agrippa Postumus, his last remaining grandson, whom Augustus had exiled, a reconciliation that might have thwarted Tiberius's succession. (If Livia did use poison to secure the throne for her son, it did her little good. After Tiberius became emperor, complaining that his mother was trying to rule as coemperor, he nullified titles the Senate conferred on her, absented himself from her funeral, and vetoed her deification.)

Fifty-five years old on assuming the throne, Tiberius had distinguished himself both as a general and as an administrator while serving in the Middle East, Germany, and the Balkans. He began as a mild and capable ruler, much like Augustus. He appointed efficient governors for the provinces and balanced the budget. Whenever he received a New Year's gift, he made it a practice to reciprocate with a present four times its value—until his house was flooded with gifts, at which point he discontinued the practice.

But Tiberius was dour, melancholy, and insecure. Plagued by a skin disease that covered his face with sores, he became increasingly paranoid concerning plots against himself. In fact, Tiberius once declared that occupying the position of emperor was like "holding a wolf by the ears"—it was neither safe to hold it nor to let it go (a phrase Thomas Jefferson later employed regarding American slavery).

Tiberius's paranoia grew so great that he spent the last eleven years of his reign on Capraea (Capri), an island that had only one landing beach, the rest of the coast being sheer cliffs surrounded by deep water. One day a proud fisherman, hoping to win the emperor's favor, scaled a cliff in order to present the emperor with the giant mullet he had caught that day. When the fisherman emerged up the cliff and strode toward Tiberius, the emperor panicked, and then, in anger, ordered his guards to rub the fisherman's face with the mullet, which skinned it raw. When the man shouted in agony, "Thank heaven I did not bring Caesar that huge crab I also caught!" Tiberius sent for the crab and had it applied in the same way.

While Tiberius was hiding from potential assassins (and molesting little boys, by one account) on Capraea, his administration languished under the cruel and arrogant direction of Lucius Aelius Sejanus, prefect of the Praetorian Guard. Sejanus concentrated the guardsmen, whom Augustus had wisely dispersed around various Italian towns, in a single base in Rome.

In 31, when Tiberius became suspicious of Sejanus (who was, indeed, plotting against the emperor), he ordered Macro, one of Sejanus's subordinates, to arrest him for treason. Sejanus was strangled to death in prison, his body was torn to pieces by a mob, and Macro assumed his post. Sejanus's family and supporters were put to death as well.

His paranoia now heightened by Sejanus's plot, Tiberius executed other citizens, including children. Since Roman tradition prohibited the strangling of virgins, executioners violated little girls before killing them. Informers were rewarded with one-quarter of the confiscated estates of the persons on whom they informed, and an informer's word was almost always believed. Many victims committed suicide rather than go through the charade of one of Tiberius's show trials. No one was allowed to mourn for the victims (an old lady was executed for grieving publicly for her son), and victims were denied decent burials, their corpses dragged down to the Tiber by hooks and tossed into the river. Two minor poets were executed for their attacks on Tiberius. One historian was executed for calling Brutus and Cassius "the last of the Romans," a reference Tiberius interpreted as an invitation to regicide, and his history was publicly burned.

Some Romans remarked that Tiberius's cruelty continued even after his death. On the day that Tiberius passed away, in 37, certain individuals were scheduled to be executed. Even after the news of Tiberius's death had arrived, none of his timid and terrified officials dared take the responsibility for revoking the orders of execution. Hence the executions went forward. The people were so furious they attempted to seize the emperor's body and hurl it into the river, shouting, "Tiberius to the Tiber!" But the Praetorian Guard protected his body, which was cremated and given the proper honors.

Caligula (37–41)

Romans rejoiced when Tiberius's grandnephew and adopted son, Gaius, succeeded him. Gaius's biological father (Tiberius's nephew) Germanicus, a handsome, courageous, kind-hearted, and pious general, had been the most beloved man in Rome. It was Germanicus's soldiers who had given little Gaius his nickname Caligula (Little Boot), since, as a small boy traveling with his father and the army, Gaius had worn a miniature version of the Roman soldier's uniform. (Unfortunately, the soldiers spoiled the child rotten, perhaps contributing to his egomania.) The Roman people were overjoyed at the prospect of being ruled by "a son of Germanicus."

At first, their confidence seemed justified. Not yet twenty-five when he took the throne, Caligula released Tiberius's political prisoners and gave financial aid to those whose houses had been damaged by fire.

But then, perhaps as the result of a severe fever six months into his reign, Caligula appears to have gone insane. He began to insist that Romans worship him as a god. (The Senate had formally recognized Caesar and Augustus as gods, but only after their deaths.) Caligula was heard conversing loudly with Jupiter, the greatest of the Roman gods, and even ordering him about. He decapitated all of the statues of the gods and goddesses in Rome and replaced their heads with his own. He married one sister and had incestuous relations with all three at parties. At such gatherings he also examined every man's wife carefully and selected one for sex, returning afterwards to comment in detail on her performance. He made top officials run for miles, dressed in their togas, alongside his chariot. For his amusement he pitted decrepit old men against equally decrepit wild animals, or people with disabilities against one another, at gladiatorial contests. When butcher meat for the wild animals proved too expensive, he fed them criminals. When a crowd at the races cheered for the team he opposed, he cried, "I wish all you Romans had only one neck!" Once, at a banquet, he suddenly erupted in peals of laughter. When the two consuls seated beside him asked politely if he would share the joke, he replied, "It occurred to me that I have only to give one nod and both your throats will be cut on the spot!" He gave his favorite horse a jeweled collar, a furnished house, slaves, a marble stable that outshone the nearby Senate building, and troops to maintain absolute silence around the stable while the horse slept. He even planned to make the horse a consul. A balding man, he became enraged at the sight of handsome men with full heads of hair and would often order the backs of their scalps shaved. He often dressed as a woman (sometimes as Venus) and practiced horrible grimaces before a mirror. He once summoned three senators, half-dead with fear, to the palace at midnight. They were escorted to a stage, where Caligula suddenly burst out, dressed in an unusual outfit, began to sing and dance to the accompaniment of flutes, and then departed, leaving the senators more baffled and appalled than when they had arrived. He once prepared to invade Britain in order to accomplish what Julius Caesar had not, but lacking the courage required in a military operation, he halted the soldiers on the French coast and ordered them to gather seashells, which he then returned to Rome as "plunder from the ocean."

Disdaining the long hours of administrative work his office required, work he considered beneath a god, Caligula devoted his time to lavish entertainment. Having exhausted the vast treasury left by the frugal Tiberius on palaces and other grand (often ludicrous) projects, Caligula forced many aristocrats to declare him their heir and then killed them. He pressured others into bidding ridiculous amounts they could not afford at palace furniture auctions. Everyone and everything was taxed. Caligula also established a state brothel at which even boys and married women were required to work.

Some Romans began to suspect that Tiberius had been killed by Macro, prefect of the Praetorian Guard, with Caligula's approval. According to one account, after Tiberius fainted, Caligula falsely assumed he was dead. Caligula then removed the imperial ring from Tiberius's finger and accepted the congratulations of a group of senatorial sycophants. When someone announced that the emperor had revived, the sycophants scattered in panic and Caligula stood paralyzed with fear. At this point, Macro saved the day for Caligula by smothering Tiberius with a pillow. By this act, Macro won Caligula's gratitude, though no one ever possessed it long; Caligula later ordered Macro's execution. If this account of Tiberius's death is accurate, the manner of his demise may have constituted poetic justice, since the bitter Tiberius had allegedly made Caligula his heir as a kind of cruel joke on the Rome he had grown to hate, sneering, "I am nursing a viper for the Roman people."

In 41, officers of Caligula's own Praetorian Guard killed him. In an offhand remark, he had accused two of its commanders of plotting against him. Fearful, the commanders had begun to plot in earnest. One of the officers (ironically, a descendant of Cassius, Caesar's assassin) was all the more anxious to kill the emperor because Caligula had repeatedly humiliated him by giving him passwords that made him look ridiculous. The commanders and their fellow assassins killed Caligula as he left the Palatine Games at about noon. They stabbed him thirty-one times, eight more wounds than Caesar had received. Arriving late, Caligula's guards killed several assassins and a few innocent senators. Searching the palace, they then found Claudius, Caligula's fifty-year-old uncle (Germanicus's brother) and one of the few surviving members of the imperial family, trembling behind drapes. They proclaimed him emperor.

Claudius (41–54)

Because of a speech impediment, a tendency to drool, a facial tic, and a limp, Claudius had long been considered an idiot. (Like many other peoples, the Romans equated physical disabilities with mental incompetence and associated both with a divine curse. The Romans greatly valued physical toughness in males.) Even the kindly old Augustus would not sit next to Claudius at the games. Caligula had kept his Uncle Claudius around the palace to serve as the butt of his jokes and had once ordered him thrown into the Rhine fully clothed. Ironically, the widespread perception of Claudius as an idiot may have saved him from the numerous executions and assassinations that had claimed the rest of the Julio-Claudian males, thereby allowing him to become emperor by default.

After Caligula's assassination, the Praetorian Guard proclaimed Claudius emperor against the wishes of many senators, who wanted to restore the republic. Evidently, the senators were willing to be ruled by a madman but not by an idiot. The soldiers of the Praetorian Guard, who preferred their lucrative and comfortable lifestyle protecting emperors in Rome to fighting barbarians on the frontier, required an emperor to guard. The average guardsman received three times the pay of the common soldier.

Nero (54–68)

Claudius's fairly competent administration of the empire, which included the conquest of southern Britain, ended when his fourth wife, Agrippina the Younger—who was also his niece, the daughter of Germanicus—poisoned his mushrooms in 54, so that Nero, her son by a previous marriage, would become emperor. Nero was Agrippina's son by Gnaeus Ahenobarbus. Ahenobarbus was allegedly so cruel he once deliberately whipped his horses and ran over and killed a boy while passing through a village. He also gouged out the eye of an eques who criticized him in the Forum. But at least he was shrewd and honest: he once declared that any child born to himself and Agrippina was bound to have a detestable nature and become a public menace.

Claudius had adopted Nero, thereby placing him ahead of his own son Britannicus, who was almost four years younger, in the imperial succession. Like most emperors who did not murder an inordinate number of people, Claudius was later deified, prompting Nero to joke that mushrooms were "the food of the gods."

Only sixteen when he took the throne (is there anything more frightening than a teenage emperor?), Nero poisoned Britannicus within a year and buried him without ceremony. (There is probably no substance to the legend that when Nero first became emperor he was so softhearted he wept on having to sign a death warrant, saying, "I wish I had never learned to write.") Nero then tried to poison his overbearing mother three times, supposedly in retaliation for her opposition to his second marriage, but each time Agrippina learned of the attempt and took the antidote beforehand. Nero then rigged her bedroom ceiling to collapse, but she learned of that plot as well. He then had the ship aboard which she was cruising the Adriatic sabotaged so that it would fall apart at sea. The crew drowned, but she swam ashore. Not realizing that the disaster was the result of a murder plot, one of Agrippina's panic-stricken friends cried out, "Help me! I'm Agrippina, mother of the emperor!" Hearing this, several sailors involved in the plot began to smash the woman in the head with a pole and with anything else immediately available, thereby killing her.

Finally, in 59, Nero took the direct approach with his mother. He accused her of treason and had her killed by two soldiers. One clubbed her in the head. When the other moved to stab her with a sword, she cried, "Here," pointing to the womb that had borne so ungrateful a son. Nero's only comment on seeing his dead mother was that she had a nice figure. Some Romans believed that there had been incest between the two, initiated by Agrippina for the purpose of maintaining power over her growing son.

Nero also killed his aunt for her money, had his first wife executed on a false charge of adultery, kicked his second wife to death while she was pregnant for complaining when he came home late from the races, and killed his third wife's husband in order to marry her. He even drowned his stepson, a mere boy, for playing at being emperor.

But Nero was perhaps hated and feared most for his notorious concerts, at which he played the lyre and sang. Attendance at these concerts was mandatory, and no one was allowed to leave them for any reason before they were finished, though Nero sometimes sang for hours. At his first concert, Nero even disregarded an earthquake that shook the whole theater, singing to the bitter end. Women gave birth in the concert halls at some of Nero's performances. Others feigned death in order to be carried out. Some men even jumped down from the rear walls, risking disability or death in their desperation to escape Nero's caterwauling. Not surprisingly, he was showered with all sorts of undeserved musical awards, yet remained so envious of all previous award winners he had their statues taken down and hurled into public lavatories, no doubt surprising those using the facilities. In Nero's defense, he did make one contribution to the arts that more than compensated for his crimes against music: he expelled all of the mimes from Rome.

Nero often prowled the streets of Rome at night, in disguise, attacking people and committing robberies. While in disguise, he was once almost beaten to death by a senator whose wife he had molested on one of these adventures. He once raped a Vestal Virgin. He had a youth castrated and took him for his bride at a marriage ceremony, prompting Romans to joke that the world would have been a better place had Nero's father taken such a bride. Nero never wore the same clothes twice and traveled with a vast train of carriages pulled by mules shod with silver.

In 64, two-thirds of Rome burned in a fire that lasted six days. Contrary to popular myth, Nero could not have been playing the fiddle while Rome burned, since that instrument was not invented until many centuries later. This legend probably arose from the equally dubious, contemporary rumor that he had been watching the flames from the Tower of Macenas while singing his own wretched poem, "The Sack of Troy." In truth, Nero was at Antium when the fire started. Rushing back to Rome, he provided temporary housing and low-cost food to victims of the fire. But Nero also falsely charged that Christians had started the fire and executed them in a grisly fashion.

Discontented with Augustus's modest abode, Nero then constructed a vast and gaudy palace called the Domus Aurea (Golden House). Adjoined by lakes and filled with gold, precious gems, and ivory, the palace featured a 120-foot statue of Nero as the sun god, hidden perfume sprinklers, and a revolving dome that showered flowers on diners below. When the gigantic palace was completed, Nero deadpanned: "Good, at last I can begin to live like a human being!"

The ostentatious palace fueled rumors that Nero himself had ordered Rome burned so that he could rebuild it to his own glory and rename it "Neropolis." Some Romans alleged that on the night of the fire, men who claimed to be acting on orders had been seen throwing torches and preventing others from extinguishing the fire.

The extravagance of Nero and his friends led to higher taxes, the devaluation of the coinage, and the quasi-judicial fleecing of rich victims. Nero told one magistrate: "You know my needs! Let us see to it that nobody is left with anything." He even stripped temples and melted down their images.

When Nero began to hint that he intended to kill all the senators, their fear finally got the better of their cowardice. By 65, the Senate, the Praetorian Guard, some military leaders, and perhaps even Nero's former tutor, the Stoic philosopher Seneca, were all conspiring against the emperor. Discovering the plot, Nero forced many of the conspirators, including Seneca, to commit suicide. Nero frequently added insult to injury by ridiculing the faces of his victims when their heads were brought to him. While holding the head of one victim in his hands and staring into his face, he said, "How could I have been afraid of a man with such a long nose?" Free speech was in such short supply during Nero's reign that Pliny the Elder decided to assemble a dictionary, since it was the only type of literary work he could think of that would not get him executed.

In 67, Nero put aside his toy chariots, made of ivory, and decided to enter the Olympic chariot race, despite the fact that he was no athlete but an effeminate man with carefully coifed blond hair and sideburns. The Olympic Games were not scheduled for that year but they were held anyway, so that the emperor could compete. Although Nero fell from his chariot and never finished the race, the judges wisely awarded him the victory. For their unorthodox interpretation of the race rules, the judges were rewarded with Roman citizenship and hard cash. Indeed, Nero won 1,808 first prizes at the Olympics that year, including several for competitions in which he did not compete.

By 68, Roman armies in Gaul, Spain, Armenia, Britain, and Judea were in revolt. (On hearing of the initial revolt in Gaul, Nero was upset only that the rebellious commander had called him a bad lyre player.) A multitude of troops now marched on Rome. Nero tried to recruit a loyal army, but no volunteers came forward. His maids even absconded with his bed linen. On one of the emperor's statues someone scrawled a reference to his phony victories in a host of musical and athletic contests: "This is a real contest for once, and you are going to lose!" After the Senate condemned Nero to death by flogging, he sighed, "What a great artist the world is losing!" and stabbed himself in the throat.

THE LEGACY OF AUGUSTUS

While it is true that the mild and capable administration of Augustus proved crucial to Roman acceptance of the imperial system of government, thereby making possible the reigns of Caligula and Nero, it is also true that Greco-Roman civilization might have been exterminated by a further succession of civil wars if not for Augustus. The peace, prosperity, and order he restored to Rome, a civilization that had been thoroughly exhausted and demoralized by a full century of chaos and violence, were vital to the survival of that civilization and, hence, to the eventual shape of Western civilization.

PAV LVS

IACO BVS

11

✝

Paul of Tarsus:
Christian Evangelist

Though Saul Paulus of Tarsus was a Jew who wrote in Greek, he was also a Roman citizen. Not only does Paul's Roman citizenship qualify him to be one of the twelve Greeks and Romans discussed in this book, but it also serves as a good illustration of the Romans' uncommon willingness to incorporate people of diverse cultures into their empire. Other than Jesus Himself, no person was more crucial to the survival of Christianity and to its eventual conquest of the Roman Empire than Paul. His evangelism to the Gentiles, which centered on the doctrine of justification by faith, allowed the new religion to spread rapidly throughout the vast empire. Furthermore, his eloquent epistles to various Christian churches and individuals came to comprise a sizable and important part of the New Testament, expounding Christian theology to future generations.

THE HEBREW PROPHETS AND THE MESSIAH

The Hebrew prophets (c. 850–500 B.C.) spoke often of the coming of a Messiah, who would lead the world into a golden age of peace and prosperity. In the late sixth century B.C., Isaiah predicted:

> A shoot shall come out from the stump of Jesse [King David's father], and a branch shall grow out of his roots. The spirit of the Lord shall rest on him, the spirit of wisdom and understanding. . . . With righteousness He shall judge the poor and with equity the meek of the earth. . . . The wolf shall live with the lamb, the leopard shall lie down with the kid. . . . On that day the root of Jesse shall stand as a signal to the peoples; the nations shall inquire of Him,

and His dwelling place shall be glorious. . . . Thus says the Lord God, "See, I am laying in Zion a foundation stone, a tested stone, a precious cornerstone." (11:1–2, 4, 6, 10; 28:16)

In a more famous phrase, now inscribed on the United Nations building, Micah prophesied concerning the golden age the Messiah would produce: "They shall beat their swords into plowshares and their spears into pruning brooks; nation shall not lift up sword against nation, neither shall they learn war any more" (4:3). Micah further predicted that the Messiah would be born in Bethlehem.

But perhaps the most influential of the messianic passages was Isaiah's discussion of the "Servant" in chapter 53. Referring to God's promise to Abraham, "In you all the families of the earth shall be blessed" (Gen. 12:3), Isaiah foretold the arrival of a "Servant" who would suffer for the sins of others. The work of the Servant would go far beyond Israel. Though imprisoned, tried, and killed as an innocent man, He would not cry out in bitterness or self-pity, but would voluntarily take the sins of others upon Himself and go to the slaughter as willingly as a lamb. Isaiah even implied that the Servant would be resurrected, an idea then alien to Judaic theology. Over five centuries later, Jesus began his ministry in Nazareth by reading these passages and announcing, to scandalized gasps: "Today this scripture has been fulfilled in your hearing" (Luke 4:21).

Equally significant to the development of Christianity was Jeremiah's prophecy of a "new covenant" between God and the Hebrew people (31:31–34) involving the forgiveness of sins and based more on a reformation of the heart than on an empty adherence to the laws found on the stone tablets in the Great Temple. Paul and other Christians later wrote that the new covenant had been fulfilled in Jesus, based on Jesus' statement at the Last Supper: "This is my blood of the new covenant" (Matt. 26:27). Jeremiah claimed that the new covenant must replace the Sinai Covenant between God and the Hebrew people, which had, in turn, replaced the original, private covenant between God and Abraham.

Christians would later claim that the Jews had rejected Jesus as their Messiah because they had failed to realize that the powerful Messiah and the suffering Servant were one and the same and that there were *two* comings of the Messiah. Jesus the Messiah had come first as the humble, suffering Servant who died for humanity's sins, but would come again as the powerful Messiah to judge and to rule the world.

JESUS

Jesus of Nazareth was probably born in or before what our medieval dating system inaccurately terms 4 B.C. He was born during the reign of King

Herod the Great, who, historians now believe, died in 4 B.C. From the biblical description of the shepherds out watching over their flocks, it is doubtful that Jesus was born in the winter. December 25, which was not celebrated as Christmas until the fourth century A.D., had been the birthday of Mithras, the god of a rival religion. (It is difficult to convert people to a new religion without allowing them to retain their traditional holidays.) The title "Christ" derives from the Greek *Christos* (Annointed One), and is a rough translation of the Hebrew *Messiah*.

After a three-year ministry, Jesus was crucified around A.D. 28–30. The moneylenders and the Pharisees, a sect of devout Jews whom Jesus had criticized, persuaded the Sanhedrin, the council responsible for local government, to arrest Him. Shocked by the blasphemy they perceived in Jesus' claim to divinity, but lacking the authority to execute Him, the Sanhedrin turned Jesus over to the Roman procurator Pontius Pilate for crucifixion. Most Jews expected the Messiah to be a military leader like King David, not a divine being equal to God, able to forgive sins, as Jesus frequently did. The Sanhedrin claimed that Jesus had proclaimed Himself "King of the Jews," a treasonable offense. Pilate reluctantly ordered the crucifixion.

Jesus' followers claimed that He rose from the dead and appeared to them before ascending into heaven. He promised to return one day, to judge humanity and to reign in peace and justice, first for a 1,000-year period, and then for all eternity.

PAUL (c. A.D. 1–67)

Christianity probably would have perished if not for the apostle Paul. His family, which was prosperous enough to have acquired Roman citizenship, had originated in the town of Gischala in Galilee but had moved to Tarsus in southeastern Asia Minor. After learning tent making from his father, Paul, an intelligent and spirited boy, had begun rabbinical training under Gamaliel I, one of the greatest rabbis of the day. A second-century account described Paul as having been short and bald, with crooked legs and a hooked nose, but also as having possessed "the face of an angel."

Like most Jews and like all of his fellow Pharisees, Paul initially considered the Christians blasphemers. In fact, he became a leading persecutor of them. Paul began imprisoning Christians on the authority of the chief priest and voting for their execution. The Jews who stoned Stephen, the first Christian martyr, laid their coats at Paul's feet for safekeeping, while he nodded approvingly. Interestingly, Gamaliel, Paul's mentor, opposed persecution of the Christians, arguing that if they were not of God, nothing would come of their teaching, and if they were of God, they should not be opposed.

On the road to Damascus, where Paul intended to help Jewish authorities uncover and arrest Christians, Paul saw a vision of Jesus, asking him, "Why do you persecute me?" Following his dramatic conversion to Christianity, Paul lived in the desert for three years, praying, reflecting on the implications of his vision, and reaching a new theological perspective based on a reinterpretation of Old Testament scriptures.

Paul then returned to Damascus, where he created a stir with his Christian preaching. His old allies among the Jews now wanted to kill him. They watched the gates daily to catch him in his attempt to escape the city. But one night his former enemies among the Christians, who were now his disciples, lowered him down in a large basket through an opening in the city wall.

Paul then journeyed to Jerusalem, where his preaching was received with equal violence from the Jewish leaders there. He returned to Tarsus, where he made tents for five or six years. He then spent a year as pastor of a growing Christian church in Antioch.

Against the outraged pleas of some Jewish Christians, who believed that Jesus' teachings were intended for Jews alone, Paul began preaching to the Gentiles of Asia Minor and Greece. Ironically, Roman peace and roads greatly facilitated Paul's mission.

Paul's decision to carry Christianity to the Gentiles was crucial, since the religion never flourished in Judea. Vital to Paul's success in converting Gentiles was his emphasis on the doctrine of justification (salvation) by faith, rather than through adherence to Mosaic law. Had Gentiles been forced to submit to painful adult circumcision and to the various Jewish dietary restrictions, few would have converted to Christianity.

Paul argued that Jesus' death, by paying the penalty for humanity's sins, had freed humankind from the yoke of the Mosaic law and had placed new importance on simple faith. The contract between God and humans had changed. God no longer demanded adherence to a complex and trying set of regulations and rituals. He now required only faith in Jesus. The law of Moses had served its purpose as a tutor, not only providing an ethical ideal, but also demonstrating the innate sinfulness of humans through their inability to keep it, thereby also proving the need for a Redeemer. In his crucifixion, Christ, who was without sin, became sin itself, offering Himself up as a sacrifice, so that whoever accepted Him might be held blameless before God. Through Adam's disobedience, sin had come into the world, bringing death in its train; through Christ's obedience, grace had come into the world, bringing with it the free gift of eternal life. While it was perfectly acceptable for Jewish Christians to continue to observe the Mosaic law, as Paul himself did, Gentiles were certainly not obliged to do so. Their faith in Jesus would result in an indwelling of the Holy Spirit, who would inspire them to follow the ethical teachings of Jesus, which were more than sufficient.

Peter, Jesus' chief apostle, agreed that Gentiles should be admitted into the church so long as they abstained from eating the meat of animals sacrificed in pagan rites and avoided fornication. He persuaded a synod of Christian leaders to endorse this viewpoint.

From about 46 to 58, Paul toured the eastern Mediterranean, preaching the gospel. In all, Paul traveled over 13,000 miles, much of it on foot through rugged terrain, sometimes at night. On his first missionary voyage, Paul was stoned nearly to death by a Jewish mob in Lystra. Though left for dead in a garbage heap, the determined evangelist reentered the city that evening. On his second journey, Paul was beaten with rods at Philippi. In his later years, he contracted malaria or some similar disease and lost much of his eyesight. Paul responded to all of these tribulations cheerfully, writing: "I consider that the sufferings of this present time are not worth comparing with the glory about to be revealed in us" (Rom. 8:18).

In every city, Paul began by preaching at the local synagogue, but was generally harassed by Jewish leaders, even to the point of being beaten, stoned, or imprisoned. Paul would then reach out to the local Gentiles, with whom he was generally more successful. Indeed, on his first missionary journey Paul converted Sergius Paulus, the Roman proconsul of Cyprus. It was then that Saul, encouraged by his success among the Gentiles, began to use his Greco-Roman name, Paul. Nevertheless, some Gentiles, such as the idol salesmen of Ephesus, were as hostile to his mission as were the Jewish leaders.

At around 58, Roman soldiers arrested Paul while he was in Jerusalem, after a group of irate Jews spotted him at the Great Temple. During the riot Paul was beaten severely and nearly lynched. He was imprisoned in Caesarea for two years by the procurator Felix, Pontius Pilate's successor, who refused to release Paul because he feared the Jewish reaction. Porcius Festus, Felix's successor, delayed Paul's release for the same reason.

Realizing that he was not going to be released, Paul demanded a hearing before the emperor's court at Rome, a privilege guaranteed by his Roman citizenship. No doubt relieved to have the matter taken out of his hands, Festus replied: "You have appealed to Caesar; to Caesar you shall go."

After an arduous journey, during which he was shipwrecked on the island of Malta for three months, Paul was placed under house arrest in Rome for another two years. During this time, he was manacled to a Roman soldier but allowed to receive visitors. This opportunity allowed him to build up the church in Rome. After his release, Paul preached in the capital and elsewhere.

At around 67, perhaps as part of Nero's campaign against the Christians, Paul was again arrested. This time he slept alone on the cold, dark floor of the Mamertine Prison. Spared crucifixion because of his Roman citizenship, Paul was beheaded. While awaiting execution, Paul wrote: "I am already on the point of being sacrificed; the time of my departure has come. I have fought the good fight, I have finished the race, I have kept the faith. Henceforth there is laid up for me the crown of righteousness, which the Lord, the righteous judge, will award to me on that day, and not only to me but to all who have loved his appearing. . . . To Him be the glory for ever and ever. Amen" (2 Tim. 4:6–8, 18).

Lacking the benefit of Roman citizenship, Peter was crucified shortly thereafter. Feeling unworthy to die in the same manner as Jesus, Peter asked to be crucified upside down.

THE TRIUMPH OF CHRISTIANITY

The work begun by Paul bore fruit. By the middle of the third century, Christianity was the fastest growing religion in the Roman Empire. It had spread from its original home in Judea to Syria, Asia Minor, Greece, Italy, France, Britain, North Africa, and Spain, and even beyond the bounds of the empire into Armenia and Ethiopia.

In 313, Constantine's Edict of Milan reversed two and a half centuries of imperial policy, granting toleration to Christians throughout the Roman world. Constantine was the first openly Christian emperor, though he did not accept baptism until lying on his deathbed. Constantine related that he and his troops had seen a cross in the noonday sun, inscribed with the words, "By this, conquer." That night he dreamed that Christ visited him, bearing the same symbol, and commanded him to use its likeness in his engagement with Maxentius. The next day, Constantine's rival for the throne Maxentius left the bastion of Rome and attacked Constantine with a larger force at Milvian Bridge.

Constantine's victory (312) changed history. The Christian emperor lavished subsidies on the church and exempted it from taxes. He built magnificent churches, made Sunday (the Christian Sabbath, the day of Jesus' resurrection) a holiday, exempted the Christian clergy from taxes and military service, repealed Augustus's laws penalizing the unmarried and childless (to the benefit of Christian celibates), granted citizens the right to appeal the decisions of civil and military courts to Christian bishops, and gave funds to Christian churches to support widows and orphans. He employed Christian bishops in his army units, the first known instance of the use of military chaplains. His soldiers' helmets, shields, and banners were all emblazoned with the cross. He forbade the use of his image in pagan temples, and medals depicted him in a posture of Christian devotion. He prohibited crucifixion and gladiatorial contests, two methods by which Christians had been executed, though gladiatorial contests continued to reappear for nearly another century. In the century after Constantine, imperial patronage helped increase the number of Christians from an estimated 5 million to 30 million.

In 392, the emperor Theodosius I proclaimed Christianity the state religion of Rome. Considering paganism the worship of demons, Theodosius prohibited pagan sacrifices and the worship of idols, closed some pagan temples, and allowed others to be converted to Christian use. The emperor also discontinued the Olympics, which had always served as a festival for the Greco-Roman gods and whose nudity offended some Christians. Although the emperor did not remove pagans from schools, the army, the Senate, or even the palace, the elimination of pagan public worship doomed an already feeble religion. Within three decades of Theodosius's death, the pagan religions were virtually extinct.

OTHER REASONS FOR THE SUCCESS OF CHRISTIANITY

While Paul's message to the Gentiles of justification by faith in Jesus was absolutely essential to the survival and eventual triumph of Christianity, there were many other reasons for the success of Christianity. Both Christianity's similarities and its differences with its competitors contributed to its eventual triumph.

Christianity struck a resonant chord with the large numbers of Roman subjects who adhered to some form of classical philosophy, particularly Stoicism. Unlike traditional Greco-Roman religion, both Christianity and Stoicism concentrated divinity into a single, powerful entity (in the Stoics' case, the World Soul), a reassuring concept in an era characterized by division, uncertainty, and powerlessness. By the second century, even most pagans had come to believe that the Greco-Roman gods were nothing more than the mediating spirits of a universal organizing principle.

Christians and Stoics (as well as the followers of Mithras and Isis) also shared a belief in the immortality of the soul. This was a great consolation at a time, during the late imperial period, when barbarian invasions, bloody civil wars, despotism, and recurrent epidemics severely limited life expectancy.

Many early Christians also believed in a form of predestination similar to Stoic fate, an important source of solace. During a period in which terrible things happened to good people every day, it was consoling to think that such suffering was a necessary part of a grand scheme.

Like the Stoics, Christians emphasized spiritual equality, at a time when crippling taxation and hyperinflation were impoverishing the empire and destroying the middle class, and when the courts increasingly favored the wealthy over the poor. While most contemporary religions reflected the social hierarchy, aristocrats sat as equals with manual laborers, slaves, former criminals, and other outcasts in Christian churches. Jesus Himself had been the son of a carpenter, and Paul had written: "There is no longer Jew or Greek, there is no longer slave or free, there is no longer male or female; for all of you are one in Christ Jesus" (Gal. 3:28). Although a hierarchy gradually developed within the early Church, the talented poor could rise within it.

The Christian belief in spiritual equality increased the religion's appeal to the rootless multitudes of great cities like Rome, Antioch, and Alexandria—that is, to those people most alienated from Roman society and most accessible to new ideas. Christianity was especially popular among the lower middle class and the free poor, meaning those with something to lose and in the process of losing it.

Christianity was also popular among women, who constituted a solid majority of early church members. Aristocratic Christian women gladly introduced the religion to their influential husbands, since its tenets reached even beyond Stoic egalitarianism, teaching that women were equal to men in God's eyes, that husbands should treat their wives with consideration, and that adultery was as serious a sin in a husband as in a wife. In sharp contrast to classical biographers, who focused exclusively on political and military affairs, areas of life from which women were excluded, Christian authors included female saints in their hagiography.

Slaves were also drawn to Christianity by its egalitarianism. The treasuries of Christian churches were often used to finance the manumission of slaves who were prisoners of war (a considerable number). Several emancipated slaves became bishops. The Church contradicted Roman law in recognizing marriages between free and slave. Constantine prohibited the sale of slaves away from their family members. Though Aelius Aristides' charge that Christians "show their impiety as you would expect them to, by having no respect for their betters" was more than a bit exaggerated, it expressed the outrage of aristocratic pagans at the greater degree of egalitarianism among early Christians.

But although Christianity's similarities with Stoicism and other forms of classical idealism were important to its success, its differences were equally crucial. First, the Christian faith was based on a historical figure. While Stoicism, Neoplatonism, and many other philosophies of the day were too abstract for most people, Christianity was based on a real man who had walked the earth, who had loved, and who had suffered and died. Christian theologians like Justin Martyr portrayed Jesus as the bridge that joined Plato's world of the forms with his world of the senses, the spiritual with the material.

Of course, the dual nature of Jesus as both man and God created theological problems as well. To some, the Holy Trinity of God, Jesus, and the

Holy Spirit conflicted with Hebrew monotheism. In 325, a council of bishops at Nicaea in Asia Minor upheld the Trinity over the doctrine of Arius that both Jesus and the Holy Spirit were creations of God, different in substance from Him, a doctrine that contradicted the apostle John's statement concerning Jesus: "In the beginning was the Word, and the Word was with God, and the Word was God. . . . And the Word became flesh and dwelt among us" (1:1, 14). The council declared Jesus and the Holy Spirit equal members of the Trinity and of the same substance as God. In 381, another council, at Constantinople, reaffirmed and strengthened the Nicene Creed. Although the Arian doctrine was banned as heresy, it made repeated appearances throughout Western history. Other Christians, including many Gnostics, attacked the Trinity from the other side, slighting or denying many of Jesus' human traits, a heresy that was condemned by the Council of Chalcedon in 451.

But many early converts were attracted to Christianity by the combination of humanity and divinity joined in Jesus. The Trinity seemed to represent the three greatest manifestations of God's love for humanity: creation, redemption, and inspiration. While Christ had made God visible to the world during His lifetime, the Holy Spirit, dwelling in the hearts of individual believers, made God visible in the centuries after Jesus' death and resurrection.

Second, early Christians evoked both sympathy and fascination by their willingness, even eagerness, to suffer persecution and death for their faith, a trait that originated in the conviction that a far better and more permanent world awaited them. Viewing Christians as dangerous traitors whose attack on Roman religion constituted a masked assault on the Roman state itself, Nero charged Christians with the burning of Rome in 64, executing women and children as well as men. While the "Five Good Emperors" of the second century ordered their proconsuls not to seek out Christians for arrest, they instructed them to execute those charged and convicted of being Christians. In 177, the entire Christian communities of Lyons and Vienne were tortured to death. The emperors Decius (249–251), Valerian (257–258), Diocletian (303–305), Galerius (305–311), and Maximin (311–313) launched even more vigorous campaigns of persecution. Soldiers burned an entire Christian town in Phrygia. Churches were destroyed, copies of Scripture were burned, and Christians were imprisoned, mutilated, beaten, tortured, drowned, branded, decapitated, hanged, and starved to death. Searching out, arresting, and killing all the Christians he could, Diocletian declared his intention to end Christianity. Maximin even offered tax exemptions to cities that demonstrated a willingness to persecute Christians.

Christian courage amid persecution transformed pagan opinion of them. Initially, most pagans feared and despised Christians, considering them an upstart cult of bizarre and rebellious Jews, slaves, and other rabble who worshipped a crucified criminal, plotted treason (at secret meetings where they preached the fall of the Roman Empire and the rise of a new king), practiced black magic and cannibalism (a misunderstanding of the Eucharist), engaged in orgies and infanticide (why else did meetings occur secretly and in the evening?), and endangered the unity and safety of the state by dividing families and by refusing to worship the gods (who responded by sending droughts). Others denounced Christians to get their property. Nevertheless, accustomed to broad latitude in religious matters, many Romans were horrified by the persecution of Christians. Even Tacitus, who detested the Christians, denounced Nero's treatment of them. He noted that the emperor's scapegoating of the Christians had backfired: "Their deaths were made farcical. Dressed in wild animal skins, they were torn to pieces by dogs, or crucified, or made into torches to be ignited after dark. . . . Nero provided his Gardens for the spectacle, and exhibited displays in the Circus. . . . Despite their guilt as Christians, and the ruthless punishment it deserved, the victims were pitied. For it was felt they were being sacrificed to one man's brutality rather than to the national interest." Even leading Stoic and Neoplatonic critics of Christianity, like Epictetus, Marcus Aurelius, Galen, and Celsus, were impressed by the courage of Christians. Though he had heard that Christians were cannibals, the pagan Justin Martyr nevertheless became so convinced by their courage that they possessed supernatural power he converted to the religion and became one of its leaders. Tertullian, a converted North African, summarized the effect of persecution: "The more we are mowed down by you, the more we will multiply. The blood of Christians is seed!" As the historian E. R. Dodds aptly put it: "Christianity . . . was judged to be worth living for because it was seen to be worth dying for. . . . We know from modern experience of political martyrdoms that the blood of the martyrs really is the seed of the Church, always provided that the seed falls on suitable ground and is not sown too thickly. But pagan martyrs under Christian rule were relatively few—not because Christianity was more tolerant, but because paganism was by then too poor a thing to be worth a life."

Third, capable Christian leaders attracted numerous followers. Jerome of Dalmatia (340–420) wrote an excellent history of the early church. He also spent eighteen years in isolation in Bethlehem translating the Old Testament and the Gospels into Latin, an essential tool in attracting Roman converts. Based largely on Jerome's work, the Vulgate Bible became the standard Bible for over a millennium. Jerome's 154 letters, written over a period of 50 years, exhibited a remarkable breadth of knowledge and a rare satirical wit.

Ambrose (340–397), a former governor of Liguria and the bishop of Milan, was an organizational and administrative genius, an adviser to emperors, and a man of great conviction and courage. In 390, he won the respect of both Christians and non-Christians by excommunicating the emperor Theodosius I after he massacred thousands of Thessalonicans in retribution for their murder of a couple of Roman officers. Ambrose not only refused to hold Mass in Theodosius's presence until he had performed a public penance, but personally barred the emperor's entry into the cathedral. Ambrose also excited his congregation by chanting the psalms to the tune of new eastern melodies. Ambrose's prize convert, Augustine of Hippo (354–430), the greatest intellect of the late empire and the early Church, will be discussed in the next chapter.

Fourth, the Christians were well organized. By the 50s, some local churches were organized under *deacons* (those who serve), who collected and redistributed alms, and *presbyters* (elders, the forerunners of priests), who provided religious instruction and discipline. When towns had more than one church, congregations were joined together in dioceses under *episkopoi* (bishops), a pattern modeled on Roman civil administration. Initially, the laity of each diocese elected their own bishop, though at least three bishops from neighboring dioceses had to agree to consecrate them.

By the fourth century, the life-tenured bishops had taken control of the selection process. As successors to the apostles, they were believed to have the power "to bind and loose sins" and, hence, to deny the Eucharist to the ethically or doctrinally impure. They could appoint and suspend deacons and elders and could excommunicate members of their congregations, the equivalent of a sentence of damnation.

Until the eleventh century, bishops were largely independent of the formal authority, if not the considerable influence, of the bishop of Rome—the "pope" (from *papa* [father])—though the need for centralization amid the collapse of the empire encouraged Pope Leo I (440–461) to advance the Petrine theory. First proposed by Clement around 100, this theory held that the rightful leadership of the Church belonged to the bishop of Rome, who was the heir of Peter, whom Jesus had called "the rock on which I will build my church." The doctrine had gained momentum during the fourth century, when some Christians believed the Arian controversy revealed the need for greater standardization of church doctrine through the centralization of authority.

Fifth, Christianity was based on a profoundly eloquent written work. The books of the New Testament were written from 50 to 100. By the end of the second century, the New Testament canon had gradually coalesced from among various rival works, a selection process based on the age of the books and on the degree to which they conformed to what were considered the teachings of Jesus' first followers. The Gospels of Matthew and John were selected because they had been two of Jesus' apostles, the Gospels of Mark and Luke because they had worked under Paul. As the historian Henry Chadwick put it: "The truly astonishing thing is that so great a measure of agreement was reached so quickly." In 367, Athanasius, the bishop of Alexandria, commanded the acceptance of twenty-seven books of the New Testament and no others. Ecclesiastical councils endorsed his list in 393 and 397. Against modern speculations to the contrary, the historian Paul K. Conkin concludes: "It now seems almost certain (on none of these issues can anyone be fully certain) that three and possibly all four canonical gospels were written before 100 C.E., that the churches early accepted them as genuine, that the received and critically compared texts are very close to the originals, that the authors were probably directly influenced by the apostles . . . and that other early, competing, largely Gnostic-influenced gospels had much weaker credentials on strict scholarly grounds."

The New Testament was simple yet profound. Written in plain but powerful Greek, it was one of the few works not written by aristocrats for aristocrats. The New Testament was written simply enough that the illiterate members of a congregation could readily understand it when read by the literate members. Yet, its wisdom was profound enough to dazzle intellectuals like Augustine, who wrote concerning it: "While readily available to all men, it yet kept the grandeur of its mystery under a more profound sense; by clear language and simple style making itself available to all men, yet exercising the intent study of those who are not light-minded." One of the most intriguing passages of Augustine's *Confessions* is his account of his initial dismissal of the Scriptures as inferior to the works of Cicero and other classical philosophers, an attitude he claimed revealed more concerning his own arrogance and folly—his unwillingness to learn from the humble Jesus—than concerning the Bible. Like most proud intellectuals, Augustine had assumed that works were profound precisely to the extent that their style rendered them inaccessible to the masses. But, on closer inspection, he had found that the Scriptures contained all the truths of the classical philosophers without any of the errors—and with the added benefit of the salvation conferred only by Jesus. Regarding classical works, Augustine concluded:

> Those pages do not show the countenance of piety, the tears of confession, Thy sacrifice, a troubled spirit, a contrite and humble heart, the salvation of a people, the promised city, the promise of the Holy Spirit, or the chalice of our redemption. . . . It is one thing to see from a wooded mountain top, the land of peace, and not to find the way to it, and to push in vain over tractless country . . . and it is quite another thing to keep the way which leads there, which is made safe by the care of the heavenly Commander.

Classical texts had shown Augustine the beauty of virtue and a vision of peace, but, in so doing, had only left him frustrated at his inability to attain these goods. It was the simple yet profound Scriptures, so denigrated by foolish intellectuals, that had shown him the path to salvation.

Jesus' well-chosen metaphors were particularly effective in conveying the full meaning of God's love to the ancient world's multitude of farmers and shepherds. In explaining the need for His own death, Jesus said: "Unless a grain of wheat falls into the earth and dies, it remains just a single grain; but if it dies, it bears much fruit" (John 12:24). In depicting His love for humankind. Jesus said: "I am the good shepherd. The good shepherd lays down his life for the sheep" (John 10:11). In portraying the love of God for lost sinners, Jesus said:

> Which one of you, having one hundred sheep and losing one of them, does not leave the ninety-nine in the wilderness and go after the one he lost until he finds it? When he has found it, he lays it on his shoulders and rejoices. And when he comes home, he calls together his friends and neighbors, saying to them, "Rejoice with me, for I have found my sheep that was lost." Just so, I tell you, there will be more joy in heaven over one sinner who repents than over ninety-nine righteous persons who need no repentance. (Luke 15:4–7)

Filled with such treasures, the New Testament conquered the Roman Empire.

Perhaps most importantly, Christianity was the first religion to place love at its center. While previous religions had certainly included love in their theology, no other religion had made it the chief obligation of its adherents. Jesus claimed that the Ten Commandments could be summarized in two statements: love God with your whole heart, soul, and mind, and love your neighbor as yourself (Matt. 22:37–39).

Love is the only theme that runs through every book of the New Testament. In a famous passage, Jesus declared: "For God so loved the world He gave his only Son, so that everyone who believes in Him may not perish but may have eternal life" (John 3:16). John also wrote: "Whoever does not love does not know God, for God is love. . . . Beloved, since God loved us so much, we also ought to love one another" (1 John 4:8, 11). Paul wrote: "What can separate us from the love of God? I am convinced that neither death, nor life, nor angels, nor rulers, nor things present, nor things to come, nor powers, nor height, nor depth, nor anything else in all creation will be able to separate us from the love of God in Christ Jesus our Lord" (Rom. 8:38). Paul added: "The commandments . . . are summed up in this sentence, 'Love your neighbor as yourself.' Love does no wrong to a neighbor; therefore love is the fulfilling of the law" (Rom. 13:9–10). He also wrote:

> If I speak in the tongues of mortals and angels, but do not have love, I am a noisy gong or clanging cymbal. And if I have prophetic powers, or understand all mysteries and all knowledge, and if I have all faith, so as to remove

mountains, but do not have love, I am nothing. If I give away all my possessions, and if I hand over my body to be burned, but do not have love, I gain
nothing. Love is patient; love is kind; love is not envious or boastful or arrogant
or rude. It does not insist on its way; it is not irritable or resentful; it does not rejoice in wrongdoing, but rejoices in the truth. . . . There remain but three things:
faith, hope, and love; and the greatest of these is love. (1 Cor. 13:1–3, 13)

Augustine wrote: "Let them all mark themselves with the sign of the
cross, let them all say Amen, sing Hallelujah, let them all be baptized, go
to church and build basilicas—there is nothing which distinguishes the
children of God from the children of the devil but only love." A pleasant
and universal emotion, love has proved an excellent basis for religion—
and not just in the brutal days of the late Roman Empire.

Christianity possessed a sense of warmth and benevolence absent from
the cold duties of Stoicism and the other classical philosophies. Although the
Christian duty to love one's neighbor was far more difficult to obey than
the classical obligation to merely avoid injuring others, the former duty was
far more emotionally fulfilling. Paragons of classical virtue were admirable
fellows in many ways: honest, hard-working, and self-disciplined—men of
iron integrity, near gods by the standards of their day. But there was little in
them to touch the heart. The classical ethic was justice, not love or mercy.
Men like Cato the Elder would not fail to give others their due. But they
would not smile while doing so and would not give an ounce more. And one
could be certain that they would insist on their own, and would defend it
with a righteous violence if necessary.

By contrast, converting to Christianity meant joining a family that offered physical, economic, and emotional support in an exceedingly troubled time. Early Christians shared their wealth freely with widows, orphans, the elderly, the unemployed, the disabled, and the ill. They placed
their lives at grave risk caring for victims of the plague and other natural
disasters, while pagans fled. They ransomed one another from barbarian
captors, distributed bread during famines, and visited prisoners and min-
ers, the most wretched of all slaves. One group of Christians in Rome even
sold themselves into slavery to raise the money to ransom their brethren
from prison. They provided for the burial of the poor and were hospitable
to travelers. Even the hostile emperor whom the Christians called "Julian
the Apostate" complained: "These godless Galileans feed not only their
own poor but others, while we neglect our own." The Christian sense of
community, reinforced by common rites, a common way of life, and the
common threat of persecution, gave Christians a sense of belonging that
was probably more important than the material security membership
in the Christian Church afforded. Tertullian said, "We hold everything in
common but our spouses"—the reverse of the rest of Roman society, he
joked, where most people shared nothing else.

While the ethical codes of Christianity and classical philosophy were similar, they differed in a few significant ways, and the Christian and classical conceptions of the purpose of ethical behavior differed markedly. The historian Forrest McDonald once explained the difference between a "man of religion" and a "man of honor" (in this context, an orthodox Christian and a classical philosopher): "The one considers vice as offensive to the Divine Being, the other as something beneath him." To the classical philosopher (the man of honor), virtue was rewarded in this life, through self-respect and the respect of others. By contrast, the Christian (the man of religion) sought his reward exclusively in the next life, expecting only persecution for his virtue in this sinful world, in imitation of Christ, and considering the love of praise a vice. In Christianity, the quest for heaven replaced the classical quest for honor and fame.

Christians differed from classical philosophers even more markedly in praising humility. While the Greeks and Romans never considered vanity a vice, and classical heroes like Odysseus were an exceedingly vain lot, Christians considered pride the greatest sin, constituting a form of blasphemy. Vanity also conflicted with the Christian emphasis on the insignificance of success in this world when set against the tremendous importance of the eternal afterlife. Christianity taught that God had not only lowered Himself to become a man, but had even adopted the humble status of a carpenter's son. What right to vanity had any mere human then? In the Sermon on the Mount, Jesus declared: "Blessed are the meek, for they will inherit the earth" (Matt. 5:5). Paul commanded: "Do not become proud, but stand in awe" (Rom. 11:20). Augustine concluded: "And therefore it is that humility is specifically recommended to the city of God as it sojourns in this world and is specially exhibited in the person of Christ its King, while the contrary vice of pride, according to the testimony of the sacred writings, specifically rules its adversary the devil." Augustine argued that classical virtue, through its impious substitution of self-admiration and the applause of others for a recognition of one's sinfulness and a plea for divine help, could itself become a vice, a proud form of self-love. Like Jews, Christians were shocked by the classical notion that the gods differed from mortals only in their greater powers and in their immortality. Lacking any doctrine of original sin and raised on the traditional stories of selfish, petty gods, pagans claimed: "Man is a mortal god, and god an immortal man." While the Judeo-Christian tradition proposed a much larger gap between the nature of God and that of humans than the classical tradition, it proposed a much smaller gap in sentiment, claiming that the Judeo-Christian God, unlike the selfish Greek gods, loved humanity.

But orthodox Christians (including this author, in the interest of full disclosure) would be far from satisfied with an exclusive emphasis on these purely natural causes of the rise of Christianity. Rather, orthodox

Christians insist that this great movement was primarily the work of the Holy Spirit touching human hearts. Christians believe that from the time of the Holy Spirit's first appearance to the apostles at Pentecost (Acts 2), when individuals from different nations each heard the apostles speaking with great eloquence in his own language, the Holy Spirit began acting as the guardian of the Church until the Second Coming of Christ.

THE LEGACY OF PAUL

Christianity has so influenced Western culture that it remains imbedded in the values and attitudes of even those individuals who no longer believe its doctrines. Although, in practice, Christians have often been deficient (in some cases, extremely deficient) in implementing the high ideals that are central to their religion, those ideals have almost certainly made Western society more humane than it would otherwise have been. While some modern historians disparage Christianity as the cause of crusades, inquisitions, pogroms, and witch hunts, none of them can cite a single verse from the New Testament that endorses these horrid perversions of Christianity. On the contrary, Jesus instructed his disciples, "Love your enemies. . . . Pray for those who persecute you" (Matt. 5:44).

While the contributions of Christianity to Western history are too vast to list here, the American Revolution and the abolition of slavery are two of the most important. The Great Awakening (c. 1730–1760), a Protestant revival movement, was as crucial to the American Revolution as was classical republicanism. Most of the soldiers who filled the ranks of the Continental army and the state militias did not have access to the classical education of the more affluent Founding Fathers, but they did hear, on a regular basis, sermons that emphasized the need to escape British corruption and to form a new nation that would serve as a "city on a hill," a model to the world. (The latter term was first used by Jesus in the Sermon on the Mount—"You are the light of the world. A city that is set on a hill cannot be hidden" [Matt. 5:14]—and then employed by John Winthrop to inspire the original Puritan colonists with a sense of mission.) Though his own theology was unorthodox, Thomas Jefferson testified that prorevolutionary sermons "ran like a shock of electricity" through Virginia. Inspired by the revivalism of the Great Awakening, America's clergymen were among the first and the most ardent proponents of American independence.

While devotees of nearly all religions have owned slaves at one time or another, it was a group of British and American evangelical Christians who led the movement that ended slavery in the modern West. The first great victory of the abolitionist movement occurred when the British Parliament ended slavery in all British possessions in 1833. This achievement was the product of Herculean efforts by William Wilberforce and other evangelicals. In the United States, the Second Great Awakening produced a raft of abolitionists, including William Lloyd Garrison, Theodore Weld, Lewis Tappan, Sarah Grimke, and Harriet Beecher Stowe. Though initially so unpopular even in the North that they were threatened continually with violence, these evangelicals persevered and gradually secured enough sympathy for their cause that Abraham Lincoln, though fighting the Civil War to save the Union, was able to envision the Emancipation Proclamation as a measure that would bring support, rather than dissension, to the Union war effort.

If Paul of Tarsus had not carried Christianity to the Gentiles, it would not have survived to play its crucial role in Western history. The liberty of many, perhaps all, Americans might never have been secured, and the nation's controversial but essential role as a city on a hill—which, in recent times, has culminated in the spread of democracy throughout much of the world—might have gone unfilled.

12

✣

Augustine:
Christian Theologian

A Roman citizen from the town of Hippo Regius (now Bona) in North Africa, Augustine was the greatest theologian of the early Christian Church. Augustine's greatest theological treatise *The City of God* not only helped Christianity overcome a potentially devastating crisis at the time of its publication, but also made Augustine the dominant Christian theologian for half a millennium. Augustine's writings also exerted a significant influence on the Protestant reformers of the sixteenth century. His intensely personal *Confessions* remains one of the classics of Western literature.

THE DECLINE OF THE ROMAN EMPIRE

Political Decline

Augustine's contribution to the success of Christianity cannot be understood without reference to the decline of the Roman Empire, a process that had been under way for a full century and a half before his own time. Some of the more unorthodox theories of recent times have held that Roman civilization died from disease, from lead poisoning (lead pipes carried the Romans' water supply), or from a cold spell in the global climate, which produced famine. But, while it is often difficult to separate cause from effect in a society as gravely ill as that of the late Roman Empire, the cancer that ultimately killed the empire appears to have been political. Constant warfare between rival generals seeking the throne undermined the Roman economy and sapped the sense of patriotism that had been the Romans' greatest source of strength.

Ironically, it was during the reign of an emperor named Commodus (Lucius Aelius Aurelius Commodus; 180–192) that the Roman Empire began going down the toilet. Commodus was the son of the virtuous Marcus Aurelius but shared few of his father's traits. (One Roman wrote of Marcus: "He inflicted only one injury upon his country—he had a son.") Commodus brutalized and murdered his subjects and confiscated their property. He enjoyed performing as a gladiator, using a javelin and bow to kill hundreds of wild animals and people in the amphitheater. Like Caligula, Commodus demanded that his subjects worship him as a god and, like Caligula, he was finally murdered by his own Praetorian Prefect—in combination with Commodus's mistress and a professional wrestler. The mistress poisoned Commodus's wine and the wrestler entered the emperor's bedchamber and strangled him as further insurance against his recovery.

After Commodus's assassination, the virtuous Pertinax (Publius Helvius Pertinax; 192), who had been a friend of Marcus Aurelius, became emperor. His reign lasted only eighty-six days. When the Praetorian Guard marched on Pertinax, he went out to meet the guards and to remind them of the sanctity of their oath to him. For a few moments the guards bowed their heads in shame. Then someone raised his sword and leveled the first blow against the emperor. Others followed suit. After Pertinax was killed, his head was paraded around on a lance. Since there was no obvious successor, the Praetorian Guard offered the empire to the highest bidder. Julianus won the auction, but a horrifying civil war ensued.

The North African general Lucius Septimius Severus (193–211) prevailed in that civil war by flattering and betraying his rivals and by offering his army in Dalmatia (what is now Yugoslavia) a bribe twice that which Julianus paid the guards. Once in power, Severus reorganized the Praetorian Guard and transferred control of finances, the provinces, and the law to his Praetorian Prefect. While Severus dramatically increased the size of the army, he failed to increase its effectiveness; Scottish tribesmen easily repelled Severus's ill-fated invasion of their homeland. While at York (in northern England), Severus summarized for posterity the reigning philosophy of third-century emperors: "Take care of the Army, and everything else will take care of itself."

Though Severus had criticized Marcus Aurelius for allowing his worthless son to become emperor, Severus made the same mistake with his own son Caracalla (211–217). Caracalla's real name was Marcus Aurelius Antoninus; "Caracalla" was a nickname derived from the long,

Gallic cloak or tunic he popularized. Unlike most emperors, who commissioned idealized figures of themselves, Caracalla encouraged his artists to depict him as a fierce character in order to reinforce his image as a ruthless and cruel ruler. Having ambushed and murdered his younger brother and coemperor and having slaughtered thousands of his brother's followers, Caracalla bankrupted the state in order to bribe the army, a double folly that did not prevent a soldier from assassinating him.

Marcus Opelius Macrinus (217–218), Caracalla's kinsman and successor, was selected emperor by the army, not the Senate, and was defeated and replaced by the adolescent Antoninus (218–222), who clearly modeled himself after Caracalla, his father. Antoninus dressed in the style of a Persian monarch, draping himself in flowing robes of silk lined with gold and studded with gems. He also wore a tiara, mascara, and make-up. He adopted the name "Heliogabalus," after the sun god, whom he claimed as his patron. The science of pleasure was the only one cultivated by Heliogabalus. The Praetorian Guard, some of whose members Heliogabalus had executed, assassinated him and hurled his body into the Tiber.

Alexander Severus (222–235), Heliogabalus's cousin, became emperor at the age of seventeen, but Alexander's grandmother Mamae really controlled the government, with the advice of sixteen senators, during the early years of his reign. In 235, unhappy with Alexander's decision to bribe the Alemanni, a Germanic tribe with whom the Romans fought on the Rhine, the army put him to death.

In the forty-nine years between the death of Alexander, the last emperor of the Severi dynasty, and the reign of Diocletian, there were twenty-six emperors, only one of whom died a natural death. Nearly all of these emperors suffered violent deaths at the hands of the very soldiers who had placed them on the throne. There was no suitable system of succession, and "barracks emperors" (army commanders) terrorized the people. Taking advantage of the chaos, parts of Gaul and Syria were temporarily successful in seceding from the empire. Even in the late third and fourth centuries, when the imperial succession was more stable, warfare between rival generals and their armies frequently distracted Rome from defense against invading tribes.

The Economic Decline

The inability of the emperors to control the army contributed greatly to the economic crisis of the late empire. Emperors sometimes had to tax the people at an extremely high rate in order to pay the ever-increasing bribes required to pacify the army and its generals, though no amount ever proved sufficient to ward off the ceaseless coups. When, in 212, Caracalla decreed that every free man in the Roman Empire was now a citizen, it was largely so that he could gouge the new citizens with the inheritance tax (a tax reserved for citizens), which the emperor then doubled. Added to this formal tax was an informal levy: corrupt officials frequently demanded protection money from citizens. As the historian Edward Gibbon once put it: "The Roman government appeared every day less formidable to its enemies, more odious to its subjects. The taxes were multiplied with the public distress; economy was neglected in proportion as it became necessary; and the injustice of the rich shifted the unequal burden from themselves to the people. . . . They [the people] abjured and abhorred the name of Roman citizens, which had formerly excited the ambition of mankind."

When even high taxes proved insufficient to raise the required revenue, the emperors (beginning with Severus) devalued the coinage, a form of taxation by inflation. The resultant hyperinflation caused the hoarding of silver, which led to the further devaluing of the coinage, which further accelerated the inflation. By the fifth century, Rome's "silver coins" consisted of less than 2 percent silver, and the imperial government was refusing to accept its own money as taxes, requiring goods instead. The goods were distributed to the soldiers as "bonuses," since inflation had decimated their wages. Hyperinflation discouraged all forms of economic activity and caused a decline in the population of western cities, as members of both the middle and lower classes were forced to move to great estates, where they became the serfs (*coloni*) of aristocrats.

Contrary to popular belief, feudalism did not begin in the Middle Ages but in the late Roman Empire (though the empire's collapse greatly reinforced it, as each region was forced even further into military and economic self-sufficiency). In the early fourth century, the emperor Diocletian required the sons of guildsmen to remain in the same towns and to perform the same occupations as their fathers, as part of an attempt to ensure the collection of taxes. Soon after, Constantine declared that no colonos or child of a colonos could leave the soil. Before long, a daughter or son could not marry outside the guild. While the emperors were not always able to enforce these edicts, they constituted the beginnings of the medieval caste system.

Other factors contributed to the Roman economic decline, of course. The end of territorial expansion prevented the acquisition of new resources and markets, thereby limiting economic growth. Furthermore, Rome made very few technological improvements in manufacturing, transportation, or agriculture. The primary means of land transportation remained the small oxcart, which limited the amount of goods that could be transported. Some roads were allowed to fall into disrepair. The decline in land transportation meant that inland provinces became more and more isolated and primitive. (Even in the best of days it had generally been cheaper to transport goods from one end of the Mediterranean to the other by ship than to haul them a mere seventy-five miles inland by cart.) Large estates moved to greater and greater self-sufficiency as the transportation of goods became less reliable, thereby further reducing trade and harming the cities. Formerly absentee landowners now fled the cities to take up permanent residence on their estates. With a few exceptions, the general quality of crafts declined.

Possessing an abundant supply of labor, the owners of large estates felt little need to improve agricultural technology and techniques. Indeed, there had long been a widespread belief that labor-saving devices were bad for society because they left potential troublemakers idle. When an engineer had offered to haul some columns up to the Capitol at reduced expense using a labor-saving device he had invented, the emperor Vespasian (68–79) paid him but declined his offer, explaining, "I must always ensure that the working classes earn enough money to buy themselves food." Like most Romans, the emperor had considered unemployment the inevitable result of any labor-saving device.

The Psychological Decline

The chaos, destruction, and inflation produced by civil war undermined traditional Roman confidence and patriotism. Many Romans deserted both the army and politics. By and large, they turned to religion for consolation. The cults of the Roman Bacchus (Dionysus), the Persian (originally Indian) Mithras, the Phrygian Cybele, and the Egyptian Isis all achieved popularity within the empire.

Like the other religions, Christianity profited from the psychological crisis. But Christianity also helped to destroy the empire by turning many intelligent and desperately needed Romans from a life of political leadership to an ascetic lifestyle focused on the next life. (Christianity may also have exacerbated the economic crisis; much of the late empire's private, and some of its public, wealth gravitated to the Church, which was exempt from the taxes needed to fund military defense and whose clergy were exempt from military service. Indeed, some pagan aristocrats even joined the Church and became bishops to escape the fighting.) As Peter Brown put it: "Perhaps the most basic reason for the failure of the imperial government, in the years between 380 and 420, was the two main groups in the Latin world—the senatorial aristocracy and the Catholic Church—dissociated themselves from the fate of the Roman army that defended them." While the demoralized senators insulated themselves as best they could from the collapse of the empire, the Church looked beyond this life to the next.

The crisis had its effect on Roman art. The outer, material world was no longer seen as a source of beauty and truth but of confusion and illusion. Romans turned inward toward the spiritual world. Portrait busts now depicted men with a distant glance, as though they were looking beyond this world to eternity. Late Roman art became less realistic, more abstract. Individual detail gave way to the depiction of general types, as artists concentrated on portraying universal, abstract truths.

The Military Decline

These political, economic, and psychological crises produced a military crisis that proved fatal to the empire. The absence of the confidence and patriotism that had always formed the foundation of Roman military success forced the emperors to rely increasingly on foreign enlistees and mercenaries, a common sign of a declining power. Roman soldiers of the late imperial period were so undisciplined they sometimes refused to wear armor and helmets or carry heavy weapons and, when forced to do so, deserted. In some instances, Romans even severed one of their own thumbs to avoid military service. As Gibbon put it: "The introduction of the barbarians into the Roman armies became every day more universal, more necessary, and more fatal." Although earlier emperors had employed foreign enlistees and mercenaries, non-Romans (mostly German tribesmen) did not constitute a majority of the Roman army until the third century. In general, the foreigners were less patriotic and less reliable than Roman citizens. They did not fight to defend a country or an ideal, as the early Roman soldiers had.

As a result of the psychological crisis, the Romans suffered a series of military disasters. In 231, the Persians, having overthrown the Parthians, defeated the Romans and terrorized the eastern part of the empire. In 251, the Germanic Goths crossed the Danube River into Dacia (Romania), defeated a Roman army, terrorized the Balkans, threatened Italy, and brought trade in the eastern Mediterranean to an abrupt halt through piracy. Learning from their success, Roman pirates grew in number, reducing trade still further. In 267–268, the Heruli, a Germanic tribe from southern Russia, plundered the coasts of the Black and Aegean Seas, burning Ephesus and Athens. The Athenians now huddled around the Acropolis as their ancestors had during the Dark Ages of Greece over a thousand years earlier. The Persians and Germans had revealed Roman weakness, but the empire remained standing for another two centuries, when a more lethal threat appeared.

Two emperors, one a persecutor of Christians, the other a convert to Christianity, managed to slow the decline of the ailing empire to some degree. A Dalmatian of humble origins, Diocletian (Gaius Aurelius Valerius Diocletianus; 284–305) personally toured the empire, recruiting good generals and fighting from frontier to frontier, as Marcus Aurelius had done. He divided the Roman army into mobile and stationary units, establishing a line of well-supplied camps from Egypt to Persia. Diocletian also launched a campaign against Christianity and the other rivals of traditional Roman religion in a desperate effort to revive what he considered the greatest incubator of patriotism: the Roman religion.

Diocletian divided the empire into four prefectures, each to be ruled either by one of two emperors (an *augustus*) or by his *caesar*, an apprentice and designated successor to that emperor. Each of the *tetrarchs* (the emperors and their caesars) would establish his government close to the frontier—at Nicodemia (in northwestern Asia Minor), Milan (in northern Italy), Sirmium (on the Danube), and Trier (on the Rhine). Too distant from the empire's threatened frontiers, the city of Rome ceased to be an administrative center. Diocletian visited Rome only once during his reign. Keeping control of the western empire, Diocletian appointed Maximian, his favorite general, emperor of the eastern empire.

Unfortunately, Diocletian's division of the empire worsened the economic situation. Four lavish new courts replaced the one previous court. Taxes grew and inflation worsened. Diocletian's maximum wage and price laws (301), enforced on pain of death, had to be abandoned when they served only to create a black market (or, in some cases, no market at all). His decree that municipal council members must pay any taxes they were unable to collect from their communities encouraged harshness in tax collection and reduced participation in government still further, as the affluent used every means at their disposal to evade service in municipal councils. The lower class increasingly saw the central government as an oppressor that seized whatever they produced and left nothing.

The fiction of senatorial rule propagated by the early emperors had vanished completely, as the later emperors insisted on being called *dominus* (lord), a word previously used to designate a master over slaves. Diocletian adopted the title "Jovius" (a form of Jupiter), wore a Persian-style diadem, and employed eunuchs, an eastern institution that previous Roman emperors had viewed with disgust. The same Rome once regarded as an exciting heroine, worthy of the most heroic sacrifice, was now seen as a mean, old hag, hardly worthy of consideration.

In 312, Constantine (312–337) defeated Maxentius, son of Maximian, at Milvian Bridge outside Rome, thereby becoming emperor of the western empire; in 324, Constantine defeated Licinius to become sole ruler of the Roman Empire. In 330, recognizing the wealth and importance of the eastern empire, Constantine transferred the empire's capital to the Greek city of Byzantium, which he renamed Nova Roma (New Rome), but which later became known as Constantinople. Constantinople's location on the Turkish Straits allowed the emperor to direct wars on both the Danube and Euphrates fronts. Nevertheless, the great expense of converting the town into a capital worthy of the Roman Empire weighed heavily on the treasury.

In 372, the Huns, a large, nomadic tribe of superb horsemen who had originated in central Asia, crossed the Volga River in what is now Russia and defeated the Ostrogoths (eastern Goths) of the Ukraine, setting their fields and villages aflame. The fierce Huns lived in wagons, wore fur caps and goatskin leggings, shot bone-tipped arrows, and ate, slept, and deliberated on horseback. Surviving Ostrogoths were forced to join the rampaging Huns as allies.

Some of the terrified Visigoths (western Goths) then received Roman permission to cross the Danube and settle in Thrace. Rather than combining with the Visigoths to oppose the Huns, the Romans oppressed the starving Visigoths, selling them dogs as food at ridiculous prices. Some of the Visigoths even had to sell their children into slavery to survive. The generally tolerant Romans never made a serious attempt to assimilate the Germans, whom they considered barbarians, as they had so many other peoples. This was a mistake, because the Germanic tribes were beginning to perceive their relative power and the Romans' relative weakness.

The Visigoths finally erupted in rebellion and, with the help of the Ostrogoths and of some Romans, devastated much of the Balkans. In 378, the emperor Valens was killed and lost two-thirds of his army at Andrianople while attempting to put down the Visigothic rebellion. Theodosius I (378–395), Valens's successor, was forced to accept the migration of more Visigoths into the empire and to recognize them as part of the Roman army.

After Theodosius's death in 395, the Visigoths, led by Alaric, occupied Illyricum and plundered Greece virtually unopposed. The Roman soldiers belatedly dispatched to oppose them stripped the Greeks of their remaining goods. Roman citizens were beginning to wonder which side constituted the real barbarians. The Romans appeased Alaric temporarily by recognizing his control of eastern Illyricum.

In 410, Alaric and the Visigoths besieged Rome, causing so severe a famine in the city there were rumors of cannibalism. Alaric demanded all the gold, silver, and silk cloth within the city. When asked, "What do you intend to leave us?" he sneered, "Your lives!" When his demands were refused, Alaric entered a city gate that had been opened for him by slaves and domestics at midnight. The Visigoths murdered or enslaved many Romans, but left after only six days to plunder southern Italy.

The Western world was shocked. Foreign conquerors had not entered Rome since the Gauls had occupied part of the city eight centuries earlier. Alaric died the same year, but his successor carved out a sizable kingdom for the Visigoths in southern Gaul and Spain, a kingdom the Romans were forced to recognize in 419.

In the 420s, the Germanic Angles and Saxons were allowed to settle in Britain, only to rebel and conquer the province two decades later. In the 420s, the Alemanni and Franks crossed the Rhine and settled in Gaul.

In the 430s, the Vandals, a Germanic tribe that had already assumed control of parts of Spain, conquered most of North Africa. They destroyed cities and tortured people to locate their hidden wealth.

In 447, Attila and his Huns, who had since forged an empire from the Baltic Sea to the Danube River, plundered Illyricum; only the Huns' lack of siege equipment and experience prevented them from capturing Constantinople. The eastern emperor Theodosius II was forced to cede land south of the Danube to the Huns and to pay them tribute.

In 452, the Huns sacked Milan and advanced on Rome. Called "the Scourge of God" by many Romans, Attila had murdered his own brother to secure sole control of the Huns' empire in 445. Dressed in flowing robes, Pope Leo I came out to meet the leader of the Huns. The pope managed to convince Attila, who had great reverence for priests of every religion, to turn away from Rome. A church legend claimed that the apparitions of Peter and Paul appeared before Attila and threatened him with death if he did not heed the pope's plea. Some historians suggest that the venereal diseases rampant in Attila's army were a major factor in his decision to depart.

In any case, Attila's decision to turn away from Rome was short lived. He was planning another invasion of Italy when he died of a burst artery in 453. Immediately after Attila's death, the Huns' empire collapsed due to infighting. For centuries, the Huns seem to have been leader-driven— invincible when well led, but not particularly formidable otherwise. While some Huns joined the Romans, others joined the burgeoning number of tribes plundering the empire.

In 455, the Vandals sailed across from North Africa and sacked Rome, hauling away nearly all of its remaining wealth, public and private. Among the items the Vandals looted was the Menorah (the seven-branch candlestick) and other items the Romans had taken from the Great Temple of Jerusalem almost four centuries earlier. The Vandals also enslaved many captives, often separating families. Deogratias, the Christian bishop of Carthage, sold his church's gold and silver plate to purchase the freedom of some of these captives.

Every spring thereafter, the Vandals, accompanied by Roman converts to piracy, sailed forth from Carthage with a massive fleet to plunder a different part of the empire (e.g., the coasts of Spain, Italy, Illyricum, and Greece). Once, when asked by the pilot what course he should steer, Genseric, the leader of the Vandals, replied: "Leave the determination to the winds; they will transport us to the guilty coast whose inhabitants have provoked the divine justice." Gibbon noted dryly: "But if Genseric himself deigned to issue more precise orders, he judged the most wealthy to be the most criminal."

The usual date assigned for the fall of Rome is 476. In that year, Odoacer, the Herulian commander of the Roman army (by then most of the army was German), demanded that one-third of Italy be allotted to his men in reward for their service. When Orestes, who was acting as regent for his young son Romulus Augustulus, refused, Odoacer dropped the pretense of Roman rule and seized control of the city. Orestes was put to death and Romulus was sent into exile at a villa near Naples. Thus did Rome begin with one Romulus and end with another.

Only the western empire fell. The more prosperous, populous, and geographically secure eastern empire continued, though greatly diminished by the Arab conquests of the seventh century, until the Turks conquered it in 1453. Constantinople (now Istanbul), the capital of this Byzantine empire, remained one of the largest, most splendid, and most learned cities in the world.

AUGUSTINE'S ACCOMPLISHMENTS

It was within this context of a rapidly declining empire that Augustine of Hippo (354–430) became the greatest intellect of the late empire and the early Church. The son of a Christian mother and a pagan father, Augustine had become acquainted with Manichaeism while studying rhetoric at Carthage and had been a Manichaean for nine years before his conversion to orthodox Christianity in 387. Named after Mani, its third-century Mesopotamian founder, Manichaeism was a combination of Zoroastrianism and Gnostic Christianity that spread westward to the Roman Empire and eastward to the gates of China. It envisioned existence as a constant struggle between good and evil. God was a benevolent being whose limited power absolved him of any responsibility for evil in the world. Though human souls were the product of this good God, their bodies, which distracted them from the good, were the product of the evil Satan. This view differed from Christianity, a religion that considered the body a good creation of God that had been corrupted by the fall of Adam and that hardly placed Satan on the same level as God. Christians viewed God as creator of the whole universe and Satan as a mere fallen angel—a disgruntled employee.

While bishop of Hippo Regius in what is now Tunisia, Augustine wrote the *Confessions* (397–401). Addressed to God in the style of the psalms, this deeply personal book began with an account of Augustine's past sinful life and conversion to Christianity at age thirty-two and ended with a series of passionate philosophical reflections. Augustine's somber self-criticism, enlivened by a tremendous eloquence and talent for metaphor, marked a radical break with the classical past and the inauguration of a new Christian literary tradition. In language remarkable for its combination of reason and passion, he flouted the conventions of contemporary Christian conversion literature by portraying conversion as merely the beginning of an arduous journey, not as a panacea for earthly troubles.

Augustine's stinging indictment of himself represented no less than an indictment of the classical world and of humankind in general. Augustine rebuked himself for a life spent pursuing all the fleeting and ultimately unsatisfying pleasures of the material world—sex, prestige, wealth, and even smug intellectualism—rather than seeking the lasting and satisfying pleasures of the spirit. He had frequented the immoral Roman theater, had fathered an illegitimate child by a mistress ("a union of wanton love, in which a child is born but not wanted, though when born it compels one to love it"), had been swollen with ambition for wealth and fame as a teacher of rhetoric (a "vender of verbosity"), had heeded the ridiculous superstitions of the Manichaeans, had consulted astrologers (whose few accurate prophesies occurred by chance), and had wasted his talents pursuing the vain commendations of a self-deluded intellectual elite. Seeing his former vanity in the scientists of his day, Augustine wrote:

> Through impious pride, falling away from and lacking in Thy great light, they foresee an eclipse of the sun, but they do not see their own eclipse in the present—for they do not search conscientiously for the source of the talent which they have, whereby they search out these things. . . . They say many true things about creation, yet they do not seek the Truth, the artificer of creation, with piety and therefore do not discover Him. Or, if they do make this discovery, in knowing God, they do not honor Him or give thanks to Him as God.

It was better to be termed ignorant by the intellectual elite for possessing faith than to secure their praise by emulating their arrogance. Had not Paul written, "The wisdom of the world is foolishness to God" (1 Cor. 3:19)?

Augustine concluded that, although earthly pleasures were both good and necessary (the taste of food was a necessary incentive to eating, just as sexual pleasure was a necessary incentive to procreation), their very goodness rendered them enormously susceptible to abuse. One must be on constant guard against them, since they so quickly and easily became ends in themselves. Augustine himself had become so corrupted by lust that he had been reluctant to pray for chastity, lest his prayer be answered. After Augustine had attempted to achieve chastity on his own and failed, he finally heard "the voice of Chastity" whisper to his tortured soul concerning the chaste Christians he often saw: "Can you not live as these men and women do? In fact, do these men and women live by their own powers and not by the Lord their God? . . . Why do you stand upon yourself and so have naught to stand on?" Overwhelmed by the realization that his stubborn quest to become virtuous without divine assistance was, in fact, the greatest of his many sins of pride, Augustine's tears "burst forth in rivers," and he cried out to God, who healed Augustine through the Holy Spirit.

Augustine published *The City of God* (413–426), his greatest theological work, in response to the Visigoths' destruction of Rome in 410. Pagans cried that the destruction of the city represented the wrath of the Roman gods against Christians and others for abandoning that old-time religion: paganism. In *The City of God*, Augustine ridiculed this theory, noting that other empires had arisen without the help of the Roman gods and that the earlier paganism had failed to prevent similar disasters, ranging from the fall of Troy to the Gauls' destruction of Rome (390 B.C.) and the bloody civil wars of the late republican period. In granting material goods, such as empires, to the wicked as well as the good, God acted mysteriously, but probably intended to show that temporal goods should not be valued too highly. Those who valued temporal, alienable goods like wealth and power over such eternal, unalienable goods as faith and love were condemned either to a perpetual desire for them or to a perpetual fear of their loss.

Augustine also criticized the Roman gods for denying their followers immortality and for failing to provide the Romans with moral instruction. Indeed, the Roman gods had personified vice itself, as even the Romans were forced to admit. After all, at the same time that the Romans had vividly recounted the immoral acts of the gods in their plays, they had made it a capital crime for a playwright to slander any citizen on the same stage by attributing the same actions to him.

Augustine pleaded with the Roman people to redirect their enormous energy and genius for territorial conquest toward the quest for spiritual triumphs. Perhaps remembering Paul's statement, "In all these things we are more than conquerors through Him who loved us" (Rom. 8:37), as well as the Book of Revelation's frequent promises of glory for "him who conquers" sin, Augustine wrote: "This, rather, is the religion worthy of your desires, O admirable Romans. . . . Lay hold now on the celestial country, which is easily won, and in which you will reign truly and forever."

Augustine contended that there were two worlds, the Earthly City and the City of God. The dark Earthly City, animated by the love of self, had begun with the fall of Adam and Eve, a fall from truth and unity to falsehood and division. Just as the souls of Adam and Eve were divided by sin, their progeny were divided against one another by selfishness. As punishment for humans' stubborn pride in seeking to be their own satisfaction, God granted their wish, abandoning them to themselves. Thenceforth, humans were doomed to die in body as they had willingly died in spirit, condemned to death because they had forsaken eternal life. The punishment for humanity's rebellion against God was the rebellion of their own bodies against their souls, the transformation of human bodies from good and faithful servants into cruel and erratic masters. The tree from which Adam and Eve ate, in defiance of God's law, was called the Tree of Knowledge because by eating of it they learned, for the first time, the true value of the life they were now to lose.

Planned by God to repair the damage caused by Adam and Eve, the bright, celestial City of God, animated by the love of God, had been constructed through the death and resurrection of Jesus. Citizens of both the Earthly City and the City of God occupied the same world. In their blindness, the citizens of the Earthly City created strife by competing with one another for the finite material goods of the temporal world. By contrast, the wiser citizens of the City of God lived in harmony, sharing the limitless goods of the spirit. While the former were enslaved by their very lust for rule, the latter were truly free. While the former valued earthly things as ends in themselves, the latter merely accepted them as necessary to survival during their brief "sojourn on earth." The opposing values of the two cities divided them irreparably, often leading to the persecution of the righteous by the worldly. But while the worldly wallowed in the futility of their earthly existence until their day of destruction arrived, the righteous awaited positions in the true kingdom of love and justice.

Augustine referred to God's elect as "resident aliens" in the Earthly City, a status his readers well understood. The elect were uprooted and homesick during their period of exile from God's kingdom. Though they had to make peace with their temporary residence for practical reasons, it would never feel like home.

History was both an endless cycle of the rise and fall of futile civilizations and a divinely propelled progression toward an otherworldly utopia. Augustine assured his readers that the decline and fall of civilizations had been a natural occurrence in the Earthly City since Adam's fall, indicating no particular divine disfavor. Only the heavenly City of God was eternal. Introspective, intellectual, imaginative, and articulate, Augustine continues to delight readers of all faiths.

THE LEGACY OF AUGUSTINE

The immediate impact of Augustine's *City of God* was crucial to the survival of Christianity. At a time when Romans may well have been tempted to blame Christianity for the sack of Rome by the Visigoths, and for the general decline of Roman civilization, Augustine persuaded many Roman intellectuals that the unthinkable, the collapse of the Roman Empire, was, in fact, natural and inevitable. In place of loyalty to the worldly empire that so many people over so many centuries had mistakenly considered eternal, Augustine substituted fidelity to the spiritual Kingdom of God, which he presented as the only truly everlasting empire. The City of God, the New Jerusalem, displaced pagan Rome, the so-called Eternal City, as the ideal—even as Rome itself was becoming the seat of the Christian Church.

Augustine's theology dominated the early medieval period. Jeffrey Burton Russell once aptly summarized Augustine's influence on medieval theology: "Philosophy and theology were for six hundred years after Augustine's death largely devoted to the elaboration of his thought." Not until the high Middle Ages, when the Scholasticism of Thomas Aquinas, a merger of Christianity with Aristotelian philosophy, gained prominence, was Augustine's theology displaced.

Augustine's influence on Martin Luther, John Calvin, and other Protestant reformers was equally great. Luther, who began his religious career as a Catholic monk of the Augustinian order, claimed he derived his doctrine of justification by faith alone from the psalms, from the apostle Paul, and from Augustine's *Confessions.* Luther was impressed by the fact that Augustine, like the psalmist and like Paul, had found no hope in himself whatsoever, but had relied solely on God's promise of salvation.

Yet Catholics continued to cite Augustinian passages—especially those acknowledging the authority of the church hierarchy—that were more suitable to their own theology than to that of the Protestants. Augustine's writings were so rich they could provide fodder for both sides during the Reformation.

Christianity both profited from the chaos, violence, and demoralization caused by the empire's decline and accelerated that decline by drawing some of its greatest minds, like Augustine, away from its affairs to the contemplation of the afterlife. But once the Church had thoroughly defanged its pagan rival, classical philosophy, the Church salvaged it and placed its most useful elements in the service of a Judaic cosmology to form the theological foundation of Western culture. At the forefront of this movement were monks, men who, in the very act of withdrawing from a dying world, preserved its record. But that's another story.

Brief Bibliographical
Suggestions for
General Readers

There are many well-written histories of, and historical commentaries on, ancient Greece and Rome that are geared to general readers. A few of these include: R. H. Barrow, *The Romans* (Penguin, 1949); John Boardman, Jasper Griffin, and Osway Murray, eds., *The Oxford History of the Classical World* (Oxford University Press, 1986); A. R. Burn, *The Pelican History of Greece* (Penguin, 1966); M. I. Finley, *The Ancient Greeks* (Penguin, 1963); Michael Grant, *The Founders of the Western World: A History of Greece and Rome* (Scribner's, 1991); Edith Hamilton, *The Greek Way* (Norton, 1930); and H. D. F. Kitto, *The Greeks* (Penguin, 1957).

Somewhat more specialized but highly readable works include: C. M. Bowra, *Periclean Athens* (Dial Press, 1971); Averil Cameron, *The Later Roman Empire, A.D. 284–430* (Harvard University Press, 1993); G. C. Field, *The Philosophy of Plato* (2d. ed.; Oxford University Press, 1969); Yvon Garlan, *Slavery in Ancient Greece* (Cornell University Press, 1988); Judith P. Hallett, *Fathers and Daughters in Roman Society: Women and the Elite Family* (Princeton University Press, 1984); Victor Davis Hanson, *The Western Way of War: Infantry Battle in Classical Greece* (Knopf, 1989), and *Carnage and Culture: Landmark Battles in the Rise of Western Power* (Doubleday, 2001); Tom B. Jones, *In the Twilight of Antiquity* (University of Minnesota Press, 1978); Joachim Latacz, *Homer: His Art and His World* (University of Michigan Press, 1996); Robert J. Lenardon, *The Saga of Themistocles* (Thames and Hudson, 1978); G. E. R. Lloyd, *Early Greek Science: Thales to Aristotle* (Norton, 1970); R. M. Ogilvie, *Early Rome and the Etruscans* (Humanities Press, 1976); H. P. L'Orange, *Art Forms and Civic Life in the Late Roman Empire* (Princeton University Press, 1965); Sarah B. Pomeroy, ed., *Women's History and Ancient History* (University of North Carolina Press, 1991); Simon Price, *Religions of the Ancient Greeks* (Cambridge University Press, 1999); B. H. Warmington, *Carthage* (Penguin, 1960); Colin M. Wells, *The Roman Empire* (Stanford University Press, 1984); and Thomas Wiedemann, ed., *Greek and Roman Slavery* (Johns Hopkins University Press, 1981).

Well-written works concerning the rise of Christianity include: Stephen Benko, *Pagan Rome and the Early Christians* (Indiana University Press, 1984); Peter Brown, *Augustine of Hippo: A Biography* (University of California Press, 1967); Henry Chadwick, *The Early Church* (Penguin, 1969); E. R. Dodds, *Pagan and Christian in an Age of Anxiety* (Cambridge University Press, 1968); and Robin Lane Fox, *Pagans and Christians* (Knopf, 1987).

The last two decades have witnessed the publication of a plethora of books concerning the classical influence on Western civilization, especially on the Founding Fathers of the United States. Such works include: Paul A. Rahe, *Republics, Ancient and Modern: Classical Republicanism and the American Revolution* (University of North Carolina Press, 1992); Meyer Reinhold, *Classica Americana: The Greek and Roman Heritage in the United States* (Wayne State University Press, 1984); Carl J. Richard, *The Founders and the Classics: Greece, Rome, and the American Enlightenment* (Harvard University Press, 1994); Jennifer Tolbert Roberts, *Athens on Trial: The Antidemocratic Tradition in Western Thought* (Princeton University Press, 1994); M. N. S. Sellers, *American Republicanism: Roman Ideology in the United States Constitution* (New York University Press, 1994); Garry Wills, *Cincinnatus: George Washington and the Enlightenment* (Doubleday, 1984); Susan Ford Wiltshire, *Greece, Rome, and the Bill of Rights* (University of Oklahoma Press, 1992); and Caroline Winterer, *The Culture of Classicism: Ancient Greece and Rome in American Intellectual Life, 1780–1910* (Johns Hopkins University Press, 2002).

Nearly all of the great classics of Greco-Roman and early Christian literature can be found in good English translations in paperback editions published by Penguin. The Loeb Classics contain older translations that are less amenable to modern readers but also feature the original Greek or Latin on the opposite page from the translation. Some other worthy translations include: Robert Fitzgerald, trans., *The Odyssey* (Doubleday, 1963) and *The Aeneid* (Random House, 1981); Richmond Lattimore, trans., *The Iliad of Homer* (University of Chicago, 1951); and Sir Arthur Wallace Pickard-Cambridge, trans., *Demosthenes' Public Orations* (Dent, 1963). Those interested in brief, charming, prose summaries of the plays of Aeschylus, Sophocles, and Euripides can consult H. R. Joliffe, *Tales from the Greek Drama* (Bolchazy-Carducci, 1984).

Those interested in learning the classical Greek language can consult Vincent C. Horrigan and Raymond V. Schoder, *A Reading Course in Homeric Greek* (2 vols.; Loyola University Press, 1945). Though the strained efforts of these two Jesuit priests to reconcile Homer with Christianity are often distracting, their linguistic instruction is exceptionally clear, and their charming quotations from famous lovers of Homer, one per lesson, inspire the beginning Greek student to continue his or her work. Robert J. Henle's *Latin Grammar* (Loyola University Press, 1958) is excellent for beginning students in Latin.

Photo Credits

Map of Greek political alliances about 431 B.C. on page 5 from *Civilization Past and Present*, 8th ed., vol. 1, by T. Walter Wallbank et al., p. 58. Copyright © 1981 by Scott, Foresman, and Company. Reprinted by permission of Pearson Education, Inc.

Imaginary portrait bust of Homer, marble, early 2nd B.C.E., on page 6 from the Louvre, Paris, France. Photograph copyright © Erich Lessing/Art Resource, NY. Reprinted by permission.

Portrait of Thales of Miletus on page 16. Copyright © Bettmann/CORBIS. Reprinted by permission.

Themistocles, Greek politician (c. 524–c. 460 B.C.E.), detail of head, on page 28 from Museo Archeologico Nazionale, Naples, Italy. Photograph copyright © Scala/Art Resource, NY. Reprinted by permission.

Bust of Pericles, Athenian statesman (c. 495–429 B.C.E.), on page 58 from Museo Pio Clementino, Vatican Museums, Vatican State. Photograph copyright © Scala/Art Resource, NY. Reprinted by permission.

Bust of Plato, Sala delle Muse, on page 94 from Museo Pio Clementino, Vatican Museums, Vatican State. Photograph copyright © Scala/Art Resource, NY. Reprinted by permission.

Head of Alexander the Great (3rd B.C.E.), from Pergamon, Turkey, on page 114 from Archaeological Museum, Istanbul, Turkey. Photograph copyright © Erich Lessing/Art Resource, NY. Reprinted by permission.

Map of the Roman world 133 B.C. on page 129 from *Civilization Past and Present*, 8th ed., vol. 1, by T. Walter Wallbank et al., p. 87. Copyright © 1981 by Scott, Foresman, and Company. Reprinted by permission of Pearson Education, Inc.

Scipio Africanus (priest of Isis), Roman marble bust on a modern base, on page 130 from Musei Capitolini, Rome, Italy. Photograph copyright © Erich Lessing/ Art Resource, NY. Reprinted by permission.

Julius Caesar, Roman bust, on page 158 from Museo Archeologico Nazionale, Naples, Italy. Photograph copyright © Giraudon/Art Resource, NY. Reprinted by permission.

Bust of Cicero on page 178. Photograph copyright © Archivo Iconografico, S.A./CORBIS. Reprinted by permission.

Profile of Augustus of Primap on page 190. Photograph copyright © Araldo de Luca/CORBIS. Reprinted by permission.

St. Paul, detail of the vault mosaics, on page 214 from Archbishop's Palace, Ravenna, Italy. Photograph copyright © Scala/Art Resource, NY. Reprinted by permission.

Saint Augustine by Antonello da Messina (?1430–1479) on page 232 from Galleria Nazionale, Palermo, Italy. Photograph copyright © Scala/Art Resource, NY. Reprinted by permission.

Index of Translations
for Large Quotations

p. 30   Tyrtaeus on war: Bradley P. Nystrom and Stylianos V. Spyridakis, eds., *Ancient Greece: Documentary Evidence* (Dubuque: Kendall, Hunt, 1985), p. 118.

pp. 54–55   Athenian speeches on the Persian offer: M. I. Finley, ed., *The Portable Greek Historians*, translation of Herodotus' *Histories* by George Rawlinson (New York: Viking, 1959), pp. 214–15.

p. 89   Pericles' Funeral Oration: Finley, *Portable Greek Historians*, translation of Thucydides' *History of the Peoloponnesian War* by Richard Crawley, pp. 267–70.

p. 90   Thucydides on the plague: Finley, *Portable Greek Historians*, pp. 275–77.

p. 97   Socrates' *Apology*: accusation against his opponents, Nystrom and Spyridakis, *Ancient Greece*, p. 70; conclusion of Socrates' speech, author's own translation.

pp. 109–10   Epicurus on virtue and pleasure: first two sentences, Diogenes Laertius, *Lives of the Eminent Philosophers*, translated by Robert Drew Hicks (Loeb Classical Library; London: W. Heinemann, 1950), 2:657; last sentence, John Boardman et al., eds., *The Oxford History of the Classical World* (Oxford: Oxford University Press, 1986), p. 372.

p. 118   Demosthenes' *Phillippics*: Demosthenes, *Demosthenes' Public Orations*, translated by Sir Arthur Wallace Pickard-Cambridge (London: Dent, 1963), pp. 134, 143, 291, 298.

pp. 183–84   Cicero on nature: Maryanne Cline Horowitz, "The Stoic Synthesis of the Idea of Natural Law in Man: Four Themes," *Journal of the History of Ideas* 35 (January–March 1974): 6, 9–10, 12–15.

p. 184   Cicero on natural law: Dagobert Runes, ed., *The Selected Writings of Benjamin Rush: Physician and Citizen, 1746–1813* (Philadelphia: University of Pennsylvania Press, 1934), pp. 181–82.

p. 199   Virgil on the happiness of farmers: Dorothea Wender, ed. and trans., *Roman Poetry from the Republic to the Silver Age* (Carbondale: Southern Illinois University Press, 1980), pp. 59–60.

p. 202   Horace on the happiness of farmers: Gilbert Chinard, ed., *The Literary Bible of Thomas Jefferson: His Commonplace Book of Philosophers and Poets* (New York: Greenwood Press, 1969), p. 32.

pp. 202–3   Horace on civil war: Horace, *The Complete Odes and Epodes*, translated by W. G. Shepherd (New York: Penguin, 1983), Epodes nos. 7 and 16, pp. 55, 62.

p. 226   Augustine on the superiority of Scripture: Augustine, *Confessions*, translated by Vernon J. Bourke (Washington: Catholic University of America Press, 1953), pp. 139, 194.

p. 243   Augustine on the scientific elite: Augustine, *Confessions*, pp. 104–6.

All translations from the Bible are taken from the New Revised Standard Version.

Index

About the Author

Carl J. Richard is associate professor of history at the University of Louisiana at Lafayette and author of *The Founders and the Classics: Greece, Rome, and the American Enlightenment.*